VOICES

Memoirs from Herstory Inside
Long Island's Correctional Facilities

VOICES

Memoirs from Herstory Inside Long Island's Correctional Facilities

First American edition published by Herstory Writers Workshop, Inc. 2009
Revised, expanded edition published by Herstory Workshop, Inc. 2012

Copyright © 2012 by Herstory Writers Workshop

Thirteen-digit ISBN: 978-0-9821385-9-5
Ten-digit ISBN: 0-9821385-9-8

Front and back cover photos: Clarence Sheppard
Front-piece photo: Vanessa Greene
Other photos in this journal are by Linda Coleman, Clarence Sheppard, and Vanessa Greene

Layout and design: Alan Gold

The quilt on the back cover was made by members of Herstory Inside and presented to Lonnie and Linda as a gift in 2007, along with the message: "We wanted to show our gratitude to you for giving us back our voices."

Herstory Writers Workshop, Inc.
2539 Middle Country Rd. FL 2
Centereach, New York 11720
Phone: 631-676-7395
Fax: 631-676-7396

www.herstorywriters.org

CONTENTS

PART ONE

MEMOIRS FROM HERSTORY INSIDE, 2007-2009

Edited by Linda Coleman and Lonnie Mathis

INTRODUCTION

"Maybe one day my story will have an impact on someone else's life. . . ."
— Angelita

WELCOME to our expanding collection of VOICES: Memoirs from Herstory Inside Long Island's Correctional Facilities. It is our privilege to offer these stories to you and our great gift to have been privy to the confidences and extraordinary efforts of these women writers. Life's mysterious unfolding has brought the two of us together, through the writing of our own memoirs in Herstory Workshops,[1] and then later, team teaching in Suffolk County's correctional facilities, beginning in Riverhead with the launch of Herstory Inside in 2004, and launching the project in Yaphank within the next couple of years.

Some of the women who write with us are rival gang members who come to know one another's hearts for the first time, as week after week and month after month they work to shape their stories. Others are members of the same family—by prison rules not allowed any physical contact as they pass on their way back and forth from the tiers. It is through writing alongside one another that they learn the secrets that have locked

---

[1] Founded in 1996, Herstory Writers Workshop provides opportunities through guided memoir writing that empower women from all walks of life (regardless of age, race, religion, financial status, or sexual orientation, whether incarcerated or free) to turn their intimate stories into works of art crafted so that others can hear. Herstory is committed to providing an environment of intensive instruction which, in addition to creating literary works, upholds our values of empathy, inclusiveness, self-guided healing, safety, and the search for social change in the expression of voices that historically have been most profoundly silenced. For more information about Herstory and the Herstory Prison Project, visit our website at www.herstorywriters.org

generations into patterns without a way out. In fact, many of the offerings in this issue of our journal are about family relationships, the wishes and cries of children to mothers and fathers, as well as those of mothers to their children. We hope that these writings, along with the letters we've chosen to include, will shed light on the process that begins their libera-tion from those generational patterns—working in the sort of communion rarely found anywhere, the sort of community most of us wouldn't expect to find behind prison walls.

Why read the stories of the women in this magazine? They are not easy stories to read. They are each riddled with darkness, but also with light— the light of each woman's resilience, her humanity, her intention to heal and resume her roles as mother, daughter, partner, and citizen in a pro-ductive way. We believe that each of us wants to be of use to others! But when life events land you in prison, the chances of resuming these roles, and of healing wrongs of commission or omission, become increasingly difficult. Statistics tell us that 70 percent of those incarcerated once will return to prison. Seventy percent equals a failed experiment in anyone's book, and yet we continue to throw away the key on millions of parents and their children[2] who are also "doing time" in their absence.

We are strange beings, we humans—powerfully creative, potentially wise, compassionate and loving, and then alternately capable of the darkest abuses inflicted upon ourselves or on others of our kind, even those we love the most dearly. Those of us who have not experienced physi-cal violence, abuse, and attack often have an avid curiosity about how others survive it, what scars are left—physically, mentally, spiritually—we want to look, can't help but look, unless it's too gruesome, too disturb-ing, and then we have to turn away. We can't take it. We'd rather not carry the knowledge that such events happen every minute somewhere on the planet, especially when we are powerless to stop them. While it's true that we have no control over the many assaults that occur even as we read this—each of us in our own way has the power to effect change in both future occurrences and the healing of those perpetrators and victims

---

[2] As of February 2008, 2.3 million adults were incarcerated in the United States, or 1 in 100 Americans. 1.2 million women are either incarcerated or on parole. Of this population, 70 percent are nonwhite. If recent incarceration rates remain unchanged, 1 in 15 persons will be incarcerated sometime in their lifetime. *Sources: New York Times* and Department of Justice statistics.

after the fact. But no change will occur without awareness first. Not just awareness of statistics—those too easily become lost in the fog of number- less faces—but instead through the intimate communications of another, through the various paths that bring these experiences into our hearts and minds. That is the great offering of art in its many forms—to allow us to experience the "other" and to see a part of ourselves in each author.

Now in our sixth year as facilitators for Herstory Inside, supported by the guidance and vision of our founding director, Erika Duncan, as well as the generosity of our funders,[3] we have worked with over 600 women par- ticipants, helping them to craft memoirs that will speak to the "Stranger/ Reader"—someone (as we tell our students) "who doesn't intrinsically care about what happened to the narrator, unless the narrator finds a way to draw her in."[4] We know that the women represented here (and many oth- ers we were unable to include) certainly achieved that intimacy in their contributions to this journal and to our weekly writing workshops, where side by side they read their work aloud. We invite you now to join them as well and to bear witness to each of their life stories.

While there is a good deal of prison writing in circulation, we believe that the Herstory process is unique in guiding women, often over several months (or for those who have continued in our bridge groups on the outside, years) of working weekly with them on a particular piece of writ- ing, towards crafting work that will speak to a larger audience. The Her-

[3] The Long Island Fund for Women and Girls provided the initial seed money for this project.

The Long Island Unitarian Universalist Fund in the Long Island Community Foundation took over the major portion of the funding of our ongoing prison project.

The Hagedorn Fund in the Long Island Community Foundation has provided Herstory with the core funding which has helped make this project possible.

The Have a Heart Community Foundation has provided supplemental funding, as have many of our individual donors.

In 2009, the Long Island Fund for Women and Girls funded a special initiative through an Education and Activism grant detailed below.

For a complete list of Herstory funders, see the inside of the back cover.

[4] This definition of "Stranger/Reader" is quoted from Erika Duncan's recently released teach- ing manual, *Paper Stranger: Shaping Stories in Community,* which can be purchased through our website.

story process is specifically designed to engage reader empathy, to write of one's experience in a way that will inevitably bring the writer and the reader together in relationship. This is a process that demands "going real deep" as one Herstory Inside writer put it, and in an environment fraught with daily assaults and indignations, incessant noise and disruption, and with many prohibitions to vulnerability, we are continually inspired by the courage and trust these women bring to this process—courage to "go deep," trusting that we facilitators will fiercely maintain our number-one rule of non-judgment—no judgment at all, except about the work itself.

Since the publication of our first issue of Voices, *over five hundred copies have been distributed, many to women in prison. With the publication of this second issue, we have also begun a new Education and Activism initiative through a grant that has allowed for the development of social justice-oriented programming, using both issues to help create forums for discussion of their contents with those officials and departments that interface with this population of women most frequently, including mini-courses for students of criminal justice, corrections officers, and judges. Formerly incarcerated women from Herstory Inside have joined us in our first few presentations to students, bringing their audiences to a stunned and tearfully alert attention with the reading of their work aloud, and applauding them with embraces and requests for autographed copies of this magazine's first issue.*

As you read, we want you to know how we've chosen to edit this volume. We believe that the language of American English is constantly enriched by the diversity of the people who speak it. Honoring this belief as our guiding principle in working with every writer who comes to us in the Herstory process, we have only lightly edited these pieces for some mechanics such as spelling and punctuation. We have deliberately refrained from making changes in syntax, vocabulary, or grammar in order to preserve the beauty of the writer's unique voice and rhythm.

We hope that these stories will shatter whatever prejudice and stereo-types you may hold about women in prison. We hope that with this new awareness you will begin to question the sanity of incarceration versus less expensive and statistically more effective rehabilitation options. And finally, we hope that if a woman with a "record" comes to you, either looking for a job, or as your neighbor, that you will keep your heart and your mind and your spirit open to her.

Our special and on-going thanks to Lieutenant Darlene McClurkin, Captain Helen Geslak, Jon Scherr, and all the Rehab Staff at RCF for their ongoing cooperation and support, to all of our funders, and to our teacher and guide, Erika Duncan, who has made all of this possible for so many women with "songs unsung."

Linda Coleman and Lonnie Mathis
Herstory Facilitators and Editors
October, 2009

THE DARE TO CARE

TOO OFTEN when someone is in jail, the first question that comes up is "What did that person do?" It comes up before that person is allowed a face or a voice or a story that is her own creation. In the case of women especially—and beyond this for those coming from backgrounds of poverty, violence and discrimination—we must train ourselves to reframe our questions, thinking from the onset "What happened to them? Who are they, and what can they teach us?" If we were to make a commitment to linger until the story of each incarcerated woman found its rightful space—resisting all temptations to rush toward resolutions, wisdom or repentance that might not yet (or ever) be part of her truth—what might we be able to learn from the process? What would happen if we were to welcome with wide-open arms, not the stories we might wish for, but those that come out when we give the permission to drop all pretending? Could this make a difference, not only to those who find healing in bringing their past selves back to life on the page, but to a society that doesn't know what to do with its own violence and pain?

The Herstory project began with a simple dare that I extended back in 1996, when I asked a group of would-be memoirists to find a moment in the larger stories that they wished to tell that would evoke empathy in such a way that the "Stranger/Reader" would be a stranger no more. What I was asking, although I couldn't have articulated it at the time, was that the "dare to make another person care" be passed along from one woman to another in every aspect of the writing process, with each workshop member playing the role of helper/listener and writer in alternation. It would take another thirteen years (at the time of this writing) to develop the multiplicity of tools that would allow us to engage over 2000 women in what would become a life-changing journey, involving community building, skills mastery and the fight for social justice alike.

Although the making of art was our mission, healing quickly became an important by-product, as each writer discovered a forgotten and often more lovable part of herself she had banished or left behind. This was particularly important for women who had experienced major trauma, who hadn't yet developed much love for themselves, as they set about the task of creating caring in the circle of listeners who extended the dare: With each line that you write, let me come inside you. Let me walk in your shoes!

Now just try to imagine what that "dare to make another person care" meant to women who had been incarcerated—discarded not only inside their own hearts, but by family and the larger society? Imagine how foreign this must have sounded at first, but also how it startled the women into a whole new way of thinking and acting. Imagine the dare being enacted around the written word, of all things, in an environment where the majority of women were convinced they had no writing skills. However, I will argue, it was the very oddness of the mandate, as well as the depth of the expectation ("You can do it!"), that in the end brought such powerful results.

By the time Linda Coleman and Lonnie Mathis went into Suffolk County's jails—seven years into the Herstory project—we had a pretty good idea of the power of our empathy-based method with women coming from all walks of life. However, we could not have imagined the family, community and healing that it would create "in a place where," as one member put it, "there was none." We hope that this anthology will give you a bird's eye view, not of solutions, but of possible ways to build family where it has been ruptured, to build bridges, and to dare others to enter worlds they might otherwise have pushed away.

As you read through the works in this volume, with its introductions and intermingled letters so beautifully arranged by our prison facilitators and editors to tell the larger story, do know that almost all of the writings you find here are only small pieces of much larger works in progress. For some of the women represented, the writing journey will be moving forward from the point that the pieces in this volume left off. For others there will be weeks and maybe months ahead of developing a single sentence, fraught with meaning, into pages and chapters of memories, visions and dreams. For the work of Herstory is very much about connecting the pieces, about staying with difficult moments on the page until new illuminations filter through or new channels to chart how in life one moved from here to there. The work of **HERSTORY INSIDE** *takes this to a special level, as women carry not only their beginnings of "books"[1] in their* *regulation pebble-covered notebooks, but the writing tools that will allow them to sustain those beginnings, whether they are in recovery programs on the outside, working in one of our Bridge Workshops,[2] or facing years of long-term incarceration in high security facilities upstate.*

This publication is the first step in a larger Education and Activism Initiative, in which we will be bringing the writings of the women with whom we have worked to corrections officers, judges and lawyers, as well as students of criminal justice, sociology and law—hoping to reach those who most immediately influence decisions around incarceration, parole and re-entry; hoping that our method and what we have learned about healing and creating community through writing might be of use to others who are trying to find solutions.

In his groundbreaking book, The Wounded Storyteller,[3] *Arthur Frank writes: "One of our most difficult duties as human beings is to listen to the voices of those who suffer. . . . Listening is hard, but it is also a fundamental moral act. . . . The moment of witness in the story crystallizes a mutuality of need, when each is for the other."*

In closing I invite you to "listen" as you read the words of the wounded storytellers who provide us not with answers, but with ever so many feelings and questions with which we must grapple if we are to truly be there, as Frank so eloquently puts it "each [one] for the other."

Erika Duncan
Founder and Artistic Director of Herstory
August 2009

---

[1] One of the things that is particular to the work of Herstory with prison populations is the fact that each writer is dared to imagine that she is actually writing a book-length memoir, with its pieces put together in a way that will give her space to tell her whole story. We have been amazed and gratified by the number of women in prison who take us up on this dare and for whom the books continue to be a lifeline long after they are transferred out of the facilities where we are working.

[2] Several years into the prison project, we instituted special workshops in which women coming out of our prison workshops would be able to work with women in the larger community. These workshops, taught by the facilitators the women came to know in jail, provide bridges not only for continuing the writing experience but provide empowerment, friendships, job networking and a general sense of being part of a new world.

[3] Arthur W. Frank, *The Wounded Storyteller: Body, Illness, and Ethics.* Chicago and London: University of Chicago Press, 1995.

WOMEN IN PRISON FACT SHEET[1]

UNITED STATES

- As of June 2008, 207,700 women were in state or federal prisons or local jails, just under 10% of the total U.S. prison and jail population (more than 2.3 million)

- Nearly 115,800 women were in state or federal prisons alone, more than 7% of the total U.S. prison population of over 1.6 million.

- At yearend 2007, there were more than 1.27 million women in prison or jail, or on parole or probation in the U.S.—over 17% of the total number in the U.S. (more than 7.3 million).

- In the early 1980s, one in every 77 adults in the U.S. was under correctional supervision. Now, that figure is one in 31. For adult women, the figure is one in every 89.

- From 1995 to 2008, the number of women in state and federal prisons nationwide increased by 203%.

- Roughly 49% of women in state or federal prisons at yearend 2007 were white, just under 28% were African American, and almost 17% were Latina.

- African-American women are incarcerated at three times the rate for white women; Latina women at almost 1.6 times the rate for white women.

- As of 2005, almost 65% of women in state prisons were incarcerated for drug, property, or public order offenses.[10] Nearly one in three reported committing their offense to support a drug addiction.

---

[1] From Women in Prison Project, Correctional Association of New York, 135 East 15th St., New York, N.Y. 10003. www.correctionalassociation.org

- 62% of women and 51% of men in state prisons are parents of children under 18. More than 64%of mothers in state prisons lived with their children before prison, compared to over 46% of men.

- 4% of women in state prisons, 3% of women in federal prisons, and about 5% of women in jail nationwide reported being pregnant at the time of their incarceration.

- Women prisoners are more likely than male prisoners to have histories of physical or sexual abuse.

- In 2004, 73% of women in state prisons either have symptoms or a diagnosis of mental illness and/or were receiving treatment from a mental health professional in the past year, compared to 55% of men.

- Nearly 30% were receiving public assistance before arrest, compared to 8% of men. About 37% had incomes of less than $600 per month prior to arrest, compared to 28% of men.

- More than 725,400 were released from federal and state prison in 2007. The federal government estimates that more than two-thirds of people released from prison are rearrested within three years.

- Since 1982, U.S. corrections expenditures increased 660%, from $9 million to over $68.7 billion.

NEW YORK STATE

- From 1973 to 2009, the number of women in New York's prisons increased by more than 580%. During the same time period, the state's total prison population increased by nearly 388%.

- Since 1997, the state's female prison population has decreased by more than 30%. The total prison population has decreased by nearly 13%.

- As of mid-January 2009, women's facilities in New York State had over 746 empty beds.

- As of January 2009, 2,618 women were incarcerated in New York's prisons—about 4.3% of the state's total prison population of just under 61,000.

- An additional 29,240 women were on parole (nearly 2,580) and probation (just over 24,080).

- As of January 2009, women made up just over 8% of New York's total parole population (nearly 31,500) and almost 20% of the state's total probation population (almost 122,200).

☞ More than 83% of women sent to New York's prisons in 2008 were convicted of non-violent offenses.[28] Of women sent to prison for violent felony offenses in 2008, 84% were first time felony offenders.

☞ Almost 65% of women under state custody are first felony offenders. About 35% have either never been arrested or convicted of a crime prior to their current offense, compared with almost 22% of men.

☞ It costs $44,000 to incarcerate a person in a New York State prison for one year.

☞ Almost 68% of the state's female inmates are women of color: more than 45% are African American, almost 20% are Latina, and more than 32% are white. Women of color comprise only 30% of New York's entire female population.

☞ More than 62% of women on parole in New York State are African American or Latina. For women on probation, more than 46% are African American or Latina.

☞ As of January 2009, nearly 30% of women in New York's prisons were incarcerated for a drug offense—43% are serving time for first-time felony offenses.

☞ More than 77% of women under state custody for a drug offense are women of color.

☞ Just under 88% of women incarcerated in New York State prisons report having an alcohol or substance abuse problem prior to their arrest, compared to more than 82% of men.

☞ An estimated eight in 10 women in have experienced severe abuse as children and an estimated nine in 10 have endured physical or sexual violence in their lifetimes.

☞ As of January 2007, more than 42% of women in New York's prisons had been diagnosed with a serious mental illness, compared to nearly 12% of male inmates.

☞ About 55% of women under state custody are from New York City and its suburbs. Nearly 41% are incarcerated at Albion Correctional Facility, about eight hours away from Manhattan.

☞ The median minimum sentence for women in New York State prisons is 36 months.

- Almost 73% of New York's incarcerated women are parents, compared to more than 58% of men.

- Almost 80,000 children have a parent in New York's prisons, including nearly 5,240 children with an incarcerated mother.

- Nearly 54% of women prisoners do not have a high school diploma, compared with nearly 46% of men. More than 35% of women under state custody read at an 8th grade level or below.

- Approximately 12% of women in New York's prisons are HIV positive, a rate of infection double the rate for male inmates and 80 times higher than the rate in the general public (.15%).

- Over 22% of women in New York's prisons have Hepatitis C, a rate nearly double that for male inmates (about 13%) and over 14 times higher than the HCV infection rate in the general public (1.6%).

- More than 27,260 people were released from state prison in 2008: 25,407 men and 1,855 women.

- Three years after release from New York's prisons in 2003, women had a recidivism rate of about 30%. Men had a recidivism rate of about 40%.

- New York State spends more than $2.8 billion annually on corrections. More than 31,000 people work for the state prison system.

ADDICTION

DRUG AND ALCOHOL ADDICTION ravage the lives of the vast majority of incarcerated women. In New York State prisons, just under 90% of incarcerated women have an alcohol or substance abuse problem prior to their arrest (see Women in Prison Fact Sheet). Of the women who come to write with us, most have battled with crack, many with alcohol, and some with heroine-often at the expense of losing not only their freedom, but often their children as well, either temporarily or permanently to foster care. Many want to use the writing process to help them confront the darkest moments of their addiction, both to look with sober eyes at the havoc and despair it has caused them and those they love, as well as to hear the excuses they've used to continue.

There is an infinite well of grief expressed in this process, as each of these women writers have managed to evoke so vividly, both in these selections, as well as in the excerpts of Dehlia Ahlstrand's Windows and Prayers, and Ricarda Renee Diamond's I, Me, Who Is Thee?, both featured in the Parents and Children section.

The U.S. Department of Health and Human Services reported in July, 2009 that 9.7 percent of adults aged 18 or older needed treatment for a substance use problem in the past year. That is only the number that found their way to asking or being mandated to get help; many millions more have not yet found their way into treatment.

In the last thirty-five years, the rate at which the U.S, places its citizens in jails and prisons has skyrocketed—largely as a result of the increase in the incarceration rate for drug offenses. However, there is scant evidence to suggest that high rates of incarceration affect drug use or deter drug users. In fact, states with high incarceration rates (like New York, with its Orwellian Rockefeller Drug laws) tend to have higher *rates of drug use.*[1] *This year, the U.S. Sentencing Commission has finally enacted changes in the sentencing guidelines for certain drug offenses, particularly addressing the sentencing disparities that have put thousands of African-Americans in prison for years for crack, while those (largely white) offenders, holding similar amounts of powder cocaine, do far less time. Some of these are the very women you will meet in these pages.*

---

[1] *The Vortex: The Concentrated Racial Impact of Drug Imprisonment and the Characteristics of Punitive Counties.* Justice Policy Institute Report, December 2007.

Here I Am Again

Jill Toyas

While Jill didn't work with us for very long, she dove into her writing work without hesitation. A dedicated mother and recurrent offender secondary to alcohol abuse, this piece beautifully describes the despair and self-hate of the mother/addict fallen and arrested once again, leaving the burdens of running a home and life on the shoulders of her children. After her release, Jill worked in the Centereach group. When we contacted her for permission to include her piece she was quick to offer it in hopes it might help another.

I'M IN JAIL AGAIN. These words travel through my brain like a banging gong drowning out all else. Jail again. How did I let this happen? I am an intelligent person. Certainly not a criminal. My crimes are self-hatred, fear, inadequacy. Certainly I am not the only person guilty of these. I was arrested and handcuffed to my pain. I was brought here and locked in with my addiction—a creature that has been hunting me for my entire adult life. I have been running through this jungle of life with it in hot pursuit. I feel its hot breath and low growl behind me keeping me running, running from everything important, everything I care about. This creature, addiction, has brought me to this place. A place where I have no control, where boredom and helplessness fill all the hours in a day.

They shackle me and load me into a bus. I watch my freedom slipping away with each passing tree and car on the expressway. Several hours ago I frantically tried to get in touch with my children, only to leave voicemails. "Kym, Kris, it's Mom. I'm sorry, but I'm going to jail again. I don't know when I will be able to call. I'm sorry. As soon as I can I'll get in touch . . ." The machine cuts off and the phone is dead. Just like I feel inside. Every nerve inside my body seems numb. I stare out the window, so many thoughts racing through my brain. The kids, my job, the bills, my cat, my life . . . Where did it go? Just then I see exit 62—*my* exit. I think about what is going on there. The panic, the turmoil I have caused, again. The phone calls my daughters are making to each other. I can almost hear the disappointment in their voices. "Did she call you yet? I don't know what to do! I can't believe she is doing this to us again."

How did I get here? I was okay—happy family, a job. All that's gone now. I am going to jail again.

The bus stops. Once again I enter the locked gates of SCCF. I can't feel anything. It's like I am underwater, like when I used to play tea party in the pool. Trying to understand the words the other person was saying as bubbles rushed to the surface. Only this is no game. I'm not in a pool, I'm in jail again. There are no bubbles coming out of the officer's mouths. There is only scorn and disdain. They make me feel so small. Once again I have no rights, a non-person. I am ushered into this cold, intimidating building. Although I have been here before it all feels so new. My body is searched as I stand against the wall, legs spread and barefoot. They feel me and look into places I don't want them to look. I feel humiliated. I am fingerprinted and photographed all over again. I'm told to shut the fuck up, asked if I am retarded. I'm taken to a room where I have to undress in front of a bunch of strangers. All my possessions are taken from me. The ring I haven't taken off since my lover gave it to me is placed in a bag. My clothes and shoes, also taken. A pile of green clothes are handed to me. We all dress in front of each other. Not much is said by the officer—I am just another loser. I can't possibly be different than any other woman in here. I think I am. I thought I was. After last time, I vowed never to see these walls again. Now here I am putting on my "greens" and getting my eyeball photographed.

I am finally allowed to use the phone. Part of me is afraid to speak to them. After two rings Kris picks up. "It's me," I say. I hear the rest of them in the background shouting out questions. I can picture them all standing around the kitchen where I stand. Justin's soulful face, heartbreak all over it. Kym twisting her long red ponytail, and Kris always in control—anger and sadness flashing in her big hazel eyes. "I can't believe it Mom, I thought we were done with all this shit," she spits into the phone. "How long this time? 90 days! Oh my god!" Her voice suddenly changes to panic. "What are we going to tell people? What about the rent, your job? I can't believe you're in jail again!"

With my head pounding and my knees shaking all I can say is, "I know . . . I'm sorry," and the conversation turns toward giving her the information she will need to do the banking. Now I feel like the child. My 21-year-old daughter has to take control of my life. Scrape up the mess. Because her mom is in jail *again!*

The conversation ends with an abrupt click and I stand there holding the receiver pushing down the urge to cry. "Okay, Toyas, let's go!" the officer shouts. She hands me the laundry bag full of the basic necessities for jail life. I remember them well. I am ushered into the elevator and taken downstairs. The officer that greets us says, "Okay, ladies, here is your location. Remember it." Mine is pod IEN26 top bunk. I remember the girls talking about the pod last time, but I don't know what to expect. We head down the corridor until we reach the door. When it's opened, bright lights flood the corridor and I hear the roar of the inmates. We enter the pod to the sound of catcalls "new girls," "fresh meat", they laugh and whistle, then they forget about us. I climb the stairs to my new home. Only this is no home. A 6′ × 12′ cell with the metal toilet I remember with a shiver. Linda greets me and helps me make my bed. She is tall with long dark hair. She appears to be in her 40's. She begins to fill me in on pod life.

"Breakfast is 6 AM. You take your cup and here is a bread bag for your cereal." I must have looked confused because she says, "Don't worry—you'll see in the morning".

We chat awhile about our crimes and our lives. She is addicted to crack and steals to pay for it. She has no family and lives in a tent. My mind wanders to my family. I know that they are probably sitting in the living room discussing their strategies. And wondering how I let this happen again. It's lock in now, and after putting all my things away I get ready to go to bed. Now comes the tricky part. There is a ladder on the bed but no matter how I try I can't get up there. I feel so weak and out of shape. I'm too old to be in jail again. Linda offers to help—she puts her hand on my butt and pushes! I don't care—I'm up there! I lie down on the slab they call a mattress and try to sleep.

I'm in jail again. I want to cry but tears won't come. I'm numb. Sleep comes finally. I don't dream. There is nothing.

A letter from a son growing up without his mother

Dear Mom,

Nothing against you but I really didn't want to write you. I
got a lot of things I feel stressed about, including the fact you're
locked up in jail. I love you to death and you know you're my Mom
and best friend, I just wish you could pull yourself together. You
really need to be a part of your grand kids life. My sister needs
help with them kids she got. You need to get out of New York,
because you stay in trouble there. I know you care about me
and your daughter so you gotta take care of your responsibility.
We all getting old, but we still miss our mother. I kept all your
letters you wrote and played hard every football game like you
told me. I played as if you were in the stands and me a waiting
your approval. I'm thinking about going to Campbell University. I
really like the Coach @ the school. It's a new program and they
sponsored by Adidas. I'm going to the pros. I feel it in my heart.
I do believe you can beat them drugs. I've never tried them
and I never will. I'm making straight A's in school. I still remember
when you told me how important academics were. I'll never forget
when you wouldn't let me go to practice cause I didn't finish my
homework.
Grandma still old fashion as far as rules go. I don't do anything
bad, but she just never content. She has started drinkin alot and
be tripin hard. I'm almost @ my breaking point. I really aint got
nobody (that's how I feel). I just play sports because it lets me
get away. It's like everyday I get a little colder. I'm just ready
to go, but at the same time I'm not rushing it. I really don't care
about my dad situation. I understand that I'm gonna be the man I
wanna be. Well I'm runnin out of words so I'll talk to you later.

I love you. Your son.

Don't get down on your self
Keep your Head up

trouble don't last always.

The Lesson

Sandy Beltran

A young single mother of one, Sandy was willing for so long to let others take care of her, even at the expense of being abused by those closest to her. When the abuse turned on her son, however, she fled with him and now is trying to make ends meet on her own. Her time with us at RCF was her first incarceration and she chose to write about her arrest, a story that brings her in an eerie full-circle from the child being taught a lesson, to the woman living the lesson.

"WHAT PRECINCT is this?"

"The 4th precinct," the officer said.

"Oh," I said with my head down in shame. I have been here before and I was twelve years old at the time. My aunt used to work here and she brought me here once. Her name was Beth and she was a police detention attendant. She was five feet tall, if that, always kept a short hair cut, never wore makeup . . . let alone a smile, and she was big-busted and that's how you could tell she was a woman. She brought me here to this precinct when I was younger as a lesson in life to never wind up here. Right now I think it was a jinx.

I remember my visit here like it was yesterday. It was the midnight shift too. I walked in nervously holding Beth's hand and we had to get buzzed in. I was so small I couldn't even see who was over the counter. I got introduced to all of the officers and they were really nice. She gave me the grand tour—the cells, where they take the mug shots, and I even got my fingerprints taken. Then we sat in her office. I looked up and saw the cameras that were videotaping the inmates. At that time nobody was there yet but soon enough a woman showed up. This woman was complaining from the minute she came in. She kept saying that she didn't belong there. She had shabby hair, a very sad face and kept coughing a lot. Beth then had to search her and asked the inmate to remove her clothing. I turned my face in embarrassment but couldn't help but listen to it all.

"Strip, squat, and cough!"

The lady was sobbing the whole time. After the strip search was over Beth locked her in the cell. She didn't let her keep her shoes, jacket, or belt for safety reasons. Beth sat down next to me in the office and started lecturing me on why most of the prisoners belong here and what crimes they have done, "Basically almost everything has to do with drugs. Drugs are the path of destruction . . ." A statement that I never forgot.

While we were talking I heard the lady in the background yelling that she was cold and she was begging for some warmth. Beth went to a closet and pulled out a plastic coated yellow foam thing. She kept crying though, to the point that auntie told her a few times to be quiet and she didn't say it so nice. She told the woman, "Shut up or I'll make you shut up," which didn't surprise me because she spoke to me the same way.

I was concerned and scared but auntie reassured me. "They all act this way. They broke the law and this is where they belong. If you stay good you will never have to worry about coming here."

The inmate kept crying though and she began to throw up too. I couldn't take it anymore. I began crying and I begged Beth to get her help and to call the ambulance. Beth looked at me with a concerned look and said, "Okay, but I know the lady is fine, and she'll be back soon with nothing wrong." She gave me a kiss on the cheek and told me to stop crying. About an hour later Beth got a call and it just so happened that the lady died on the way to the hospital. I wanted to leave immediately, this place was scary. I felt a desperation to run out of there but Beth didn't let me. She had to finish her shift. I was so mad that she had made me come here. She told me to fall asleep on a cot she had up against the wall and eventually I did.

That was a long time ago and now I'm 25 walking in here. Wow. Where's auntie when I need her now? I bet she wouldn't help me anyway.

The female officer came out and told me to go in the picture room. It was just the way I remembered it. As she took the picture I saw my reflection—it wasn't the reflection of a seven-year-old, that's for sure. I looked drained, my hair was unkempt. I couldn't even smile for the picture. I got my fingerprints taken. The next step was to go to the cell area. Before I walked in I glanced at the office hoping I would find auntie there but I knew damn well she was retired.

"Strip, squat, and cough!" I obeyed, teary eyed, but I did it as fast as possible. Damn it's cold in here, and I can't even keep my shoes or jacket. I'm supposed to be at work right now. This is ridiculous. Locked up in this little cell and I'm claustrophobic. All I can do now is pray. "Oh God, I'm sorry . . . Please just let me go home tomorrow and I'll be good and please don't let me die in here . . ."

Oh my God, it's so cold in here I'm shivering. I hollered to the officer that I was cold, but I didn't get a response. I kept hollering so loud that it turned to sobbing and I got a flashback of that lady sobbing and sobbing. It was like déjà-vu . . . like I could hear her echo . . . like I felt her spirit. The officer finally came and threw me this plastic coated yellow foam thing and told me to shut up.

I shut up and lay down on the hard wooden bench and covered myself up. I was still shivering but I tried not to think about it.

And then a thought came to my head—if she only could see that this criminal was once a child.

A Letter from Adeline

Adeline Acevedo

 *Addy is one of our earliest students and a featured writer in the first issue of* Voices. *The letter below is the first of many, many pages sent to us during an upstate bid several years ago. She has, since her release almost a year ago, joined a weekly Herstory workshop in Huntington and has assisted Herstory with public presentations through our Education and Activism Initiative where women from Herstory Inside speak and read publicly to those most likely to interface professionally with incarcerated women.*

Addy continued to work on her writing while doing time upstate. In spite of many obstacles and a history fraught with early physical and sexual abuse, Addy clearly is actualizing the beautiful and generous intentions described in this letter.

12/31/05

AND SO BEGINS our correspondence . . . Addie.

Dear Linda & Lonnie,

Hello Ladies. I hope you both had a Merry Christmas and Happy New Year. It's New Year's Eve!

I started writing reflections on my now feelings sitting here. I want to write about my contemplations and epiphanies, on what my past has been, my present, and on what I want to make of my future. I want my words to inspire someone else who has lost a child after loving them, to be able to move on without turning to negative influences. I want to touch young kids like late teens and children, so that they never touch heroine. I want to touch them into knowing that anything can go wrong in an instant in the hustling game, to know that a normal average everyday next door neighbor kid can lose themselves to the point of being far gone. And that they can always come back from the dead and stop dying on a daily basis. That is going to be my mission in life, and, of course, to live my dreams and write.

You two have really touched my life . . . everything I write sets me freer with every page. I want to be truly free, cause this cross I carry is too heavy. I'm done dying everyday. I feel like I've died a million deaths already and haven't even truly lived. I want to take my disappointments and turn them into a success story. I felt very different growing up and want other young teens to know that they are not crazy for going through it, they're just sick. And that it's okay to feel all those emotions and learn to handle them instead of Dying inside. And to have self esteem and know that they can grow up to be anything they can imagine in this world.

I know I'm gonna be alright thanks to you guys being my strength when I was weak. You believed I could write the words I have put on paper, and for that I thank you a million times. I am going to write some things over to send to you, and can you write comments in Red?

They are going to give me 8 months on 1/11/06 when I go to court. I'll only do like 5$^{1}/_{2}$–6 months out of that. I have 15 days in already. I'm okay with this for myself, but my mom has leukemia now and will soon start chemo, so that leaves my kids out for a while. I don't want that. I need to be there. But I've learned that you can't do anything about what you simply can't do anything about. So I'm taking it easy, and breathing, cause I know late is better than never, right?

Well I am going to keep writing now until I run out of supplies. Supplies are low though because they took 5 marble notebooks from me, and all my story ideas. I really need those books—it's crucial to my writing.

I would like to thank you both for everything you are doing for me—you are my support team, my two-woman army.

Love,
Adeline
A. Christina
K. Acevedo
A.
ADDIE

Cracked

Nina Wilson

For those readers unfamiliar with the effects of crack cocaine, it is a substance that causes instant and short-lived
euphoria, loss of appetite, insomnia, intense craving for
more crack, and often an increasing paranoia. Typically
users go on binges lasting up to three days or more without sleep or food, ever seeking (and failing to find) the
level of euphoria they experienced in the initial hit.

Few will forget the images that Nina brings to the page as she takes a
hard look at the depth of desperation that crack addiction brought her to.
Her writing poured from her week after week as she used the writing process
as a cleansing of sorts. With each depraved and harsh image she wrought on
the page, she moved from seeing herself as a disgusting and worthless "crack
whore" to recognizing how sick she had become, how controlled and domi-
nated by this drug.

On her "Page One" we met Nina as a little girl being left on the road by
her family at her new foster home. Confused, alone, and afraid, she wondered, "Why aren't they taking me?" For so many women in prison who ask
the question "How did I get here?" the answer almost always takes them to
the lost, abandoned, wounded children they once were.

FOR SOME REASON I thought that hanging out there was normal. I really thought that there was nothing wrong with me smoking crack, weighing approximately 130 pounds, wearing the same
clothes for two to three days, eating every two days and only if I
didn't have crack, and still thinking I looked real good. How sick
was I? I could only go out at night because I was on the run from
parole.

I thought back to last Wednesday when I went to report to my parole officer . . .

"Nina Wilson."

I stand and walk to the door where I greet Mr. M., a medium build Caucasian with gray hair.

"How are you, Miss Wilson?"

"I'm not alright," I reply. "I need help. Yes, my urine is dirty. I want to stop."

So he says, "Nina, get yourself in a program before you come back. If you don't, then just come in anyway."

"Thank you, Mr. M," I reply.

But next week never came.

Now I'm not only addicted heavily to crack, I'm homeless because I don't want parole to catch me and lock me up. But the ironic thing about this is I'm not running from parole to stay free, I'm running from parole to keep smoking. How deep is that?

"Nina, someone's sitting there."

"What?" I said to Willie.

"Sister, I'm sorry, but my friend is going to sit on that crate."

Now I'm looking at this man I call my brother like he has two heads—a man who used to weigh about 220 pounds but due to the crack use was now about 120 soaking wet. I'm looking at him because I cannot believe that with all of the love I show him as a brother that he's telling me I can no longer have a seat, on a crate, in an abandoned house . . .

So I decided to just go in the back behind the house and smoke by myself. I found a log to sit on, and took a hit off my pipe. Right away, the tall grasses all around me got real creepy, making ruffling sounds as if someone was making their way through the woods towards me. So I stood up trying to listen more closely, and heard a sound like someone stepping on twigs. I started to tip-toe backwards and slowly passed the doorway to the house just as someone opened the door. Terrified, I turned and ran . . .

As I flicked my eyelids to gather my eyesight, I realized that I'd been asleep. As I regained full focus on my surroundings, I looked to the right of me and my stomach turned with disgust at the dark, wrinkled body of Richard laying next to me smelling like stale wine and piss. I looked at his rough calloused hands with finger and toe-nails that curved over the skin and were permanently black. Tears welled up in my eyes because once again I was lying in this bed filled with grit and dirt because this trick does not wash. I'd been so desperate to get a hit that I'd degraded myself once again to sleeping with this man, knowing he had at least $1500 dollars in his wallet. This parasite had been all over my body. Because I had not been to sleep in days, I'd left myself open for anything he wanted to do to me. I hadn't cared if I'd caught crabs, herpes, or most of all Aids, just to let me get a hit.

As soon as I heard him stir I sat up as gently as I could. My body had shit stuck to it from the filth in the bed—food, dirt, liquids. I brushed off as best I could but everything was gritty and dirty, even his wash rag. How long had I been here? What had he done to me? Then I remembered. I'd left Willie at the abandoned house and as I was running up the street I saw Richard's brown Cadillac turning the corner. At that point I was so tired it did not matter who was coming or going, I just needed some rest. As the car came near I put my hand up for him to stop. He pulled up and I opened the door. The stench from his body engulfed my nostrils with the smell of ammonia. I almost gagged. There was no conversation needed between the two of us—no greeting, no eye contact, no nothing. We both knew what we had in common—nothing but his money and my "acting-as-if-it's-in" sex. The reason that I call it that is because I do not let his penis enter me. I do a hellofa job acting "as if."

Before we got to his house, I fell asleep. His house was only four blocks away so I know I was tired. How I got inside his house, I can't tell you. How my clothes came off, I can only imagine. The real questions were—did he penetrate me? Did he cum inside of me? I was sick to my stomach just by that thought alone. So I slowly bent my head down to see what I feared with all of my heart. I had white dried up spots on my thighs. My eyes welled with tears as I put my hand on one spot and then the others. Some were still sticky wet. I snatched my hand back in horror and began to sob quietly to myself. In spite of what was going through my mind, I had to know if he came inside of me, so I slowly eased my hand to my pubic area and used fingers to check to see if I was wet inside. I sighed in relief that I was not wet, but the disgust was still there.

It was at that moment I realized that I needed to get help for my drug addiction.

When Richard woke up, the first thing he did, as always, was to check for his wallet and then his front pockets—as if someone was going to steal from him as stingy as he is. I checked to see if I even got the money for whatever he did to me the night before but as I only had eight dollars and change in my pocket I said, "Richard, I'm ready to go." He already knew that meant I wanted my pay. He turned his back as usual and peeled off a $20 bill. Before he gave it to me he licked his two fingers and rubbed the bill to make sure there wasn't a second one stuck to it. The man was pathetic, but what was I if I just got out of his bed?

I asked him if I could use his phone. As I expected he started his sermon, "I don't let no one use my phone . . . no one tells the truth . . . they call long distance . . ." Before he finished I walked to the phone and snatched the receiver off the hook. I've only been dealing with this man for fifteen years to hear the same thing. So I dialed 411 and they gave me the connection to Talbot House, a detox where people can go to get a new start on a life without drugs. The receptionist answered and I stated I needed a bed. She asked some screening questions and then said, "Can you be here by 2 PM?"

I looked at the clock—it said 7:15 AM. At this point, I was desperate, and deep down inside I really wanted to stop using, the pain was so great and there was nowhere else to turn. At the same time, I got butterflies in my stomach as I felt the three remaining rocks in my pocket and I lied and asked her if she could give me a later time.

"Nina," she said, "Do you want the bed? Do you want to stop using?" She had to know what I was thinking.

"I want the bed. I'll be on the next train out of Wyandanch."

"Good . . . then call when you get in and we'll pick you up."

I hung up the phone. "Take care Richard," I said and left. He was still talking shit about his phone.

I walked out into the morning air. I still did not feel the freshness because I was so filthy. I was too embarrassed to be seen so I

took all of the back streets through Wyandanch to the railroad station. I reached the train station and the schedule on the door said
that the next train eastbound was at 11:45 AM. I had four hours.
There was a dumpster across the street and I took the crack and my
pipe out of my pocket and threw everything away. And then I went
and sat down in the platform booth and cried.

Later, as I waited for the train, I walked up the platform and
every few steps I would look for that distant single light. I looked
down at my clothes and saw there was a wet spot on my once white
shirt, and the acid washed jeans I wore had dirt lines in them, dirt
circles the same size as each coin I had in my pocket. My appearance alone was enough to make me want to run to a place to hide.
And my hands—if anyone would have seen them they would have
thought I was a car mechanic. Just looking at myself gave me a
feeling of disgust. I folded my shirt up making it a belly shirt so I
could hide the wet spot, held my head up, and proceeded down the
platform towards the depot to buy my ticket before I let my negative
thoughts deter me from my primary purpose of getting help.

Finally, I saw it coming so I walked to the very end of the platform where I would be in the first car with the operator in it. The
train pulled up to a stop and before the doors opened, thoughts
came to me: "Nina, how are you going with no toiletries, no change
of clothes . . . you know there are probably some fine guys there."
The bell of the door opening snapped me out of those meaningless
thoughts. I've learned from prior treatment that that was my disease trying to stop me from getting on the train. I stepped through
the doors and grabbed onto the pole so that I would not change my
mind, and I was grateful to God and felt a huge sense of relief when
I heard the bell signifying the doors closing, and only then did I
dare to let go and find a seat.

As I walked through the aisle, people looked at me in utter disgust, but at that point I was the happiest woman alive because I'd
made it onto this train to save my life.   ✎

Breathe

Tina Taylor

Tina dives into the deep end in her writing. The very first pages she read aloud to us were of an incident of being drugged, tied, and raped at the age of twelve. Her short pieces have been in high demand in our groups—everyone wants a copy! She is mature beyond her years and always offers a motherly support to other group members.

BREATHE . . .

Shh . . . wait for it, ahh . . . here it comes, calm.

I taste it now. Swallow my problems again down they go down, down.

They're gone, gone for now. I feel at peace, relaxed.

Breathe . . . am I breathing?

Rush, I feel it running through my veins from head to toe.

Oh, there's nothing like it. Wait don't go!

Chaos is back. Pain, sweat, pain. Scream but no one hears you.

Breathe . . .

Got to get it, have to have it. Make me whole again, make me better.

False illusions, I'm not whole, I'm not better

Breathe . . .

Do I have enough to make it through the day?

What's your next move?

Better make it fast, do what you have to do. Do it now!

Another piece of me dies. I have to drown it, have to stop this pain.

Breathe . . .

Quick fix, everything is gone, gone for now bound to return again.

Stop this madness, this vicious cycle.

Round and round I go. I can't take much more of this . . . Help!

Breathe, breathe . . .

Here comes the pain again, strong and hard like a wave that I just can't stop. It's going to knock me down, down from where I started. Look at me now. Who have I become? I'm a shell of what I once was.

Breathe . . .

Jails, institutions, and death. That's what it is. This is how it ends. What's your next move?

Breathe . . .

VIOLENCE AGAINST WOMEN

WHEN WE BEGAN *our work with incarcerated women, we had no way of knowing the extent to which violence of all kinds had shaped their lives —sexual abuse as children, beatings carried forth from childhood into their adult relationships with men (all too often confused with "proof of love"), and as victims of rape. Virtually all of the women that we work with have experienced one or all of these attacks. According the Centers for Disease Control, one in four women will experience domestic abuse at some point in her life. In more than half of those cases, children are also involved and abused. **Domestic violence is the leading cause of injury to women between the ages of 15 and 44 in the United States, more than car accidents, muggings, and rapes combined.***

While the statistics are shocking, they do not let us inside of the re-lationships and experiences of abused women the way these stories do.[1] Tynetta King and Felicia Corbett struggle with their own attachments and affections for their abuser; Samantha Sarro, sexually abused at a young age, is also confused by her body's responses that betray her. Janine seeks relief from her emotional pain through drugs and repeated attempts at suicide. And two letters, side by side, were written by one woman (afraid to reveal her name in the event that her former abuser might find her and retaliate)—one letter to her abuser and one to the mother who aban-doned her after finding out.

It is a powerfully liberating experience for these women to speak out,

---

[1] These comments and citing of statistics are not intended to demonize men, however brutal the behavior of the men in these circumstances. A full understanding of these relationships is well beyond the scope of this journal. We know from accounts of counselors who work closely with incarcerated men that many of them have also experienced rape, as well as other forms of sexual violence and brutality as children, and we would gladly seize the opportunity to work with incarcerated men as well, or to train others to do this work with them.

to be heard by others, to be supported through the transit of grief, and rage, confusion and shame that always accompanies the telling. But while many have spoken of these events before (though many have not), it is in the process of writing and rewriting, having to revisit scenes repeatedly until each moment of the text can speak to the Stranger/Reader, and then to be heard through reading the work aloud in our small and safe communal circle that the healing takes place.

Many of the women who write of violence and abuse have classic signs of post-traumatic stress disorder. Current research[2] now points to just such a process (of repeated telling and retelling of causative incidents) as the only treatment that holds promise for recovery from PTSD. While that was news to us, it is clearly apparent that something extremely powerfully therapeutic takes place in this writing process.

---

[2] American Psychiatric Association, *Psychiatric News*, December 7, 2007 (vol. 42, no. 23): 1.

In the Eyes of Love

Felicia Corbett

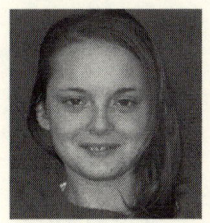

Many of the women we work with are young—still in their adolescence. Perhaps none have been as "young" as Felicia—her petite stature, her bright-eyed pixie face always in a smile, her stubborn pleasure and pride in writing her story. "Wait till you hear what I've got for you this week!" she'd announce proudly when we'd first arrive at class.

As street-wise as these young women may be, they are still children in many ways, in need of parental guidance and love. Felicia is one of those drawn into drugs and enamored with a sentimental sweet-talking brute of a man, Primo, who was as intent on killing her as he was on loving her.

Women who love men who abuse them are often asked, "Why do you stay? How could you love him?" We asked Felicia, "What did you tell yourself to allow you to stay?" When we first met Felicia she was clearly still "in love" with Primo. But week by week as she did her work of going deeply and honestly into tender and heart-felt moments of love shared between them, juxtaposed with those moments of fear and brutality, that love began to fall away. In part because of the reactions she witnessed from other women in class to the brutality and contradictions in her story, a new awareness came to Felicia.

I WOKE UP to soft kisses all on my face and lips. I could feel the soft skin of his cheek rub against mine as he brushed his face softly against me. I smiled but didn't turn around to face him keeping my eyes closed, not wanting him to stop yet. He whispered *"I love you"* ever so gently causing a tickle in my ear. I could feel my stomach turn into a billion little knots as the excitement of how much I loved him ran through every vein in my body. Finally I turned around, wrapping my arms around his neck, and began to kiss him on the lips.

"Good morning, baby," he said.

"Good morning," I replied.

He pulled away from me and reached over to the night stand. "I made you breakfast baby, look!" On the plate were four perfectly made golden pancakes with butter syrup. "Thank you baby," I said as I reached for the plate. I couldn't get the grin off my face as I thought how I had finally found the love of my life and the best man walking.

"I win again as usual! Let's play again," Primo said.

"Oh hell no! Let me see that score sheet. You're such a cheater," I said back to him.

He started laughing, "No, you're just a sore loser." He tickled me and we started to play-fight on the bed.

"I love you Felicia." He looked at me but the phone rang before I could reply.

"I'm going to go meet B. to get dope. I'll be right back," Primo said.

"No I don't wanna be here when you get back. Let me go with you!" I said as I looked at him, pleading.

"No I'll be right back—just wait here," he said walking down the hallway to the front door.

I rushed to barricade the bedroom door after he left. I lay down on the bed, tense from the fear that was overwhelming my body as I continued doing hit after hit off my crack pipe.[1] I'm so tired, was the last thing I remember thinking to myself before I dozed off.

BOOM! I jumped and turned to look behind me. The pole that was barricading the door was now sticking through it. The door had been kicked open.

---

[1] Crack users often experience increasing paranoia as they ingest more and more crack, searching for the euphoria of the initial hit.

"Why the fuck wouldn't you open the door?"

"I was sleeping," I replied. My heart dropped as I thought to myself, "Oh no, Lord, please not again!"

He looked at me with a look that let me know he was not in his right state of mind.

"Who was in here while I was gone?"

"No one!" I replied.

"Don't lie to me!"

"No one, Primo, please don't do this!!"

He grabbed my throat, "I'm going to ask you one more time—lie to me one more time and see what happens!"

I looked into his bright green eyes with fear for my life and began hysterically crying . . . "No one. . . . please, Primo . . . THE BABY. . . THE BABY!"

"You don't deserve my baby," he said as he repeatedly kicked my stomach and stomped on my face. Finally he walked out of the room.

I glanced at the clock . . . 12:15 AM. "It's my birthday," I mumbled to myself as I held my hands together, filled with blood.

The pain was unbearable but all I could do was think how badly I wished things could be how they used to be.

I felt the blanket get pulled off of me. "Good morning, Beautiful, happy birthday! Everyone to the living room!" I turned over to see it was a well known officer, Silver Fox. He was doing his weekly check up. Being that we were living in a crack house, he would frequently show up to run everyone's names for warrants. His face turned as pale as his silver hair, his nose and cheeks became rosy red, then tears began to run down his face. "Billy! Billy!" he screamed to his partner. I heard Billy's footsteps come running down the hallway. He came to a sudden halt as he looked at me and his jaw dropped. He looked at Silver Fox who was now kneeling by my side of the king sized bed.

"Oh Lord! What did he do? Why did he do this? Does he know you're still alive?"

I looked at him puzzled, "Are you crazy? What are you talking about, Billy?" I said.

"No, are *you* crazy?" Silver Fox said, cutting me off. "He's going to kill you. Get up! Have you seen yourself yet?"

I walked into the bathroom and looked in the mirror. My face was covered in dried blood. My lip was completely split in half and almost as swollen as my two black eyes. My temple was swollen up like a baseball. I was the perfect example of a horrifying Halloween mask, not to mention my left elbow was near to impossible to move.

I looked over to Silver Fox and Billy. "Where is Primo?" they asked.

"I don't know," I replied.

"Are you sure you don't want to go to the hospital?" Billy asked.

"I'm sure," I said. "I just want to go lay down."

"Okay, let us drive you to your mom's then. You need to get away." Silver Fox wiped his eyes, then looking at the end table on my side of my bed, he picked up my crack pipe and poked my pillow with it. Blood ran out from the pressure of the pipe against the pillow. He looked up and said, "No you're coming to the precinct and pressing charges. You have no choice." I grabbed what I could then and followed them to the squad car. I sat in complete silence as we drove to the precinct. I thought back to the first time I'd met the two of them and the advice they'd given me then . . .

". . . I love you, Felicia," Primo said, one of the first times we were together. He held me from behind and his soft, simple touch caused me to quiver as he lightly ran his lips on my neck. I took a deep breath, closed my eyes.

"I love you too," I replied. He grabbed me closer holding me tight. I turned around looking into his eyes, and then began to kiss him. *I love this!* I thought to myself. *I never felt like this for anybody. He is definitely the one.*

He laid me down caressing my soft skin. "I want you to have my baby," he whispered in my ear.

I looked at him in disbelief. He tipped his head, as if looking for approval, so I nodded causing him to smile, bend down, and hug me tight.

"I never wanna lose you. I want to be with you for the rest of my life," was the last thing he said to me before he began to undress me and turned off the light.

KNOCK-KNOCK! "Primo open up . . . I know you're in there!"

He sat up and put on his boxers before opening the bedroom door. "Can I help you?" Primo asked the officer.

"Yes," the officer replied. "We have a warrant for your arrest. So can you please put some clothes on and come out into the living room?"

I was confused as I lay there holding the white sheet over my naked body. "Get dressed, young lady, and come out into the living room also, please."

What's going on? I thought as I got dressed. I walked into the living room. Primo was leaning against the wall, cuffed.

"So you're Primo's new girlfriend?" Silver Fox asked me.

"Yes," I answered.

"Well, run while you can, 'cause he's known for beating his girls," he said.

I looked at Primo who gazed at me with his puppy eyes.

"So are you going to beat her, too, or are you going to kill her?" Silver Fox asked Primo.

"No, she's different," he said before they escorted him out of the house.

We pulled up at the one story brick house. Silver Fox and Billy got out of the car and gave me hugs making me promise to be good. I walked up to the door, trying the door knob. It was open so I walked right in. I didn't see anyone so I opened my mom's bedroom. She was sleeping with her back to me on her side. The lights were off but the sun made it that much brighter as it shined through the big bay window beside her bed and bounced right across to the closet mirror. I could see her blonde hair coming out of the top of the blanket and hear her lightly grinding her teeth. I hesitated on waking her up because the grinding usually meant she'd gone out the night before and didn't get to bed till late. I walked toward her anyway because I was too anxious to wait. I wanted to see her reaction. Maybe she would finally pay me some mind . . . hug me and actually tell me she loved me instead of just shaking me off as usual. I hoped she wouldn't start screaming at me for being at the house or for waking her up.

"Ma . . . Ma . . . Wake up!"

She turned over and looked at me. "What are you doing here? And what happened to your face?" she said calmly.

"Primo," I said.

"Oh . . . well, don't wake your brother up because I really don't feel like having him come in here making me get up."

"Okay," I said. I walked out of the room stunned but not surprised by her reaction.

I went into the bathroom, turned on the shower and began to cry as I undressed myself and then stepped in. "WHY? WHY?" I mumbled to myself as I wiped my face lightly to wash off the dried blood.

Looking at my ring on my finger made me think of the Primo that I once knew, the man who'd proposed to me. I fought with myself as I tried to run the wash cloth over my face. It felt tender and sore. I sat down on the bottom of the shower floor letting the water run onto my body as I cried hysterically. I felt so miserable. I was starving but couldn't move my mouth to eat. I was in unbearable pain physically and suffering from a broken heart, and wondering why my mother just looked at my face and reacted as if it was normal. She must not care about me, I thought. When will someone care about Felicia? I'm so sick of everyone hurting me. When will I be loved?

Flashbacks ran through my mind of Primo hitting me with his closed fists . . . remembering the feeling of temporarily losing my vision and hearing as a result . . . of him holding knives to my throat, trying to choke me . . . of my mom beating me with coffee mugs for missing the school bus and her boyfriend getting frustrated, being drunk, and throwing dishes across the house at me . . . of me as an 8-year-old child trying to take my own life.

The house phone rang as I was drying myself off. My cell phone number showed up on the caller ID. I knew it was Primo because he had my cell phone. Should I answer it or not? What should I do? I heard my little brother's voice pick up one of the other house phones.

"Hello . . . No she don't live here no more."

Oh my God! Yes I am here! "Who is it, Nicholas?" I said to let him know that I was there. I could hear his little footsteps running all over the house trying to find me as I was fighting to get my clothes on my damp body. Nick was still talking to Primo. I heard him ask, "Why aren't you here too? Are you coming over?"

I opened the bathroom door reaching for the phone. "Hello," I said.

"Hey, baby . . ." he said as if nothing was wrong. "I lost you forever, didn't I?"

I didn't reply, leaving a scary silence over the phone line.

"I heard that Silver Fox and Billy brought you over there—you didn't write anything on me, did you?" he asked me.

"You almost killed me, Primo. Of course I did . . . are you crazy?"

Shocked, he replied, "I can't believe you would do that to me! I love you! You know that, right?"

"No, I don't, Primo . . . not anymore at least."

He asked me if he could see me and I told him no, that I wasn't ready for that yet as I opened the bathroom door. "I love you . . . do you still love me?" Primo asked.

"I don't know, Primo. I don't know anything right now. I just need some space."

I heard my grandmother's bedroom door open and her going into the kitchen. I left the bedroom and followed her oxygen line to the kitchen table where her little five foot body sat. Her short brown hair came to the same height as the back of the chair as she sat down to the table with her mug of hot tea in her hand.

"Hey, Nan," I said. She swung the rolling chair around holding onto the table so that she wouldn't roll away, being that her feet didn't reach the floor. She was wearing her favorite pink robe with a set of pink flower pajamas, her light green eyes were always so comforting.

"Oh my goodness! What happened to you?" she said, breathing heavily.

"Primo," I told her.

"He's a loser. You need to stay away from him! Does your mother know you're here?"

"Yes," I told her. I told what my mother had said, how she'd reacted. She shook her head in disbelief that the evil woman she had raised, my mother, was her daughter, and told me to go lie down in her room . . . she was up for the day. I thanked her, giving her a kiss on the cheek and telling her I loved her before I walked away, getting my cell phone out of Nicky's room and going into my grandmother's completely pink room that used to be mine. Once I lay down, my mind started to wonder . . .*Why would he leave the phone here? Now how will I contact him if I want to talk to him? Where will he be staying? He must really love me if he's still not mad at me after me going to the cops on him. We have been through so much together. What will I do when he gets locked up? Will he ever want me again?*

I forced myself to look at my face in the mirror and began to cry.

"IT WILL NEVER BE THE SAME . . . IT WILL NEVER BE THE SAME AGAIN!"   ✎

Love Bites

Samantha Sarro

By many estimates, over ninety percent of women incarcerated have been sexually abused and/or assaulted in childhood. Many of the stories in our first edition of Voices brought the horror of that experience vividly and brutally to the page. In this issue, Samantha's story is the only one included that describes her own experience, though we discovered unwittingly after our choices had been made that over ninety percent of the writers in this second issue were also victims of childhood sexual abuse.

With long blonde hair and pale blue eyes, Samantha is a tall, full-bodied girl with a soft, little girl's voice. What is arresting about Samantha's piece is the seductive way she brings to the page the difficult truth of body arousal both during the abuse and as an aftermath that persists years later. Samantha worked hard on this piece, in large part as a way of protecting her own daughter from the same path.

"**I** WANT to be red!"

"Okay fine—it doesn't matter what color you are, I'm still going to win."

And what do you know, just like clockwork, he won again. He asked if I wanted to play another game because he kept winning Battleship. Of course I said yes. We always had fun together, always something new, so I was so happy to play whatever with him. Him and I were like two peas in a pod. He was so cool, plus he was the only person that lived with me that would play with me. David was like a grown-up to me because he was so much bigger and older—he was 16 and a "bad boy," stealing and lying to everyone else—but not me, we were special friends. This was the first time I ever got to play Truth or Dare with him.

"I dare you to pat your head and rub your tummy at the same time."

His turn. "I dare you to get naked."

"UH-UH."

"Consequence!"

"What's that?"

"What you have to do if you don't do your dare."

"I can't do my dare."

"Yes you can."

"But what if your mom comes?"

"She wouldn't. Come on! I'll do it too."

He tells me how pretty I am, and how much he likes how I look naked. Next thing you know, we're kissing, and he's on top of me. He gently presses his lips against mine for a long time and hugs me while doing so. I like the way he kisses me. I was told that this kind of stuff was only for husbands and wives, not friends. But David always gave me attention, so it's alright cause its him. But wait—he's kind of hurting me! I start to cry but he whispers some things in my ear and I decide to just be quiet. As soon as it started, it was over. I'm soaking wet between my thighs and a little bloody. He told me its okay. It means my body liked it. He said the pain is natural. The first few times it will hurt a little but he promises it will get better.

That was how our physical relationship began. Anytime that we were left alone or could sneak away, David and I would try more and more. Finally, one day, in the middle of the unmowed grass of the backyard, his penis made it all the way in, deep inside my five-year-old body. He told me that if I ever told anyone, nobody would ever believe me, and even if they did, I would go to jail and be taken away forever because I let him fuck me!

I have wondered for so long why I have always been so distrusting towards men yet a perverted sex fiend. It wasn't until I walked into my jail cell and saw a book on my bunky's bed concerning sexual abuse and children that I began to understand. She didn't realize the content at first and when she did she didn't want it any longer. I asked to look at it and there went my mind! I'd never received professional counseling or therapy—my mother was told by the doctors, "She'll never remember," and with her long work hours, she didn't have the time, money, or energy.

Hmmmm . . . Time, money, or energy! The youngest of five kids and all of that had been spent a long time ago. I believe that was my cue to grow at a different pace, to be a different kind of person. The kids I knew growing up never understood the subconscious longing that I had for another David in my life. I was chasing boys at the age of nine. Wow . . . that's when it all began.

It took six weeks of sitting in jail to realize the sickness I had carried beginning 21 years ago. I read the book about childhood sexual abuse that ignited such a lustful fire in my groin it made me realize just how sick my thinking is. Short stories of children being sexually abused and violated by the adult men in their lives—one story was about a nine year old girl on a camping trip with her father. She was so ecstatic about going on a trip with him and then she wound up being raped repeatedly by her Daddy throughout the course of the weekend trip. The book was filled with similar stories of the ultimate betrayal.

After reading half the book, I decide to put it down and never read it again. As a matter of fact, it's got to go! What's wrong with me? How and why is my body betraying me like this? I lay on my two-inch-thin mattress and cried enough tears to saturate my makeshift pillow of sweat suits. "God, please help me cleanse my mind, purify my heart, and take this perversion away!

The love bites on my frail body are only in places nobody gets to see, between my thighs. I liked it when he did that. He would clean up his mess so I didn't have to run into the bathroom. He was so nice—I always thought, "I will love him forever!"

"Be careful nobody sees our secret spots," he'd say.

"I will, I don't want to get in trouble."

Bath time became real fun, because I would beg to use a lot of bubbles and would always get them. One day I stayed in too long and the bubbles disappeared. JoAnna, my older sister, came to my rescue, but not without noticing the red spots between my legs.

"What is that?" she asked.

"Um—nothing . . ."

"Oh it's something! What is it?"

"I can't tell you."

"Why?" she demanded.

"'Cause I don't want to get in trouble," I whined.

"You wouldn't, just tell me!" she said sternly.

"You promise I wouldn't get in trouble?" I pleaded.

"Yes."

"David's my boyfriend and he did it, but please don't tell. He said that I'll be taken away forever!" I confessed. "Hey, why yah crying? JoJo, stop crying! Where are you going? Come back . . . why you calling Mommy? Oh no!"

I got out of the tub to find David handcuffed to the railing of the staircase. I know he's in trouble because his mother has been doing this for the past year that we have lived together—anytime he does something she doesn't like, she screams, beats him and then she hand-cuffs him to the stairs. I felt so bad; I couldn't look him in the face. I wanted my Mommy to make everything better. I wanted to hide behind her legs, but I couldn't because she was yelling, screaming about killing motherfuckers.

I have no recollection of any further events of that day but my mother said that's when I started having nightmares—I would awake, hysterically crying.

The next day, I was so nervous sitting in the examination room at the doctor's office. The unease and fear that I was going through seemed to consume me completely. The doctor came into the room and my mother and him discussed in hushed voices what I can only assume was whatever he was supposed to be confirming. He came over to me and tried to be very friendly. He told me to "get naked" and then put his fingers on my vagina. He said he "wasn't going to hurt me"—he "needed to know if someone else did." I knew he was talking about David and I was so confused. I didn't think David was hurting me, yet everyone else was saying he did a horrible thing, that he was very bad and if he did touch me "inappropriately," he was going to jail. Then this tall, hairy-faced man (a/k/a doctor) who was touching me said the words, "She was definitely penetrated." My mother broke down frantically crying. I felt so lost, so abandoned. Who did I hurt more? I didn't want to make anyone cry. Why am I such a bad person?

Immediately from there we went to the precinct so my mother could talk to the detectives. One of them was a very nice lady and she wanted to play dollies with me. I was so happy 'cause nobody ever played dollies with me. She played with two and I played with two. She said my two were David and I. She made me a little scared—everyone's been telling me how bad he was and now I'm supposed to show her what kind of friends him and I were??? It confused me but she assured me that it's okay, she is my friend, and she doesn't know David, she doesn't know if he's good or bad. Her and I played for a while and I wound up showing her mine and David's secret game. She showed me some games with her dolls but they didn't play the way I played.

My next memory is of those detectives coming to my house and arresting David, putting him in handcuffs and taking him away. That lady said she didn't hate him like everyone else, but now she's putting those same handcuffs on him that his mother does every time he's in trouble.

Moe Trouble

Tynetta King

 *It has been a year or more since we've seen Tynetta, but we remember her serious, no-nonsense persistence in getting this story written, and her hopes that in publishing, it might reach other women in an abusive relationship, offering them the courage to finally say "enough is enough." As serious as she was about her writing process, Tynetta offered us great warmth, a dry, quirky sense of humor that always brought laughter to the group, and a compassionate support for her writing companions. We send her love wherever she is.*

T HE OVERHEAD bedroom light contrasted sharply with the gaping black hole where previously a window had held the outside air at bay. Slivers and chunks of glass lay scattered on the carpet. I stared uncomprehendingly for several seconds at this destructive nightmare. It took no guesswork to know who was responsible, and with that realization, any idea I harbored about letting this latest violation of decency slide by, dissolved in anger. I had felt anger toward him before, but nothing compared to this. I believe, at that moment I truly hated him.

I left the room, slamming the door closed to keep the cold air from seeping throughout the house. Destruction had once again touched my life. I stormed down the stairs and purposefully walked to the back door to lock it—not only the bottom lock, but the safety lock for which he did not have a key. There was no point in sitting up to wait for him so I undressed and crawled into bed. I did not expect sleep to come and I was right. I lay there with my stomach tied in knots as I recounted all the previous wrongs he had inflicted on my life. I could not forget how he had torn my family apart with his behavior, nor, if I was honest with myself, could I forgive him for doing it.

After what seemed like hours, I heard the inevitable key in the door. Then knocking. I did not move. Next came the banging and then silence. Shortly, there was rapping on my bedroom window. "Tynetta, Tynetta, are you awake? It's Moe. Let me in! The door's locked."

Let him in! God, how many times had I threatened not to let him in. But, in the end, I had always relented just one more time. This time, however, I felt no softening towards him, only that hard knot of anger in the pit of my stomach.

"Go away! Spend the night with one of your abusive friends. I've warned you time and again what was going to happen if this continued. You are not coming into this house tonight."

"Aw, Tynetta, come on! Let me in . . . I can explain."

More pleading. When I didn't respond I could hear his footsteps crunch on the gravel as he returned to the back door, which he proceeded to beat and kick, all the while cursing loudly. My poor neighbors!

I threw back the covers and grabbed my robe. Why couldn't he get it into his fucking head that he wasn't coming in? But, then, why should he? We had played out this scene a hundred times and he always ended up sleeping in my bed.

"You are not coming in. I don't care if you beat on the door all night. Come back tomorrow when you calm down and we'll talk."

"God damn you, bitch, let me in or I'll break down the door!" By now, he was doing his best to match his actions to his words. He kicked the door so violently that the metal frame started to bend inward. What did he care that it was a new energy-efficient door installed only two months ago. He was breaking it apart like he broke the upstairs window, like he broke my foot, like he broke so many other things, including my heart.

I couldn't stand to watch as the frame slowly caved toward me, so I returned to the kitchen. The clock showed 2:12 AM. I walked over to the wall telephone and dialed. The refrain "Light up your life with a call to someone you love" kept running through my mind as I listened to the background cursing and hammering. My brother Shabazz answered with a sleepy hello. I felt a stirring of resentment toward him that he could sleep while my world was once again fall-ing apart.

"Moe is at the back door kicking and pounding on it. I'm afraid he'll break it down. I don't want him in here. He's in a rage. Can you please come?"

"I'll be there in five minutes."

I replaced the receiver and returned to my side of the door. "Moe, you better leave. I called Shabazz and he'll be here in a minute."

"This is *my* house. Let me in!"

After what seemed an eternity, the noise stopped and I heard a car door slam and then there was silence. I ran into the living room and pulled the curtain aside to look out. Moe's car was gone. I felt a rush of relief and gratefully slid into a chair to wait for Shabazz to arrive. It was so quiet I could hear the clock as it ticked off the pass-ing minutes. How could one person bring such chaos into my life? The next thing I was aware of was a car pulling into the driveway. Shabazz had arrived. I undid the safety lock and tried to pull open the door, but it would not budge. "Come around to the front door Shabazz, I can't get this one open." Once again I walked through the kitchen and living room.

"Where is Moe?"

"I don't know. He left in his car just after I called you."

"Tynetta, you better call the police. He's going to end up killing you."

"I know I should, but how can I call the police on someone I love?" Those words expressed the unspoken thoughts that had run through my mind from the start of the trouble with Moe. If you love someone how can you turn against them? Wouldn't I be a fucked up girlfriend? Dare I take the first step off the cliff of no return?

Shabazz must have read my thoughts. "Tynetta, why don't you make me a cup of coffee, then call the police. I know it's hard to do this to your boyfriend. But listen to this old voice of experience. Remember, I've been there. Until you make him responsible for his own actions, he will continue to do this. How long has it been going on now in spite of all your attempts to cope with it?"

I knew what he said was true. God knows I had pleaded and threatened. Moe in turn had made promise after promise . . . all broken. My thoughts flashed to the broken window upstairs and I thought, "How much is enough?" How many times would I have to look in the mirror and see my face swollen, eye closed, or my lip busted. Even his handprint around my throat. How much can the heart endure before enough is enough? Before I could change my mind, I walked over to the telephone and dialed 911.

"Suffolk Police Department," a voice answered, followed by two clicks, which meant I was being recorded. I took a deep breath.

"This is Tynetta King calling. My boyfriend has vandalized my house and abused me." Once I started in it wasn't so hard. No shocked disapproval from the dispatcher as she continued to question me. She asked for the license number, color and make of the car, and the direction he was headed when leaving the house. She told me they would put out a bulletin. If he should return home, she requested I call them back. All so routine. As though her words were a magnet drawing Moe home, his car raced into the yard and I could hear the screech of brakes and then the slam of a door. Oh boy, here we go again.

Shabazz, who should have known better, walked out into the yard with his cup of coffee to talk to Moe. I could hear Shabazz speaking but couldn't make out the words. Moe's much louder response I had no trouble hearing. "Fuck you, you can't tell me what to do, you are not my father. My father's dead. You're nobody!"

Shabazz's low voice once again, and then Moe. "I'll fight you! I don't care how big you are!" With that Moe knocked the coffee cup out of Shabazz's hand. Having shown Shabazz how tough he was, he then walked over to his car, got in and burned rubber as he left the yard. This time I noticed which direction he went. I didn't need Shabazz to tell me what to do. I picked up the telephone. It was not fifteen minutes later, as I sat at the kitchen table holding a cup of untouched coffee, that the telephone rang. The dispatcher's noncommittal voice spoke to me. "Your boyfriend has been picked up. He was traveling 75 miles per hour when stopped. He refused to give any information. Can you please come to 109 first precinct and make your statement?"

As the seconds ticked by, I knew my next words would determine the direction my life would take—and Moe's life as well. Things could never be the same again. After six painful years, for better or worse, we had reached the turning point. ✎

No More . . . No More!

Janine Matteo

As we guide each woman towards an opening that will be the most powerful for the "Stranger/Reader," and help to propel the story forward, we give equal permission to begin with those most traumatic events or to find unexpected drama in seemingly small moments. Janine's first pages, which precede this selection, detail a painful abduction and gang rape at the age of twenty-one, when she was left for dead in the shallows of a lake. Once discharged from the hospital to the care of her abusive boyfriend "C," he has insisted on sex against her doctor's advice, resulting in a second hospitalization. Now she is home again . . .

In writing this story Janine is taking an intense look at what she's gone through—and as some of her past trauma lifts up off of her so has her relationship with her current partner and family members become more open and loving.

Janine has a long history of both physical and mental disorders. She has epilepsy for which she is heavily medicated and still she regularly experiences grand mal seizures in her cell from which she often sustains injuries. In spite of whatever condition she is in, she manages to write and to faithfully come to class.

AS THE WEEKS went by I slowly got better physically, but definitely not mentally. Every night I would have flashbacks and wake up out of a dream screaming and pleading for my life in a cold sweat. During the day while I was out I would swear I'd see their faces in a crowd. This prevented me from wanting to leave the house. I knew that C's friends all told me not to worry, that they (the men) were taken care of and would never be around again to hurt me. I knew what that meant but still questioned it because I hadn't seen it for myself. And at times I wished I could see someone hurting them the way they had hurt me. I wanted to see their faces scream in pain and horror as I did the night they brutally raped me.

Sex for me was out of the question. Whenever I tried to sleep, all I could think of or see in my head were those three guys viciously attacking me, and C, the night after I'd been discharged , forcing himself on me causing me more physical damage. I kept a knife under my pillow for protection which could have been dangerous knowing how C was when he got drunk. I could have killed him. Every time he mentioned sex I would turn him off immediately. Although I was healing nicely, I couldn't stand the thought of a man being inside of me or touching me. I couldn't sleep close to him or have him hold me. I would cringe and shiver every time he came to bed. I was grateful he wasn't pushing sex on me after that first experience we had where I'd ended up back at the hospital. I knew he was out there getting it from someone else because he didn't go a day without it and always had numerous women, but at that time I just didn't seem to care.

One night as I was sleeping, he approached me without my knowledge. I grabbed the knife instantly and swung it at him. His eyes were big and fiery and I thought for sure he would beat me for what I had just done but I didn't care. If he came any closer to me I think I would have tried to stab him. He grabbed the knife out of my hand so quickly and looked at me like I was crazy. At that moment I felt crazy. I wanted to stab him for what he and every other man had done to me all my life. He was mad and called me a stupid bitch. But for some reason he didn't hit me. I think, for a minute he realized a little of what I was going through and stopped himself. He told me I had to get help or he would have me committed. I don't want help, I thought. I want to die.

Thoughts would constantly run through my head on how I could go about committing suicide. It got so bad, that was all I thought about. I finally agreed to go to a psychiatrist, but never told anyone I was suicidal. They put me on Ativan for anxiety and Halcion to help me sleep. Perfect, I thought, just what I needed to complete my plan.

I waited for just the right day. It was a bright sunny day and C was a landscaper so I knew he would be at work until late that night. While C was in the shower I slipped a $50 bill out of his wallet. I knew he would realize it later but by then I thought it wouldn't matter. I kissed him goodbye and as soon as the door closed, I was calling every dealer I knew to get whichever one would come the fastest.

Finally, a knock at the door. I could feel the flutter in my stomach already. I opened the door and there he was. "Hey Baby," he said. "How are you doing?"

"Alright," I replied, "but could be better—and now, thanks to you, I will be."

He just shook his head. He came in and we talked as he served me. I had known him for a couple of years and used to have a crush on him. If you could ever consider a dealer your friend, he was one. He always came through when I needed something, and not just drugs. He handed me what was at the time a $100 piece of crack for the $50 and we kissed goodbye and he left.

I was sitting there enjoying my high when the phone rang. I answered it.

"Jeanine, where the fuck is my $50?" I heard. Busted.

"What $50?" I said.

"I had $250 in my wallet and when I went to buy breakfast there was only $200."

"I don't know what you're talking about."

"Alright, bitch, I'll see you when I get home tonight!" And he hung up abruptly. Normally I'd be so scared knowing what was coming for me when he got home, but this time it didn't bother me because of my plan. I continued to sit on my bed enjoying my high and playing with my dog Chubby. When the drugs were almost gone I got up and got a huge pitcher of juice and a cup and sat back down. I reached for my medicine bottles and poured both of them on the bed. I started grabbing about ten pills at a time and putting them in my mouth and swallowing. My wish was going to come true. I continued hitting my crack pipe and swallowing pills until the next thing I knew, all the pills were gone. One hundred and twenty pills swallowed just that fast. I was upstairs on my bed and had just finished my last hit of crack. The room started closing in on me and I got very dizzy as I lay back and closed my eyes.

The next thing I knew I woke up in the hospital a few days later with tubes down my throat, trying to kick and scream, but I was tied down and couldn't scream because of the tubes. Later C told me that a huge storm had rolled in while he was working and it had poured hail like rain. After a while his boss had decided it wasn't going to clear up and sent them all home. C walked through the front door the same time my heart stopped beating. He was screaming and calling 911 when a neighbor came and started CPR.

I was in a coma for a few days and then woke up very angry. I kept saying to God, "Why did you bring me back? Why do you continue to punish me? I don't want to live anymore!"

I was kept in a psychiatric ward for several weeks until finally I convinced the doctors I wouldn't try to hurt myself again. So I was released to go home, a place I loved and hated to be at the same time, knowing damn well inside, I'd keep trying until I got it right.

A letter to Janine Matteo from her niece, 2007

AG,

    I love you. I want those words to be the beginning and the end for you. When they wake you for bed check, I love you. When they call for lights out, I love you. During the wee in-between hours with your scattered photos hanging above, I love you. Keep this with you—in your heart, in your pocket, wherever you keep your most treasured thoughts and certainties. Keep it with you as you read each line, trying to recall my face and voice exactly. Keep it close as your heart aches and rages and swells. Keep it as your one real truth, and let IT keep YOU safe.

    Put this aside for now, if you'd like. Let that sink in, till you feel it in the marrow of your bones. Walk away for a while—a day, a week, a minute—read it over and over, till you've committed it to memory. It may not be as easy as you think. In all of time, no other three words have held such meaning, been evocative of such power. Let this be, from me to you, forever — I LOVE YOU.

    Go on, take a break. I'll be here when you're ready.

    Pinky swear.

✳ ✳ ✳

    Welcome back. I still love you. Are you ready?

    Clear your mind. Focus on the letters, the text, the paper, until it all blurs and comes back into focus. The edges of these papers are now your temporary universe. Nothing, NOTHING exists outside of it. It's just you and me, AG. So let's talk.

    There are things we have, you and I . . . things that are ours alone, made all the more precious in their rarity. Things that will always be part of us. Things like . . .

    Driving to the beach with the top down. Music's playing, gulls are yapping, the pavement below us gives way to crunching dirt and stones. The smell of the vinyl interior is overcome with salt and suntan lotion. The sky is so startlingly blue it makes the water look black . . .

    Being so miserably sick, barely having enough energy to roll over and vomit. My only solace is with you, sitting on that huge red couch, eating orange flavored sherbet and watching Disney movies . . .

Swimming, racing, wrestling in Grandma's pool. The chlorine's so thick the water is cloudy and dim. Timeless, endless cannonballs off the deck, splashing out as much water as we could before Poppi bellows at us from the porch . . .

Our laughter. YOUR laughter. I could live a hundred years and never hear a laugh more moving or sincere. A chorus of joy that could brighten the darkest hour. The only voice louder than Aunt Jen's. A sound that inspired. You laughed with your whole soul.

These things are ours. OURS. Forever. No amount of evil can take them from us.

But those are not the only things we have.

Asking the family where you've been. Having their eyes darken, their voices hush, as they search for a pained excuse.

Meeting strange men, strange friends. Feeling watched, guarded and uncomfortable.

Seeing the flame of your eyes start to flicker and burn out. Watching myself become less important in them.

That terrible morning after leaving my life savings in the mailbox, when I learned your secret. Having Mom slide money across the table and explain to me how I naively paid for your drugs. Having never before cried so bitterly.

Now, as I write this, crying with similar grief. Knowing that all my love cannot save you.

It occurs to me now that I'm speaking to you as if you're dead. As though I'm writing a eulogy. But you're not dead. Far from it. You may FEEL dead — you may even wish for death — but it's not over. And if He and His pale horse came for you now, you'd have nothing to leave behind you but sorrow and regret.

I don't consider myself a religious person. The Catholicism I was raised on never took firm hold of my flesh. But I do believe in Hell. Not the place or its purpose in popular mythology. Hell is real. Hell is every sleepless night this family has endured worrying for you. Not being able to solve your problems for you. Not being able to see you or hug you or laugh with you as we once did.

And Hell could be where you are now . . . but it needn't be so. I have another memory for you.

Driving again—in my car, this time, coming home from one of our many family functions. Your smile was wide, your laughter rich. Your eyes were bright, fully ablaze, and thoughtful. You were remembering as we are now. Remembering your life—the good, the bad, the hazy gray middles—and you asked me about a book. Your book. You wanted to write your memoirs. You wanted to remember, and have others learn, and you asked to share it with me. To have me write it with you. What did I say? Do you remember that?

Give me your heart and I will lend you my mind. Lend me your every scattered memory and I will string them together and make them beautiful. Together we would do this, another special thing, but this thing would be bigger. Would OUTLAST us. This would last, truly, forever.

The offer still stands, AG.

What will you do with your long, empty days? What will you do between bed check, roll call, meal times, and the quite hours in the semi-dark with your photographs? Use those moments. Use them—fill them. Make them meaningful. Write those memoirs. Write down anything—good, bad, old, new. Notes. Scribbles. Poems. ANYTHING. Keep them together. If you fear for their safety, send them to me. Write a book. Write a page. Write fifty pages and tear them into mulch. Ask me to mail you some blank pages, if you wish.

Think of who you are. Think of yourself as I see you. Warm. Bright. Smiling. Beautiful. Think of how I'm with you every day, missing you. Write, don't write, do what you will, but DO NOT LOSE YOURSELF. You've been lost in the dark too many times for too damn long.

Look about you now. That tiny four-cornered universe has grown exponentially. The walls and bars can only hold your body. Your mind and heart cannot be bound by such things. They are free. FREE. Free to do with what you will. Not what guns or drugs or pushers or dirtbags or anyone else wants with them.

And part of you is always here, with me. And I'm sad. And I'm angry. And I miss you. And I'm sorry. And I love you.

Melissa

Anonymous Letters

THE FOLLOWING two letters were written by the same woman who has survived both the abuse of a "step-dad," described in the first letter, and then the suicide death of her mother a few years later. The author prefers to remain anonymous as long as her abuser still lives and breathes, even if still behind bars—such are the nightmares both waking and sleeping that still haunt her. After she "told" on her abuser, the author was abandoned by the mother she adored (who chose to stay with the step-dad), and later, when finally re-united, watched her lose her life to drugs. In writing these letters she feels she has re-claimed a part of herself lost many years ago.

Letter to a "step-dad"

Dear ———,

Well, it certainly has been a long time hasn't it? 13 years to be exact and I hope that yours have been filled with as much pain and shame as mine have. This letter may be to you, but it's really for me. Even if it never gets sent I feel the need to get these thoughts and feelings off of my chest. Who knows? Maybe if I write these things down, I can finally be free! So, how's prison treating you? I heard that they had to stitch up your asshole the last time you were in general population. Just so you know, the mental image of you being tortured and tormented brings a smile to my face! Did it hurt or did you like it? Being the sick and twisted fuck that you are, you probably enjoyed being sodomized! I hope they left you powerless and ashamed. Tell me, did you scream as loud as I did the first time you penetrated me? Did you bleed as much as I did when you viciously ripped my 7 year old anus to shreds? Did you have to wear a Kotex over your asshole like I did? I wonder if you'll have hemorrhoids for the rest of your life like I do.

I want you to know that you have absolutely no power over me! I was a sweet and innocent child and you took that away from me! You had no fucking right! You were supposed to be the father I never had but instead you turned into the heinous monster that I wish would've never crossed my path. Not only did you hurt me, but you hurt my mother as well! You took away the only family that I ever knew! You destroyed my relationship with the only person who loved me unconditionally. She never did look at me the same, or herself even for that matter.

Before I go on, I have to know, what makes a man, who has a beautiful wife, take advantage of her only child? For years, I thought that there was something wrong with me. That somehow I provoked you or led you on. It took years for me to realize that the problem lies within you. I let you get away with the abuse because in my child-like mind I somehow thought that I would get in trouble with you. The worst part is that I believed you when you said that you would tell my mother if I told. I guess in my childish ignorance, I believed that somehow I was protecting her by enduring your brutality. So, not only did you hurt me, but you hurt my mother as well! And at the end of it all, I couldn't protect her from herself. You should know that she spent years smoking crack and trying to erase the damage that you did. I know that deep down she blamed herself for not knowing as much as I blamed myself for not telling sooner. Ultimately, she committed suicide to end her pain, mental anguish, and physical suffering. But I am here to tell you that the strong survive. I am the living and breathing proof of that. I am that much more determined to succeed, even if it's only to prove you wrong. Because of all the things you put me through, I spent most of my youth abusing my body and trying to numb the pain. Today, by the grace of God, I have realized that I have more to offer to this world than what's between my legs. I bet you thought you broke me, didn't you? You thought wrong! All you did was make me stronger. All you did was prove to me that I am a survivor and I have the strength to endure just about anything. So, in a crazy kind of way, maybe I should thank you? Yeah, right! But I will thank God for carrying me when I could not stand alone and for giving me strength when I was weary. I endured the savage beatings and the brutal sexual assaults over the years, but it made me resilient. It made my skin thick! You were trying to ruin me, but you couldn't break me! I did not, and will not allow you to get the best of me. On the contrary, the best has yet to come! I can't say that I forgive you because I'm not there yet. As I grow with God, he will have to put forgiveness in my heart for you. It won't come easily, but all things are possible through Christ who strengthens me!

I will end this by telling you that one of the greatest achievements I have made so far is putting you behind bars. I sleep well at night knowing that you will never get another opportunity to steal anyone else's innocence! Don't ever forget that what goes around comes back around! You reap what you sow, and with that being said, I pray that God may have mercy on your soul!

Letter to Mom

Dear Mom,

It's been 2 years since the day you selfishly decided to end your life! I've spent 3 birthdays and 3 Mother's Days without you and it has been far from easy. That day was the hardest day of my life. Sometimes my dreams lead me back to that day. Seeing you lying on the floor, motionless and cold is an image that will haunt me forever! I will never understand why you made the choice you made but it was yours to make. When you called that morning, you could've left a message. You could've even written me a letter. Why Mom, why did you leave me? Why did you give up on life? Even though I'm upset with you, I miss you everyday. You'll never meet my husband, you'll never see your grandchildren, and now here I am sitting in jail, needing you now more than ever and you're gone! What drove you to do it, huh? What pushed you to the point of no return? Did you call upon Jesus in your final moments? Did you think of me? Or were you too busy being selfish and thinking of your own pain! I wish you were here. I need you, didn't you know that? Even though I might not have always wanted you, I'm always gonna need my mother. Do you blame me? Did you do it just to spite me for not serving you? If I would've taken the pills from you, would you have found another way? I thought you were happy, why couldn't you talk to me? I would've helped you. I would've done everything I could for you! But now, you're gone and I'm left with all these unanswered questions! I miss the sparkle in your eyes, the brightness of your smile, and the smell of your hair against my face. I just miss you and no one will ever be able to take your place. You died thinking I was a crack- selling, coke- sniffing, unemployed failure. By the time I got a job and went to school it was too late. Now I'm an ex-crack selling convicted felon and I'm headed to divorce court. And all I need is you! Thanks Mom for always managing to disappear when I need you the most!

PARENTS AND CHILDREN

O UR LARGEST SELECTION of work, these pieces speak to the hopes and prayers, the devotion and the failures of parents and children—mostly, in this case, mothers and daughters. Each of these pieces brims with the heartache of loving, or of wanting love, or of begging forgiveness or attention from those most central relationships. As you will hear so vividly in these stories, these bonds are the vortex around which everything else revolves. We know you will hear your own voice and find your own heart expressed in many of their powerful offerings.

By lowest estimates, 80,000 children in New York State have a parent in prison. Over 5000 of these children have a mother incarcerated. As the vast majority of these mothers (over 80%) are both first-time felony offenders and are convicted of non-violent crimes (mostly related to drugs), we again have to question the wisdom of such "correctional" methods. How many permanently fractured families result from such a system? And while foster care can be a blessing to many (given the rates of incarceration), it can also be a curse, as these are very often the homes described by our women where they were most abused and unloved.

We hope that by the time you have visited with these women, with all of the women writers in this journal, you will question this system of harsh and hugely costly sentencing and family separation.

I, Me, Who Is Thee?

Ricarda Renee Diamond

A coffee-skinned, green-eyed, Muslim beauty, Renee enters a room with the grace and reserve of a queen. It is hard to imagine that she has lived her early years as a child making her own way on the streets by the age of eleven. When she first began to write with us and witnessed how powerfully her words affected others, she asked us one night after class, "Do you think I really could write my story? I've never thought, never believed I could do anything but sell crack for a living because that is all I've ever done."

Renee never smoked crack, but she successfully built a life on that income and a home for her children until she lost it all. One night during Black History Month, while incarcerated in RCF, she watched other women inmates perform in a talent show. She saw how much intelligence and potential was locked up in the jail alongside her and realized that, as a crack dealer, she had helped to put them there. Later she came to us and said, "When I go home I don't have to sell drugs for a living . . . I'm going to go to college. I can write!"

THE WEATHER was beautiful. The sunrays were shining upon my face, leaving school after a good day. The weather only added to the goodness of the day. After saying Hello to the bus driver, I headed to the back of the bus. The last seat was my regular. Looking out the window I began to think of how excited I was to be going to the doctor's with my mom. I loved going places with Mommy, wherever it might be. I was just grateful for the time with her.

Heading off the bus saying goodbye to the driver, "Hey, Ma," I greeted her with a hug. Mommy always walked me to and from the bus stop.

Looking at Mommy standing there with her pink pretty summer
flower dress on, her sea blue eyes and her pale white skin, she was
really pretty.

She placed a soft kiss on my forehead. "Hey Bambino," her voice
very low and sweet and motherly. She took my book bag and we
headed home, or should I say to the house.

Before we headed to the doctor's, Mommy called for Tia to come
from her bedroom. "Tia, come in here for a minute, Baby." Tia is
my older and only sister. She had two babies of her own at this point
already. Mommy started to speak: "Tia and Mommy's Bambino, I
love you two with all my heart. Mommy's health isn't good. So if
something were to happen to me, promise to always stick together."
With that said, me and Mommy were off to the doctors . . . her not
realizing the promise wasn't ever really made.

Mommy checked in at the window. I headed for the magazines.
All of the nurses knew me by name. They adored me. Mommy asked
Nurse Mary to watch over me for a moment, as she proceeded to the
examination room.

As I was reading the magazine my mind began to wander. I
found no more interest in the magazine. I placed it back on the
table. I entered a daze, my mind taking me back to what Mommy
said. *If anything were to happen to me.* Starting to reflect on all the
regular trips to the doctors, my stomach got an instant knot.

My daze was broken by Mommy reaching for my hand. In the
car Mommy didn't look at me once or utter a single word. Silence
along with worry filled the car. By the time we reached the driveway, Mommy's tears were nonstop and her pain very obvious. I began to cry along with Mommy, her pain instantly became mine.

We entered the house. I did as I was told. I went into my bedroom, even though I yearned to just be held by Mommy and fall
asleep to the melody of her heartbeat. I turned my TV on as low as
possible. I listened to Mommy telling Tia she is very sick . . . "Tia,
the doctors have informed me that I have AIDS along with a form
of cancer. Tia, I don't believe that I have much longer." At 11 years
old I'm unaware of what cancer or AIDS is. But I'm aware that it is
killing my Mom. This is the one condition in life I never grew an
understanding of . . . for love to equal pain.

Their voices faded and recent good memories escaped my mental
index, replaced with bad ones . . . rather heart aching horrible ones,
my first flashback hitting me. My mental is taking me back to when

I was about seven years old. That was the first time I found a dirty needle—my enemy. Myself along with the other children are jumping on the bed, playing around. I'd rather be eating dinner, along with getting attention from Carole (Mommy), but her and company are in the living room "doing what grown folks do" like always.

On the very last jump is when I saw this needle along with what appeared to be a huge rubber band. Looking back now I ask myself, Is this why Mommy was always napping? Is this the reason I was always in harm's way? Here was the answer to my many questions. My tears flowed and my physical was filled with rage . . .

This year goes by so fast. It seems as quick as a blink of an eye. Mommy is in and out of the hospital, CPS is a regular. It's routine for me to enter various foster homes as she enters the hospital, me being put in harm's way again and again. Tired of being violated in the wee hours of the night by "foster dad," tired of being beat by "foster mom," I decide that I'm going to make do on my own. I won't hurt myself. Me is all I have. I have to take care of me; after all Child "Protective" Services isn't protecting me.

Now school is a faded memory. Smoking weed is a part of my everyday.

I have been watching Tia's kids' father along with other older cats. I was extremely observant of their actions in the drug game. Tired of being hungry, needing and wanting, I was ready to put thought into action, getting money that is. I recall walking in the kitchen, the smell smacking me in my face, smelling as if nail polish remover is cooking. All the other females in the house are in the living room speaking on hair, nails, men. That girly stuff is of no interest to me. My interest is in here in the kitchen with the older cats. I grabbed a mask and joined Poppy at the stove.

"What's this, coke?"

"Yeah, but it won't be in a minute. It'll be crack. It's money and power in this pot."

"Let me stir it. Show me how to do it." Poppy shows me what I think is magic. Whipping the coke around in the pot made me feel like a natural chef. I learned how to do so in minutes as if I was born to do it. Taking the pot off the stove, placing it under cold running water, zoning into the water. It felt as if it was only me and the crack in the room. Thinking of all the moves I needed to make to be on.

"Poppy, let me borrow a pack."

"Alright, but slow down, let me dry it and show you how to cut it."

"Good looking out, Poppy."

"Alright, be careful out there, Shorty."

With that said I was on my bike headed to the "block."

I'm moving like a grown woman but at the same time thinking like a wounded child. This silent killer called AIDS has attacked my mother. Mommy cannot speak now nor can she walk—she has gone into a stage of a baby mentally as well as physically.

In between shifts on the block I go tend to Mommy. I bathe her, change her diapers and brush what is left of her pretty blond hair. It makes me feel good to help her but helpless cause I can't cure her. My wishful thinking tells me that the more crack I sell the better chances are for me to heal her.

Mommy points to the wheelchair. She directs me to the kitchen. Mommy desires so badly to be my mother. She wants to cook a meal for her "bambino." The heart wrenching truth is that she doesn't remember how. She is not mentally or physically capable of doing so. She sits in front of the stove, her head hanging low in shame. Her pretty sea blue eyes crying an ocean. Her heart is shattered along with mine. I'm unable to think of any words of comfort. The pain in my heart seals my mouth. I lay Mommy down, tucking her in, I lie beside her as close as our two bodies can get. As sickly as Mommy is, she still smells the same . . . good and sweet. My body so tired from being up for days, my mind racing beyond the limits won't allow me to sleep.

I am a child turned warrior all before my 12th birthday. There is a child captured and held prisoner inside this woman that wants to be free. This child wants to play with dolls, jump rope and go to school. This woman has to sell this pack out to survive.

I'm tired as hell, but have nowhere to go. I go to Ms. Lucy's house to get a few hours of sleep. It's a hot spot so of course I won't be completely asleep . . . one eye must always be open.

Back outside to the block. The fiends are coming so the bread is flowing. The block is moving smooth today, no arguing over sells and no blue and whites patrolling. It was August 31, 1993. The day was going okay . . . sitting on the step with my glass of Remy with some cats on the block, Uncle Ricky walks up to us. No one from the family ever comes to look for me. Before Uncle Ricky could say it I knew it. The glass left my hand. It shattered everywhere.

"Damn, Renee! What's up with you?"

I can see their mouths moving but I can't hear a word. I asked Uncle Ricky not to say what I already know.

"Uncle Ricky, please, let's just get in the car."

By the time me, Tia and Uncle Ricky reached the hospital to view Mommy's body we were told it was too late. Looking at this woman in her white nurse's uniform, my blood boiled. "What the fuck do you mean it's too late to see my mother? It's my mother!"

"It's too late. It's too late . . . " is all I keep hearing.

My vision is blurry, my chest is so tight, thought pattern cloudy, "Why? Why me . . . " is the question I'm asking this life that I'm in . . . "Mommy please, I just want to be your 'bambino'" is what I'm crying out. "Mommy please! I have something to tell you!"

The very next time I held my mother was in a white box that contained her beings. These last few days have been filled with un-bearable pain, wounds to my soul that cannot be healed. The pain along with being lost causes me to self destruct, to search for com-fort, except it's in all the wrong places . . . on the block selling crack and inside the arms of men old enough to be my father, with end results being still no direction, and my physical being used for all the wrong reasons.

Talking to this dude by the name of God, figuring maybe he do exist, he just forgot that I exist, too. "God, why was I given life? I'm not living. Who are you? Where are you? Where were you when I was being raped, when my innocence was stolen, when I was hun-gry and cold? Where are you now that I have no one? I only want to simply be loved." I need a hug after crying out and still not receiving comfort from this dude that everyone glorifies. "Yeah I didn't think you were up there. I'm on the way to my Mommy's funeral. You could at least come with me."

While entering the funeral home I don't know if I'm depressed, angry, or both. As I approach the white box which contains Mommy's ashes, there is a picture of Mommy on top. She was in her mid-twenties and her beauty was flawless, breathtaking . . . looking into this picture my physical cried quietly while my inner beings screamed out loud.

The service was very short. Only about six chairs were filled. After all, no one wanted to arrange it.

As I'm leaving the service I receive a tap on my shoulder. It's Ms. Harris, the woman who's supposed to be my grandmother.

"Here she is." She's handing me my mother in a damn box.

I couldn't get 'Grandma" to roll off my tongue. "Ms. Harris, I don't have anywhere to bring my mother."

"Well, if I take her now, I take her for good."

"Can you please just hold her until I get a respectable place to bring her?"

"No, I cannot. If you wasn't out there selling drugs, you would have somewhere to bring her."

I'm thinking to myself, The nerve of this bitch. She don't feed me. She won't be my grandmother. "You know what, lady? I don't have an argument in me. You're right. Keep her. She was never mine. Goodbye, Grandma."

From that moment on when I didn't even receive a hug from 'grandma, wasn't offered a place to live, or this nigger George, my "dad" didn't show up to be my father, I knew that this shit was real, that there was no turning back. This is when I was forced to be an adult, forced to put the little scared child in me to rest.

This was the very beginning of my addiction to this game . . . selling drugs, with a weight on my shoulders as heavy as a ton of bricks. I was headed from my mother's funeral to the hood. I needed comfort, whether it be from fiends, spending their money, or men twice my age. I was empty. Sitting on the stoop making sells, smoking a blunt and thinking on everything that had taken place in my 11 years on earth, I'm thinking, "Now what . . . ?"

October 20, 1993, my twelfth birthday. Nothing is happy about it. Another day in hell on earth. I'm a runaway from CPS, no mother, no father, no nobody. Birthday . . . hell, why would I celebrate the day Ricarda Renee Diamond was born? Let me roll another blunt . . . I'm thinking too damn much.

I'm twisted, trying to hold my composure so I can get this money. I'm filling a grown woman's shoes but as I'm on the block I'm wishing I could be home, playing with the neighborhood kids, singing "Happy Birthday," blowing out candles on my birthday cake. Instead it's only about 3 PM. I'm drunk and high as hell, posted on the block, selling crack with all these grown ass niggas. Happy 12th fucking birthday.

Waking up with the worst hangover, realizing where I'm at . . . the porch of a crack spot. My first instinct, as always, is to check my pockets and my panties for my pack. Something within me this morning wants to go see the house that I can't label home anymore. Riding up on the bike, I paused . . . the sight of the house made every hair on my body stand at attention. Once I worked up the nerve, I entered the house, looking around at what was once a beautiful three bedroom home which was so beautifully kept by Mommy. Now it's deserted and filled with pain and agony. Entering Mommy's bedroom that was once fit for a queen made me drop to my knees. From the emptiness of the house I can hear my cries bouncing off the walls. Memories started to invade my mind. I hear the laughter and the cries that once shaped this place. I see the lights blinking from the Christmas tree. I hear Mommy singing as the aroma from her home-cooked meals filled the air. My chance has been taken away. I will never be able to tell Mommy those three very important words, "I love you."

Looking around one last time, locking and closing the door to my home forever, along with locking and closing my heart. No one is allowed inside. Emptiness fills both.

Running the streets, running from reality, has become so exhausting. But I'm lost. I don't know what to do or where to go. Foster care is unsafe and these streets are cold.

Shit, Renee. What are you going to do now???

Excerpt #1 from
Windows and Prayers

Delia "Dee" Ahlstrand

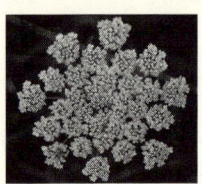

Scattered throughout the journal you will encounter a variety of short pieces by several authors. Some of these will be from the Windows and Prayers *written by Dee, who often was inspired to write while looking out of the various windows of her incarceration. A firefly wearing a worn-out soul, Dee was shy and tentative about her work in the beginning, rarely willing to read aloud. After some weeks, she began to make these offerings aloud to the rest of the group, and grew in confidence as she did so. Some of her prayers have been answered since her release—her reunification with her children, her maintained sobriety, and her completion of a college degree.*

September 10, 2008

HOW IRONIC . . . I'm sitting at a window praying to God. It is so familiar. Always praying at a window. It is such a beautiful day, a slight breeze in the air, sun still shining warm, but not too warm. Hoping some of my prayers will be answered today, that I have prayed for so many times before. Actually just one prayer—to see and/or speak to my children.

Yesterday I shared on how angry I was toward so many people. Today we spoke and read about resentment and Marion asked who has resentment? I immediately raised my hand and quickly said, "I DO!" loud and clear. She said that was great, that I admitted it, especially after what I'd shared the previous day. She said I was being "humble" . . . it felt great, like growth. I am very proud of myself. Thank you God for answering one of my prayers.

Birth of Destiny

Cara Mugavero

Many women choose to write about the birth of a child as a peak experience, but few can draw the reader into that experience effectively. Like many of the women in jail, Cara is faced with repeating the patterns of drug-addicted, dysfunctional parents, a story she artfully weaves through the telling of the birth of her first child, Destiny. In doing so, she has chosen to face her demons directly. Her stated determination to become a better mother has put her on the path of writing "her own treatment plan," which included her long-awaited participation in the DWI program at Yaphank. With the abundance of support there, she feels ready to look even more deeply into the harder parts of her story.

As we were unable to raise the supplemental funding to keep the Yaphank program going at the time of her transfer, we have included her letter of farewell to us so that you can hear in her own words how this work has helped her.

"**M**UGAVERO . . . Medical!" I hear the officer shout. I quickly get dressed and yell back, "I'm ready! Open 6." As I wait for the elevator I wonder what this is about. Maybe they're finally calling me for a sick call that I put my name on a month ago. The elevator pops open and snaps me out of my thoughts. I get in and the door closes. The elevator descends . . . 4, 3, 2, 1.

"NAME."

"Mugavero."

"You're here to see the midwife. Have a seat."

Midwife? I think to myself. What the hell is a midwife? Still not thinking much of it, I take a seat on the wooden bench. After a few minutes I hear my name called from the back.

"Hi, Cara," says a bright and cheery woman.

"Hello," I reply. But the look on my face must say something different because she wrinkles her forehead and asks, "Do you have any idea why you're here?"

"No."

"Okay, well your pregnancy test came back positive. When was your last period?"

"Come to think of it, I'm a few weeks late. With everything else going on I didn't even realize it." Tears well up as I begin to process the information I have just received. I feel a wave of emotions all at once. Happy, sad, excited, nervous, anxious, and I'm sure there's a bunch more I forgot. I give the midwife the date of my last period which was the first or second week in November. It's now the end of December and she gives me an estimated date of delivery of August 28, 2003.

"I put you on pre-natal vitamins, doubled your meal portions, and added a late night snack. Congratulations." And that was the last thing she said before rising from her seat. That was my signal that it was time for me to leave.

I called my mom to let her know I had been sentenced to a 1–3 and that I should be going upstate within 14 days. My stepfather answered the phone and told me that she was in the hospital and that she had overdosed.

"Is she okay? Is she alive?"

Alan told me that she was okay. The medics had gotten there in time. I pictured my mother lying there like Uma Thurman in *Pulp Fiction*, turning blue, foaming out of the mouth and having to get a shot of Narcan straight to the heart. It broke my heart. I silently thanked God for sparing her life. Alan told me that he would let her know I'd called. He was great and I knew in my heart that he loved her and he was doing everything he could to keep her safe. I didn't blame him. I knew that she was the one that had turned him on to the dope and that now they were just caught up. I had to remember that I wasn't that far removed from it all myself, and that only a year earlier it could have been me. I told him I'd be in touch and hung up the phone. I felt like my whole world was caving in on me and I didn't know what to do. And now it was only a matter of time before I'd be going upstate. I contemplated having an abortion. Was I ready for this? Could I do it? What if I wasn't a good mother?"

I remember it like it was yesterday. I was six years old. We lived in a blue house, the one my parents had shared before my dad moved out. I lived there with my mom, her boyfriend Carmine, and his son Joey who was eight years older than me. One night, it had to be around 11 because I remember watching *The Honeymooners* on my little 13-inch TV, I was lying in my bed and Joey was sleeping on the floor in my room. I heard Carmine call my name so I got out of bed and walked into the living room and he was sitting on the couch. As I got closer I realized he had no clothes on. He had a jacket over his lap. It was black with gold writing. My mom's work jacket. She must have been asleep in her room. He told me to come sit down next to him and I listened. He told me to touch him in his private places and I did. He even made me put his penis in my mouth. It was gross and I ran back in my room and hid under my covers. My mother never woke up. She should have known. She's my mother, but she didn't and I never said anything.

When I finally told a babysitter two years later, after we moved to a new house in Northport, my mother took his side and allowed him to stay. CPS entered my life for the first time and I was taken away from my home, from my mommy. I had no idea what an affect this would have on my life, but as I lay there in my cell, those were the thoughts I battled in my mind. I decided right then and there that I could never go through with an abortion and I was going to keep my baby. I was going to break the cycle and be a better mother to my child than mine was to me.

By the time I found out I was having a girl, I'd been clean for five months and I decided to write my mom.

Dear Mom,
    I am writing to share my feelings with you. I am going through a lot of changes being pregnant and being in prison — neither of which I ever imagined happening to me, especially at the same time. I found out I am having a girl and I am going to name her Destiny. I would really like for you to be a part of your

granddaughter's life, but I refuse to let you hurt her the way that
you hurt me. As long as you are using drugs I will not allow you
to be around the baby. We have both made some bad choices in
the past but I hope now you can do what's right. I'm going to be
a mother and I need you. Please get your act together. You can't
change my past but you can be there for my kids. If this is too
much to ask then don't even bother writing me back. I love you and
I don't want to see you hurt yourself anymore.

Love Always,

Chippy

That had been my mom's nickname for me since I was three
years old.

I had just gotten released from prison two weeks prior when I
went into labor. When I finally went to the hospital, I was four cen-
timeters dilated and 50% effaced, which is when your cervix thins
out to make room for the baby. I was admitted, and the first thing
I did was call my mom. At the time she was clean, and renting a
little apartment at her friend's house in Ronkonkoma. She didn't
have a car but her friend Bruce was going to give her a ride on his
motorcycle from exit 60 on the expressway all the way to Central
Suffolk Hospital. I was nine months clean and very serious about
my recovery. I didn't want pain medication and I made sure my doctor knew this in advance. I was deathly afraid of the epidural, so I
was going to have an all-natural delivery. The contractions started
coming stronger and every few minutes. "Oh my God, this is it!" I
thought. My doctor, Dr. Spataro, a very nice, attractive Italian man,
checked me again.

"Cara you're ready. We're moving you to the delivery room."

"But wait! My mom isn't here yet." Panic swept over me, I started
to sweat. I thought back to when I was young, after CPS made me
go to live with my dad. I was allowed visitation with my mom and
every weekend I would sit at my front window waiting for her. I'd
close my eyes, clench my fists and say out loud, "The next car that
comes is going to be her." At the sound of a car I'd open my eyes and
watch as it kept on going. She never came. I finally stopped doing
this around the time I turned eighteen.

The doctor's words snapped me out of my thoughts. "I'm sorry Cara but she wants to come out and we can't stop her."

I was moved to the delivery room and being prepped for delivery. The contractions were really hurting now. I was really starting to think that my mom wasn't going to make it. After all, she had let me down time and time again. It wouldn't surprise me. Just then, she appeared in the doorway and I started to cry. For a split second nothing else mattered but the fact that she was there. She had made it at a time when I needed her the most. As she walked up to me I could see that she was crying too. She bent down and hugged me and it felt so good. I didn't want to let go. I felt like a little girl again.

"Okay, Cara, are you ready? I want you to bear down and push really hard and slowly count to ten."

"Okay."

"Whenever you're ready go ahead."

I took in a deep breath and held it in while I started to push.

"Come on, Chip, you can do it."

"You got it, Cara, push real hard!"

Another big breath and I started pushing again. My mom was slowly counting.

"Ma you're counting too slow," I yelled.

"Cara, you have to push as long as you can."

"Okay, okay," and I tried again.

"She's got a lot of hair," said Mom.

"She's out?"

"No!"

"Another big push. We got a head."

"She out?"

"No. One big push and that should do it." This time, we both started laughing.

"Okay, okay!"

It took one more big push and everything I had and at 12:01 AM August 29, 2003, my beautiful 6-pound baby Destiny was born.

A letter from Cara Mugavero to Lonnie and Linda

Dear Lonnie & Linda,

It's Monday. I'm sitting on my bunk. I've been sitting here all day. Reading and crying. I just read the (first) journal from cover to cover and I loved it. I'm going to be lost without you when I go over to the DWI facility1. I look forward to Herstory coming every week because it's helped me to take a real, honest, look at my life and to put it on the page and be able to express it for the first time ever.

I feel like a brand new person after reading at the anniversary party. Out of all the programs I've been in and months I've spent behind bars, I have never been able to recognize the story I read and my life as one and the same. I've spent more time running from my life then actually trying to have one and I just want to thank you both so much for giving me the chance to be free of my past and start a brand new chapter in my book.

I look forward to working with you as soon as I get out. Thank you so much for helping me to be ME.

I love you guys!

Love, Cara

Excerpt #2 from
Window and Prayers

Dehlia "Dee" Ahlstrand

(9/13)

I AM SITTING HERE praying at another window again. Two sets of bars and a gate again. Each one smaller and smaller, just like my existence. If the windows get any smaller, what will happen to me? What if there were no windows left?

There are four women sitting behind me playing cards—Chantel, 19 years old and 9 months pregnant. She won't be getting out anytime soon so she will be staying here in this jail with her baby in the nursery. One of the other women (in for murder and elderly) who needs a cane to get around, speaking with excitement of the church retreat she attended today. On the floor outside a cell, is a beautiful black girl who preaches the word of the Lord, singing beautifully, gospel music, playing cards with a white girl in solitary. Three cells down is a young black woman (sweet as can be) in a cage with cells in it, who is in for an extremely violent murder. Next to me is a white woman my age in stripes instead of greens, in solitary also . . . There are all different kinds of prisoners, all with our own stories, what we are in for, how much time we got, how much we have left, who's been sentenced, who's not. It amazes me how the guards remember you, as I sit in my cell and hear, "Ahlstrand, what are you doing back?" As if I was released and came back by choice! After this stint I will never be back. **EVER!!** Meanwhile, all I want to hear is "Ahlstrand, roll up!"

Not today . . .

My Life Is All I Have

Cynthonia "Tone" Shewprashad

 *If anyone were to meet Tone (not to be referred to as Cynthonia!) as we have, her dimpled smile and gentle and loving demeanor, and then read her story, alongside her letter to her mother, they might conclude that locking young women (and men) up, thereby branding them for life, is a questionable therapy for treating the source of the problem. An entirely bright, personable young woman with obvious leadership potential has grown up with no love from the one person who mattered most—Mom. In a period of adolescent loneliness and self-doubt, she looks for family in the wrong place.*

Tone is now in prison for eight years for association with the violent crimes of a gang. Violent felony convictions are in some ways life-time sentences in this country as once released, jobs are next to impossible to find, just as gangs, we're told, often do not let former members go.

One of the common sayings among inmates is, "Do your time . . . don't let your time do you." Tone has taken this adage to heart as she looks towards her years upstate as an opportunity to complete a college degree and to set herself firmly on another path.

"**O**N THE NOISE . . ." Mr. V yells down the tier. "Then you females wonder why everyone calls you animals . . . you act like it!" he says after cutting eyes at me.

I look a few cells down the tier at Jessica as if there's an eight legged spider sitting on her head. Jess, who stands at 5'6", 165 pounds, long dirty-blond hair that drops to the middle of her back and the complexion of soy milk, with eyes that look like the Bahamas finest beaches, looks back at me and laughs. "Don't worry about him Tone, he's got the Napoleon Defect . . . you know . . . li'l dick syndrome!"

We both burst out laughing. "I know, but I hate the fact that they think that their grey suits exempts them from trouble. Shit, they need to know that they could come up in here at any time, word up!" I said loud enough for the oversized correctional officer with pants entirely too tight to hear me.

"Hey Tone . . ." Jess calls from her cell. "Did you hear from your pops?"

"Na, my sister Jasmine told me today that he's sick . . . his kidneys are acting up due to his drinking," I reply walking towards her. I'm thinking to myself how my head's been hurting all day, because when I woke up this morning I was crying due to the fact that I've been locked up for over eight and a half months and I'm missing my family. On top of that, my girl isn't answering the phone anymore because I broke up with her, and I don't know if it's because I 'm going upstate for 12 to 15 years or if it's because so many girls like me. I am a flirt, and I already know what's going to happen. In any event, my head is killing me and bringing up my pops is only making shit worse! "I don't want to talk about it, because then I'ma start thinking about home again," I said.

Now I'm sitting on a gray bin at the gate of her cell. I never really realized how small these cells are. I mean damn, I am about 5'4" and I'm as long as the bed. I can reach my toilet bowl that's connected to the sink while I'm lying on the bunk! Shit, there's barely enough room to put lotion, deodorant, gel, baby powder, shampoo, and conditioner on the shelf they give us.

Jessica interrupts my thoughts with a slap to the back of my neck. "Hey Tone, we're the same age right?"

Great, where the hell are we going with this, is what I'm thinking.

"How come your family doesn't hold you down?" she asked, getting right to the point.

"Jess, that's a long story," I said.

"On the gates . . . lock in!" Mr. V yells with a slight grin on his face, knowing he's about to go home and we're stuck here.

"I'ma tell you tomorrow, alright? I'ma see you. Goodnight."

I run back down the tier because the CO is trying to lock me out of my cell so he can have an excuse to keep me locked in tomorrow. I slide in and jump on my bunk, close my eyes and a tear falls from my long lashes. *How did my life come to this?*

"You black ugly bitch!" my mom yells. "I told you to take the chicken out, clean it, season it and pour lemon juice on it!"

"Mom, I don't know how to cut the fat off though . . . you never showed me!" I said, swallowing the hard knot in my throat and trying to fight back tears that hold so much hurt in them.

My mom comes around the table to where I'm standing and says, "You're 12 years old now. If you don't learn to use your damn head and learn how to cook then you'll never find a good man!" Then she picks up a kitchen knife from the table next to her and holds it up to my face—maybe so I can see it real good. The thing is that I'm not looking at the knife. I'm too scared to look at the knife. I look at my mom's eyes. Why does she hate me? Why does she do such mean things to me and not my sisters? Am I wrong for not knowing how to clean chicken? Maybe I should have been watching her when she did it . . . I'm always messing up. To top it off, I'm ugly and she has no problem telling me. I wish I could just disappear! I look down at the knife for one second and my heart starts sprinting faster then a cheetah in Africa! I can't hold back the tears any longer and my lips start to tremble. I bite the inside of my bottom lip.

I don't remember when everything went mute, but at that moment the sound came back to my ears and I heard my mom say, "Do you hear me??"

"Yes!" I said, hoping that it would get her away from me.

My prayers were answered when the upstairs phone rang. She started to walk towards the stairs, then she turned around and said, "Nobody wanted you . . . that's why I adopted you!"

She continued up the stairs and I heard the door slam closed. I stood still in the same spot for what seemed like the longest three minutes of my life. *Adopted?* Yeah right, I'm not adopted. This is just one of her evil ways to hurt me. I mean this is the only place I know! I'm going to ask Daddy. He has no reason to lie to me. He always tells me the truth.

I move toward the 'frig and pull out the chicken. I start to pull off all the white mushy stuff, but my thoughts keep replaying the last statement from a lady I've considered my mother forever.

Chicken . . . clean the chicken, I had to keep telling myself.

A letter from Cynthonia Shewprashad to her mother

Dear Mom,

I hope everything is well with you right now. As for me I'm maintaining, tryna keep my head up. I know this letter may come to a shock to you but I figured I'd let you know how I feel right now. Maybe if you have time you'll write back. I know things in the past have been hard for us. We've been through a lot and really I still have some questions I need closure for. Like what did I ever do to make you feel the way you feel about me? Why don't you feel like I deserve love? Tell me, Mom, do you ever feel like things could change between us? (LOL) You know that some nights I lie in my bed and daydream about me and you being cool, going to the mall and laughing or going to lunch and talking about each other's problems. Do you ever think that would happen? I find myself sometimes wishing upon a star, it's crazy! Somebody asked me the other day, "What brought you to jail?" On the surface it's because I followed up behind some bloodz and started doing stupid things, and that's what I told her but, whenever I'm in my cell I can't help but think about how I got involved with that gang. Mom, I'm not blaming you for me being locked up, but at the same time I really feel that if you would have been more caring and showed me a lot more love then I wouldn't have looked to another group of people for love.

Mom, I know you're disappointed in me right now. So maybe that's why you don't acknowledge me now, but what about all the times I did do good? All the times I had your clothes ironed for the whole week so you would never be late for work! When Michael and DeKaila came home from school and I was the one who got them off the bus, made sure their school clothes got put in the hamper, their homework was done and they took showers every night. I got them ready in the morning for school when you were late coming in from work! Mom, you never gave me credit for all the times I picked the girls up from school and dropped them to work, then picked them up again. I never complained when I helped you work with your patient and stayed there for 12 hours at a time every day and only got half of what you got! Mom,

I never cared. I just wanted to make you happy. I just wanted
for you to say, "Maybe I was wrong about her." Even though
you hated me, the only thing I wanted was for you to be proud.
I did everything for you Mom—graduated with honors, played
basketball. I even did stupid chorus. You said I needed something
to fall back on besides basketball so I took up Medical Assistant,
then I did my L.P.N. because you're a nurse and I figured you'd
like the thought of me tryna be like you. (LOL) Remember when
you would say something really mean and I would write a poem
and leave it someplace so you could find it? It worked for a few
days, for a few days you'd tell me that you were lonely, and ask
me if I wanted to come up and chill with you. I guess I'm writing
this letter hoping it would be one of my poems I wrote when I was
younger and maybe it will have that same effect. Mom, I don't
want you to be mad or upset, I just want you to think about me. I
want you to think about all the good things I've done so maybe you
could forgive me for the bad.

　　I'm not going to write a long letter because I know you
don't like to read for too long. Mom, even if you don't know the
answerz to the questions I asked, it's okay. Deep in my heart it's
always been. I guess what I'm trying to get at is that I forgive
you! I love you, Mommy!

                                        Love, Cynthia,
                                        Cee Cee

Daddy's Girl

Kelly Keane

Kelly is a little sprite of a young woman. "Not so young!" she quickly reminds us. "If only I had had this program earlier, maybe I wouldn't have made so many stupid mistakes!" Born with a cleft palate and a speech impediment, Kelly nevertheless wrote and read aloud every week, and overcame her shyness about her speech in reading her work to an audience of fifty at our last annual reading. Not only did she read, she "performed" with antics and song that so clearly demonstrated a new-found self-confidence, and the closing of a chapter that had stunted her growth for years. She is now studying to become an accountant.

October 1st

AS I'M sitting here on the steps in the backyard of the DWI trailer, the sun is hitting my face and the cold breeze is going through me. My eyes are closed, and I'm just soaking up the peaceful moment of quiet—no yelling, fighting, farting, talking and whatever else goes on in there—in those pink Pepto Bismol rooms, where we all sleep, eat, change, talk and read. What we do day after day. Sometimes it's nice to just escape for a few moments, even if it's just a few minutes in my own thoughts. I call this place on the stoop my throne, even though I know that other women's butts have sat here too. These steps remind me of the docks in my home town. I can imagine walking down the stairs, holding onto the railing, letting go on the last step, putting my bare feet right in the hot sand, and walking down to the beach, just enjoying the summer day. I can smell the sea air as I sit down right at the edge of the water, with the sun's rays shining on my face, giving me that summer glow . . . I wish I was there right now. Well, this spot serves its purpose—at least for now.

As I sit here, I'm thinking about what occurred earlier today. Tina did her life map, and it really hit home. She was sitting in her chair, looking at the collage of her life. I sat a few chairs away, just looking at her. I made eye contact—and saw the pain in her eyes, the sadness that she was about to tell. She started talking, and went into her journey. My ears tuned in like I had bionic hearing. I believe I was meant to hear her story, because the more she talked, the more I heard my story. She reminded me of me. However, I did have at least a decade on her. God, I wish I was young again. I also wish I had had this program at her age. Maybe I wouldn't be in this mess at the age of thirty-one.

As she was speaking about her family, she started on her father and his death. I started to feel the tears flooding my eyes, then rolling down my face. My mind started to race, bringing me to a place in my mind where the past lies dormant . . . the past—where there are things that I'd wanted to forget about. But my thoughts were invading, and I couldn't help it. I started to think about that day. The day my whole world ended.

It was early morning, and I heard the alarm clock going off in my dad's room. Why wasn't he turning it off? Didn't he hear it? I was getting frustrated because it was too early to get up. I still had an hour before I had to get ready for school, and I couldn't fall back to sleep. So I got out of bed, put on my slippers, slid the door open and headed to the bathroom, rubbing my eyes, still in sleep mode. As I was looking in the mirror, checking myself out, I could still hear that damn alarm clock. Why wasn't he up yet? In the morning I could usually hear him walking around the small two bedroom basement apartment. I went to check his room, and to my surprise it was empty. Where the hell was he? I knew that he hadn't gone to work early. I guessed he never came home. He was probably too drunk, so he must've crashed somewhere. Still, this didn't make sense. He never stayed out all night. Usually, he would come home, no matter what the circumstance—sometimes really late, but he'd always come home. I shrugged my shoulders with disgust, I blew it off. I went to the kitchen to get some breakfast, then plopped my butt on the couch and turned on the TV. Flipping through the channels, I landed on MTV and contemplated if I should go to school or not. Hmmmm, let's see, what should I do? Well as you may have guessed, I never made it. Come on, think about it—home alone, no dad, no school, lying on the couch, watching TV, pigging out, relaxing and getting myself into trouble without even leaving the apartment at the age of twelve! That's cool!! As I lounged on the couch watching videos, Warrant's "Cherry Pie" came on, so I jumped to my feet and broke into a dance. With a hairbrush in my hand and my dancing shoes on, I started to sing—pretending that I was in the video, rocking it out right next to the guys.

After awhile, about fifty videos and ten pounds of junk food later, I started getting bored of being a bum. Plus, I was worried about my dad. By this time, he should've been home screaming at me for not going to school. Something didn't seem right. So, I decided to call my aunt and uncle. I got my aunt on the phone and asked her to come and get me. I told her that my father was MIA—he wasn't here this morning. Plus, I wanted to hang with my other half—my twin, Keri.

See, my father has three daughters. Out of the three, I lived with him because I was the only one who got along with him. My father and I were really close—so close that one day, when he got injured on the job, I even knew before he came through the door that something was wrong. All day I kept telling my sisters I thought Daddy was hurt. They thought I was nuts, but it turned out I was right. I remember him walking through that door with a cast on. I ran up to him, with tears rolling down my face, screaming "Are you all right?" He turned to me with a smile, saying he was okay, just a broken leg, and don't worry. As I hugged him, I told him I'd had a feeling something was wrong. He put his arms around me, and I can still hear his voice telling me "You are daddy's little girl."

I was always daddy's little girl.

I hung the phone up with my aunt and went to get ready for my next adventure. I turned up the music, getting my groove on and dancing around the apartment like Tom Cruise in the movie *Risky Business*. I waited patiently for my aunt and uncle, and finally they came. We picked up Keri at school and headed back to their house in Kings Park.

It was such a beautiful day—the 1st of October. Keri and I decided to walk around the block, just bullshitting about the plans for

Friday. We couldn't wait to go to the roller rink and see the guys. We always had fun there, plus it was the spot where we escaped from the madness of our lives. As we approached the second hill, we heard a car come up behind us. Then it stopped along side of us. It was our aunt and uncle. My uncle was in the passenger seat, telling us we had to get in. We were going to grandma's house because she needed to talk to us about something. Keri and I were about to question it, but we both knew something was wrong. The look on my uncle's face said it all—sad, confused and nervous. Without another word, we got in.

At this point I was feeling sick, and my stomach started to knot up. I felt like I had butterflies in my belly trying to come out—a familiar feeling that something had happened to my dad. I knew something was wrong. As I looked out the window, I turned to my aunt and uncle and said, "My father is dead, isn't he?"

With the shock of what had just come out of my mouth, their faces turned white, like they'd had seen a ghost. They stared at the road, not making eye contact with me. My uncle said with a quiet, stumbling voice, "Grandma will talk to you guys." I could see their faces in the rear view mirror, and that told me all I needed to know. The five minute ride felt like a lifetime.

We pulled up to the house where I used to live. It looked different now—very sad, lonely, and empty, even though it was fall and the sky was bright and clear, the leaves were already changing colors, but my grandma's house was the only one surrounded by this glum, dark, gray cloud. As I walked up the steps, I felt tired, drained and terrified. My heart was beating so fast that I could almost see the outline popping through my shirt. The tears started to invade my eyes. My young body aged within a few minutes. At one time I had run up these steps—now they felt big and huge, like I was climbing a steep mountain, and it was taking all my energy. I went to reach for the screen door, but for some reason the handle seemed so far away. I felt like I was in a weird dream playing tag. I was dizzy, scared, and my hands were shaking. Finally, I got the courage to turn the knob—already knowing what was going to be on the other side.

Excerpt #3 from
Windows and Prayers

Delia "Dee" Ahlstrand

(10/9)

HERE I AM sitting at a window again. Oh dear God, thank you for creating another beautiful day. The cool wind is blowing on my face, there is a beautiful black and yellow butterfly just enjoying the day. There are men working across the lot laughing and joking around, even though they are wearing orange jumpsuits and being watched by a Corrections Officer, they too are enjoying the day, as I watch through a gate window.

It's 2:15 PM. I am so excited! In about 45 minutes the prayer I've been praying for is about to be answered. I am going to see my children! (God is good). It has been so long since I have seen them. I'm sure Joey, almost 18, and Kevin, 16, will be towering over me. And Victoria, 4, and Angelina, 2, have probably changed so much. Angelina is probably almost fully potty trained. When I hold her in my arms with her little tushy in my hands, it will be without padding because she'll be wearing "big girl" underwear. Not to mention she now wears glasses.

It's just about 3:00 . . . they should be here any minute. Victoria, I hear, has grown so much and has become such a little lady. Her hair has probably gotten so long. Oh my God, to just hold her little face and cover it with kisses is just a dream away.

Kevin must be huge because he is now on the football team of Kings Park High School. And Joey is going to Wilson Tech for Computer Science. I am so proud of them both—they truly are young men, my men. I love that they tower over me, it reminds me of when they were little and I would tower over them and take care of them.

I know in my heart, if they could take care of me, or fix me from this awful disease, they would, and they'd do an excellent job. I feel like I don't even know them anymore, it has been 5 **LONG** months since I've seen them. At least within the last 2–3 weeks I've spoken to them at least 4 times. It's better than nothing. Since I've been here at the DWI facility, I've had dreams of visits with them and they were great. It was like I really saw them, and in the morning I was always in such a good mood.

It is now 3:40 and I am still waiting at the window. Mr. Scherr came and I asked him if I was getting my visit and he said, "I'm sorry—CPS cancelled, but we are trying to reschedule." He didn't know that I knew about the visit and he hadn't told me for exactly this reason. It was almost like I could see my own pain in his eyes because he has been working so hard to set this up. As tears quickly roll down my face, I am trying to come up with a justification or reason that will make me feel better, but I am at a loss for thoughts. But I find myself still praying at that very moment because I know God is especially loving me now while I am in so much pain. Soon I will reap the benefits of recovery . . . soon!   ✎

Mother/Daughter . . .
Daughter/Mother

Lorraine Gray

 *Lorraine commands respect with her cool, unassuming remove, her controlled way of holding to dignity in the face of indignity. While Lorraine chose to begin her first page in a moment when she felt powerless and invisible, she came to see that her words were not only heard but highly valued by the other women. Older than many of her fellow inmates, others referred to her as "Miss Lorraine" in a show of respect.*

So many of these women see themselves as bad mothers, and often it is this belief that fuels their fall deeper and deeper into the well of their addictions. Lorraine's writing, along with the letter we've printed from her daughter, we are certain will remind other incarcerated mothers that often they've done something right, and that the mother/daughter relationship doesn't stop because they're in jail.

I WAKE UP Tuesday excited. It is the beginning of the week for us. Our week starts on Tuesday because on Monday we don't have visits and for some unknown reason sometimes the women don't get mail either. No one has ever explained why that is, we just accept it. This is jail—in here you just accept everything to be as it is and you don't get an explanation.

I'm excited today because I am expecting a visit from my daughter and two year old granddaughter. I know my visit is at 4 PM, but I am happy all morning. The officer calls, "Listen up ladies, these are the visits for today . . ." I don't hear my name but I don't panic. Instead, I call my daughter and she tells me that she's coming at 4 o'clock on a walk-in visit. So, I continue on my day.

At 3 PM I begin to prepare for my visit. Today I put effort into fixing myself up. I know that in the past I haven't cared enough about myself to put any emphasis on my appearance. I just woke up and existed—there I was. But today is a special day so I am going to condition my locs and give them a shiny look. I apply black mascara, not to my eyes, but to the roots of my hair. I put the mascara in the front to hide all the newly acquired gray. It seems since I have been in jail I am getting grayer and hairier! I also apply lipstick to my lips. Lipstick in jail is a homemade combination of Chapstick and a crushed colored pencil, melted and meshed back together to form a soft colorful lip balm.

Once all this is done, I am ready. I'm wearing the county-issued green shirt and pants, but when I get to the visiting room, everyone puts on a mandatory one-piece yellow jumpsuit that zips in the back. I dress quickly because it is after 4 PM, which means my visit will be less than an hour. I give the officer my name and he says, "OK, Gray, go to booth #6."

I look over at my visitors and I see two familiar faces. One face looks just like mine minus the stress and strain of time. The other face is small and beautiful. Her eyes are full of amazement. She sits with patience and tolerance. She is much too controlled for a two-year-old. She sits with her tiny hands crossed in front of her on the table. She waits for my gesture. I smile at her and she smiles back. I say, "It's okay, Sweety, you can smile at grandma."

My granddaughter is now using our visits as a way to manipulate me. She has taken to whispering to me. The first time she did it I asked her what she had been doing and she said "smoking cigarettes." That was her way of telling Grandma that her Mommy had been smoking cigarettes. Later on in the visit she whispered to me, "Mimi." I said, "Yes, sweetie," and she said, "I want ice cream." I said, "What kind?" and she said "nanilla." So I made her mother promise me she would take her for a small dish of ice cream. When my daughter agreed, my grandbaby wanted confirmation so she said "I want cream on top."

Visits are supposed to evoke feelings of happiness. My visits sometimes depress me. I feel like I have been left behind by my loved ones when they leave. This is my punishment for my stupidity. I was told that jail was a form of rehabilitation but I don't feel rehabilitated. I feel angry and upset. My loved ones are putting up a front to make me feel better.

I imagine that my daughter is suppressing her feelings of disappointment towards me because she doesn't want to upset me. When we sit and talk she has so many encouraging things to say to me. When I say things like, "The D.A. is going to give me a lot of time," she says, "Mommy, why don't you take it one day at a time." When I tell her "I don't like it here," she says, "I don't like you here either, but now I don't have to worry about you like I did when you were using." When I tell her, "I don't want to be here with these people," she says, "Mommy, Mommy, I'm grateful to see you here instead of in a grave!" Wow, why do kids have to be so smart?

God has a way of showing me things. A few years in recovery has taught me many valuable lessons. I didn't know when I was taking my five year old daughter to 12-step meetings for 15 years that one day she would be encouraging me. Now she is telling me to "hold on, keep the faith, God doesn't give us more than we can handle."

Just when I thought that things were so bleak, my daughter has stepped in and reversed roles with me. She is now the rock that I must lean on for support. This 25-year-old wife, mother, sister and loving daughter is who I now look to, to brighten my spirits in this seemingly dark and dismal time. It seems even though I think this is the worst my life could get, she is more optimistic.

I told my daughter that I don't want her to visit me upstate with the babies. I think I am saying the right thing, but she says, "No, Mommy, I have to see you." My daughter tells me that she cannot wait for her children to be old enough for her to instill in them the values her mother has instilled in her.

I am overwhelmed by her words. All the time I was talking, yelling, preaching, thinking that my words had fallen on deaf ears, she was listening and taking my advice. She just didn't want me to know at that time that she trusted and believed in my wisdom. Because of this, today I feel blessed, blessed; my life has taken on new meaning. I have learned a valuable lesson. The visits are not just for me, they are for those who truly know my heart and love me for the real person that I am.

A letter to Lorraine Gray from daughter, Lakisha

Hi Mom

We thank the Lord for giving us not what we want but what He feels we need . . .

I've just left court. Came home w/kids, trying to be strong. I wanted to write this because you may be feeling the same type of way — I know I am.

1st thing—It's Gonna be Okay.

2nd—God Never gives us more than we can Handle.

3rd—We have an End in sight.

4th—We love and support you always.

In this letter I'm gonna say sorry Mommy for the way I went about & said things to you. I don't judge you, I love you. You know I will always do my part. Please stay strong.

I know it's hard. Oh I know each day is a struggle . . . what gets me thru are my kids (wow my kids!!) and knowing that one day I can show you how good of a Mother & Person you taught me to be. I want them to think I'm as good a mother as I have.

OK, gonna go clean my house, wait for Kali to wake up. Stop looking at my spelling and take this letter for what it's for — to tell you how much I love you, to show how important you are to my family (It always starts w/you!).

LOVE YOU
MOMMY
Lakisha

OTHER SELECTIONS

WE END WITH *a few offerings we simply couldn't bear to leave out —
three of our very youngest voices—a "Teen Gone Wild" at sixteen, a young
Diva of eleven, and the soul-searching of a seventeen-year-old inmate.
And one love story.*

"Fly Girl" Exploded

Maria Turcios

 *Maria wears her hair tightly braided and pulled back from a round, smooth-skinned face with sparkling deep brown eyes, and an infectious energy that makes everyone around her want to laugh. Even in prison greens she always manages to look "fly," and even in prison facing a five-year bid upstate for association with "the wrong guys," she is invincibly good-natured and kind-hearted.*

In this section of Maria's story we meet her at sixteen years old, playing hard but, at least to her young mind, harmlessly, in the ways of the hood—dressing "fly" every day, cutting classes at school, and living for the fun she has with her friends.

We know that Maria has come to understand how outrageous this story is—but when she was sixteen and teamed up with her best friend, Erla, and her parent's credit card, she had little idea of just how big a deal it was to rack up a twenty-five thousand dollar credit card bill without her parents finding out . . . money spent on clothes and one clandestine trip to a vacation resort in Florida! Like so many of the women we meet here, Maria is full of heart and courage, intelligence, and a great sense of humor—all of which you can gleam from the beginnings of this story. She plans to make the most of her time upstate by pursuing a college degree. She would most like to study to become a nurse.

6 A.M. every morning. Alarm goes off. Another day closer to the summer and schools out. Look in the closet. What to wear today? That's the first thought on my mind since I always had to be looking fly from the kicks on my feet to the jeans on my legs to the shirt on my back to my nails and my hair. Never worried about the make-up—just made sure my Blistex was always with me because I do not like to wear make-up. I'm a natural fly girl. Never-wore-the-same-thing-twice type of girl. What did I buy yesterday? were the thoughts running through my mind when I heard *"I like my beat down low, down low. I like my top laid back, laid back."* It was T.I. as my ringtone. Bopping my head and rushing to get my cell phone. It's my best friend Erla, like always the only person in the right mind to call me at 6:30 in the morning.

"Are we going to school today?"

"Yeah I'm getting ready now. What you wearing? Because I ain't trying to wear the same shit you wearing, because you know there have been them days we had on the same shit . . . like it was planned!" I said.

"I'ma wear my constructs cause I ain't got gym today—it's an 'A' day," she said.

"Oh well, then I'm bout to throw it back and wear my red, white and gray Tims. Looks like it's going to rain today and you damn well know we ain't staying pass 4th period kuz I have a test 3rd and you got gym 5th, bitch," I told her. All we could do was laugh. "Damn, we spent mad money yesterday!" I said.

"Word! Did you tell your mom about the credit card?" she asked.

"Hell no, you crazy? She'll kill my ass and won't think twice about it," I responded.

"Yeah, you're right. Ya moms is mad bugged out. You dressed yet?" she asked.

"Yeah, I'm about to hop on the bus. You already know I'll meet you at 5 Corners."

"Alright, bet," she said while I'm pressing the end button on my sidekick 3, grabbing my Nextel and about to run out the door to make sure I got the bus.

"Smack that ass all on the floor, smack that ass, gimme some more."

It was Akon playing loud in Karl's car. As the bass is hitting my back I thought to myself, Damn, I'm high as a mothafucka right now. I want to go shopping!

"What time is it?" I asked Kenny, who had shot gun.

"1:30," he said.

"Oh shit, Karl," I said. "Stop by my house—I gotta go get the mail."

Erla just looked at me. She already knew why. "The bill comes today?" she asked.

"Yeah, sometime this week. You know I have to check the mail before anyone else does."

Karl goes, "Okay, but what we doing after that?"

"Well, 1st off, I'm hungry and I need a pair of kicks, man. They having a party at the VFW."

"Whose party?" said Erla.

"Bitch, I don't know! What I do know is mad people gonna be there," I said.

As we pull up to my house, "Hurry up," they said to me.

"Hey, Frank!" I said to my mailman, as he hands me the mail and I quick flip thru it all. I see my credit card bill, grab it out, and put the rest of the mail in the mailbox, open my backpack, and put the bill in it. I open the front door, and run to my room, throw my backpack on my room floor forgetting to close it, and all my papers fall out, not caring that the credit card bill falls on my floor. Fuck it—no one comes in my room anyways, I thought. I lock my room door, and then the front door and hop back in Karl's car and tell my friends, "How about Brooklyn?"

Dáme más Gasolina. Dáme más Gasolina. I said, "Damn, it's my house calling me. My mom probably gonna to ask me why didn't I take the meat out." I picked up. "Hola, mami."

"¿Maria Lusia a dónde está?" *Maria where you at?* she asked me, sounding really heated, and the fact she said my middle name I knew she was going to black out on me.

"Estoy en el mall, ma." *I'm at the mall ma,* I lied.

"Venga para la casa ahorita mismo." *Bring ya ass home ASAP,* she said.

Damn, I thought to myself. "Okay ma," I said as she hung up on me. We hopped back on the Belt Parkway on our way back to Brentwood. *What the fuck is the problem now?* is all I thought.

Stepping out the car, I tell everyone, "See ya later."

"Make sure you call me when you're done getting screamed at," Erla said as I'm closing the car door and turning around to give her the finger. Now as I'm walking up my driveway I'm trying to take baby steps and getting ready to hear my mother's mouth. Telling myself, *Alright, all I'm going to say to her is, "Mom, I'm sorry. I love you," hug and kiss her.* But then I said to myself, *Damn that ain't gonna work because it's always the same response from her when I forget something.* "¿Se te olvida limpiarte tu cola cuando cagas?" *Do you forget to wipe your ass when you take a shit?*

Damn, finally got to the front door, took my keys and went to unlock the door, but before I'm able to turn my key my mother is opening the door with the mean grill on. *Oh shit!* was all I thought. Before I was able to walk through the door my mother already had me by my hair.

"¿Qué tú hiciste? ¿Por qué?" *What you do? Why?* was all she kept yelling as she had me by my hair and she dragged me to my room.

All I kept thinking was, *Damn what the fuck did I do now?* As she pushed me on my room floor I seen the fire in her eyes. *Damn, I've done fucked up this time!*

Then she pulled out the stupid bill.

Walking up Freeman in the rain so mad with so much on my mind. How he put his hands on me? Why they overreacted like that? All over some fucking money! Questions running thru my mind. It starts to rain harder and so many headlights coming down the street looking like they going to hit me because it's so rainy and dark.

"Tu eres tan estúpida. ¿En qué puta cosa gastaste todo ese dinero?" *You're so stupid. What the fuck you spent all this fucking money on?* was what I heard as my father's fist connects with my face. I feel my lip gush out blood and I'm trying to find it in me not to hit my father. All I kept saying to myself was, *Maria, this is your father! You can't raise your hand at him. You know better.*

"¡Déjala ir la estás lastimando!" *Let her go, you're hurting her!* is what my mother's yelling as she is trying to get him off of me and trying not to get hit when he swings at me. But when my father's eyes met with mine, all I saw was anger. Then I thought,

I have to get away from him. So I kicked him off and ran to the bathroom.

"¡Véte de la casa! ¡No te quiero aquí!" *Leave my house! I don't want you here!* These were my father's final words. *Why didn't I see this coming when I was walking through the front door?* were my thoughts.

Honk honk honk!! A car splashed me with a damn puddle and I snapped out of my deep thoughts—wet, mad, bruised up in the face, looking like I walked into two fists and a boot. Without a clue where to head to, without any answers and definitely filled with a shitload of questions.

Leaving Wisconsin

Angelita Peete

Another child turned adult way before her time, and a fierce survivor, when we meet Angel at age eleven she's already a blunt-smoking, beer-drinking, pot-dealing Diva who does everything in life to protect and defend her loving but permissive and negligent mother. Even now, to meet Lita, always wearing her fierce bravado ("No one can hurt me anymore!"), we can still see the little girl she must have been . . . the sudden spark of her eyes at the thought of something new and exciting, or the pouting dropped lip when bored at play. We see that little girl every week, the one horribly and repeatedly sexually and physically abused by her mother's career military husband from the age of eight—the little girl who refuses to give up the idea of perfect mother love. In writing with us, she has begun to grieve and let go of the mother she never really had, and to unburden some of her rage at her abuser, and to hug us hard at the end of every class.

Angel has a strong character with strong opinions—one of them being that Herstory is an essential part of her growth and healing.

IT'S February 13, 1996, and as we travel down the highway, my upcoming twelfth birthday is the farthest thing from my mind. As I stare out the window, I'm trying to permanently etch every little thing into my memory—Oak Creek High School where I had just begun my freshman year, the Pick-N-Save me and my mom used to shop at, the Sentry where I got caught shoplifting—I want to remember it all. The corner store that sold me my first pack of Newports, the complex my friends and I used to hang out in, even the laundromat that I hated going to, I'm gonna miss everything about my little town. The sights and sounds of Milwaukee, Wisconsin have become my home over the last five years and I almost don't want to leave. My mom says this is the best thing for us. Yeah, maybe for her . . . I used to be just fine right here.

As I light my cigarette and crack my window, I catch a strong whiff of the unmistakable smell of barley and hops coming from the brewery. Damn, am I gonna miss that smell! "Do you think we can stop soon? I need a beer," I ask Patrick who's driving the eighteen-wheeler that I'm riding in. He was concentrating so hard on the road, I think I startled him.

"Ah, yeah—as soon as I get your mom's attention," he says flatly. As I look at him, I can't help but wonder what he looked like when he was my age. His 6'4" frame, his mocha complexion, his light-brown almost almond shaped eyes. He's only thirty but he looks like he's 22 with his round baby face. Mmmm, too bad he's too old for me! I wish he had a son. "Don't bother," I say, "I'll just call her on her cell."

As I reach for my phone, I take a minute to admire my shiny new toy. It's a slim little phone, with a flip-down flap to speak into. My little Samsung phone is the shit, and so am I for having it! I could just kiss the person who invented a telephone that I could take with me everywhere. As I dial my mom's number and stare at her two-door Black Chevy Cavalier that she's driving ahead of us, I wonder what's she thinking and how she's feeling. We haven't spoken much in the past twenty-four hours. So much has changed in that short amount of time! Hopefully, she just needs time, I tell myself as I glance at Patrick before pressing "send." He glances back and I can't help but notice how bloodshot his eyes appear. And why the hell does he keep sniffling? "Mom, can we stop at the next truck stop? I need some beers, and I think Pat needs some cold medicine."

"Sure, Angel, whatever you want," she says, seemingly agitated. "And tell Pat that I have his medicine right here with me," she says sounding a little more upbeat!

"Alright, Ma," I say as I end the call, relieved that her agitation seems to be disappearing. "Pat, she said that she has some medicine for you," I say a little confused.

"Great, 'cause I need some bad," he says as he sniffles even harder. Must be because it's so cold. It's brutally cold outside, the kind of cold that freezes your boogers to your nose when you breathe! Despite the freezing temperature, the mounds and mounds of crystal clear snow seem to sparkle in the sun. I sure will miss Wisconsin winters!

As we pull into the truck stop, I hurry out of the truck and look around. "Can you find my mom and tell her I went to the ladies room?" I ask in a hurry. I've had to pee for the last fifty miles!

"Sure, we'll come inside in a minute. Get everything you need now cause there's a long stretch of highway ahead of us," he says with a smile.

"Don't forget to get some medicine while you're at the car. I hope you're not contagious!" I said choking on my laugh.

"I'll be fine in a minute," he says through clenched teeth.

"Damn, it was only a joke," I say as I turn to walk away.

I feel like I'm standing onstage under the bright lights outside the truck stop. I'm rushing to finish my cigarette and then I realize that you can smoke inside. As soon as I open the door, the smell of old men, cheap cologne and stale smoke hits me like a freight train! Don't they have showers for these guys, I'm thinking as I hurry to the ladies room.

Leaving the bathroom stall I get a glimpse of my (almost) twelve-year-old body in the long mirror opposite me. I could pass for eighteen, maybe nineteen, but definitely not twenty-one. My double D breasts stand out in contrast to my slim waistline. As I sashay my way to the mirror, I must say, that my ass and hips look better than some grown women! As I look at the face looking back at me in the mirror, I notice a few lines around my eyes. Who knew you could age overnight? The past three months have definitely aged me, I'm thinking, "But I'm still fly," I say out loud with a smile and a snap! My ponytail reaches my bra strap, my brown eyes seem to sparkle, my glasses make me feel sophisticated, and my teddy bear nose and full lips would make any nigga want to kiss me! My 5'2" frame is well proportioned and my thick hips, fat ass, full breasts and juicy thighs are enough to put most bitches to shame. Not to mention my style is impeccable—from my skin tight bell bottoms to my baby tee, to the matching belt and hoodie, to the fours on my feet. Let's not even talk about how my hair, nails and toes stay fresh! Yeah, I got it going on!

Walking back down the hall, I catch the scent of homemade food, that's when I notice the Perkin's located inside the truck stop—a cute little country eatery with amazing chicken pot pies. I wonder if my mom and Pat are as hungry as I am. As I walk through the store,

I pick up a couple of different things. A pack of juicy fruit gum to keep in my purse, some Starburst and Skittles for my sweet tooth and a *Seventeen* magazine 'cause that's my jumpoff! At the beer cooler, I'm torn between Heineken and Corona. I like them both equally but I decide on Heineken 'cause I really only like Corona's with lime. I'm about to grab the twelve-pack when I realize that I'm still alone and underage. I quickly close the fridge and decide to go find the adults with ID. What the hell is taking them so long? Just as I'm about to give up my search and head for the door I notice the two of them walk in. They are both sniffling and giggling, caught up in their own little world. I guess Patrick gave his germs to my mom. "Hey, over here! Did you guys forget about me?" I ask them as they approach me.

"No," Patrick says, "I saw one of my drivers and got caught up talking is all."

"Yeah, Angel, did you get everything you want?" my mom asks me, never taking off her sunglasses. That's weird . . . she's probably still upset, but she'll be okay . . . at least I hope she will.

"Yeah, but you know I can't get what I really wanted, Ma! Oh, yeah, you guys should probably get some cough drops or vapor rub or something 'cause the two of you sick at the same time is too much for me!" I say to the pair as they continue to sniffle.

"Don't worry about us, we took some medicine. Do you want Heineken's or Corona's?" my mom asks. "Heineken's, Ma, and can you get me some cigarettes too? I only got one left."

"Yeah, yeah, gimme some cash, kid," she says with a smile as she grabs a twelve-pack.

"Ma, I'm drinking by myself," I tell her as I hand her my ten dollar bill.

"Yeah, well, it's a long ride," she replies.

As I look at my mother, I can't help but wonder why she's being so nice to me. I know she probably feels like shit about everything that's happened, but she's killing me with kindness. Oh well, I'll enjoy it while it lasts.

"Anything else?" the cashier asks my mom.

"Yeah," she says. "Let me have two packs of Newport 100's box and a box of Dutch Masters."

"Oh shit, ma, you gettin' with the program?" I ask teasingly.

"No, baby girl, I've been hip, but they're for you. We have one more stop to make in Gary, Indiana, and then New York here we come!" she says happily. I can't help but to admire my mother's beauty as she smiles. At 5'4" she's a little taller than me, but hell, we both short. Her fire red hair hangs just about to her waist in soft waves, her hazel green eyes change with what she wears, and it seems all her freckles and moles were meant to be right where they are. Her high cheekbones and full lips let you know she's not your average white woman. That is, if her ass didn't tell you first! My momma might be white but she sure has a black girl's booty! I guess that makes up for her lack of breasts. But her smile, that smile could light up the darkest night. It's nice to see her smiling again.

When we reach the truck and get inside, Patrick starts it up, cranks the heat, and asks me if I need anything from the car. "No," is my reply as he steps out to meet my mom and walk her to her car, parked behind us. I find the station on the radio that my joint is playing , turn it up and sing along . . . *I'll see you at the crossroads, so you won't be lonely* . . . is what Bone Thugz N Harmony are saying to me as Patrick hops back in the truck.

"You ready to roll?" Patrick asks with a sniffle.

"Yeah, I think I'll ride in the back awhile and get my drink on!"

"That's cool . . . just save me a cold one," he says as I plop onto the twin bed in the back of his truck and pop the top to my beer.

"Yeah!" is all I can say as the truck pulls off onto the highway and my mind takes me to another time and another place.　　✎

Missing Kasiem

Luiza Callender

 *A guarded, dark-eyed, pale-skin beauty, Luiza has grown up with an image of herself as "mentally ill," "severely learning disabled," even "stupid"—labels that she has come to challenge (just as we have) by the writing, reading aloud, and witnessing other's responses to her work. Luiza came to us with a tic of looking up in the middle of every other sentence with a furtive glance towards her teachers, clearly expecting disapproval and judgment. Finding only encouragement from all of us, she literally flowered before our eyes. With this growth, she has been able to advocate for treatment and placement that will help her to reunite with her children.*

In the story below, we meet Luiza visiting Kasiem in prison, temporarily separated from the man she loves. They are trying to maintain a friendship, as both are involved in other relationships—Luiza with a man named Chino, and Kasiem with a woman, Shallamour. Still, their love for each other jumps off the page.

As of this writing, Luiza and Kasiem are married. Even though Kasiem has still many years to serve in prison, Luiza is completely loyal and devoted to him. "There will never be anyone else for me."

WEDNESDAYS, Thursdays, and Fridays were my favorite days of the week. Those were the days of the week that I could escape and go see Kasiem. I would always be a little nervous. I had to plan where I would pretend to be in order to go see him. I would start my journey getting on the local bus to take the hour and a half ride to the Westchester County jail. Waiting in line outside the gates to show my ID, my heart would start to beat faster, my stomach filled with butterflies. The process took longer to get in than the actual visit, but it was becoming routine.

Here I sat at the little plastic table, my heart racing as I sat watching the door the inmates come out of every second. What seemed like hours was only a few minutes 'till I saw him. Damn, even in a bright-ass orange jumpsuit he still looked good! 6'2'', dreads falling past his shoulders, light caramel complexion, a stocky build with that swagger that always made my heart melt and still had me feeling like a school girl . . . a sparkle in his eye, his face becoming soft when he saw me.

"What up? How you?" was always his greeting.

"What's going on with you?" I was stuck on stupid, lost in his eyes before I could respond.

"So where does everybody think you're at?" he asked with a smirk on his face.

"They think I'm working late. What about Shallamour—does she know I've been coming to see you?"

"Yeah, I called her yesterday and told her. I explained that you were part of my life once upon a time. She can't complain. It ain't like she's been coming to see me these days." I could hear the frustration in his voice. Then there was a stretch of silence as we just sat and stared into each other's eyes. I could feel his soul when I looked into his eyes. We were holding hands, his fingers lightly caressing mine, sending a chill down my spine. I sat there missing him even though he was right in front of me.

"So," he asked, taking a deep breath, "what about this dude that you're seeing? Are you happy?" I tried to read his expression before answering him. His expression asked something different, more like *Are you happier with him than you were with me?*

His eyes suddenly looked so sad. I chuckled, "I think it's more like he's dating my parents. I'm not really feeling him too tough these days."

"So tell him to bounce, Lisa, if you don't want to be with him— what's the problem?"

"It's not that simple," I said trying not to sound defensive. "He seems to have my parents hypnotized . . . enough about him. I ain't come here to talk about him. I came here to see you!" I crossed my arms in a frustrated defiance.

Kasiem arched his eyebrow. "Damn, okay, Shorty; I was just trying to give you some advice." I threw him a "Yeah, right" look. One thing, Kasiem was not the Dr. Phil type.

We started talking about his case, his face becoming serious. "Look, Lisa I'm facing 21 years behind this bullshit. I'm not taking the DA's offer so I'm going to trial. I'm actually trying to get Shallamour to bail me out. I know I could fight this better on the outside."

"How much is your bail?"" I asked, pondering the thought that maybe I could come up with the money and be the superwoman that saves the day instead of Shallamour.

"Fifty G's, but I'd only need five G's going through a bail bondsman. Why?" his eyes desperately trying to read my face.

"I'm just asking," I said.

"Yeah. well I really hope I can get bailed out by next week," but he didn't sound so confident. As he kept talking I just listened without responding too much, trying to have him feel with me there now that things would somehow be okay.

A C.O. shouted over a loudspeaker, "Visits are now over. Visitors say your goodbyes and inmates remain seated!" As I got up to give him a hug he tilted my chin up towards his face till my eyes met his. "What?"

"No kiss?"

I reached up on my tippy toes, closed my eyes, and time stopped.

I was lost in love waiting at the bus stop. He still had that incredible hold over me. I glanced at my watch. Where is the damn bus? I left my house at 4:30 this afternoon. It's now 8: 00 at night. If the bus comes now, I'll make it home by a quarter to ten. Good, then I won't have to explain myself to anybody. I just need the bus to come NOW! Finally, I jumped on the bus and grabbed the first available seat closest to the door. I stared out the window past the barb-wired fence to the windows of the jail, wondering if any of them were cells and was he in any of them. I whispered softly, "Be safe. I'll see you tomorrow." Then I closed my eyes.

I woke up just in time not to miss my stop. I checked my watch— 9:50 PM. I flew off the bus and walked as fast as my legs would carry me to my house till I was in front of my driveway trying not to let my feet hit the dirt and pebbles. All was quiet. All the lights were out, not even a flicker of a TV. Good, I thought, everybody must be sleeping. As I turned my key in the door I damn near jumped when I saw Chino sitting at the kitchen table with the oven light on, eating a sandwich.

"How was work?" he asked, sickeningly cheerful.

"Work was work," I replied, transforming into character as I walked over to kiss him on the cheek. "What are you still doing up?"

"I was waiting for my baby—you know I can't fall asleep without you next to me," he responded as he pulled me towards him to sit me up on his lap. I closed my eyes and tried not to pay attention to the nausea climbing up into my throat.

"So then let's go to bed," I said grabbing his hand, leading him to the basement room we shared. As I climbed into bed next to him, I took a deep, deep breath. Just pretend he's Kasiem, I told myself. With that thought planted in my head, I could feel him kissing the back of my neck, tracing his fingertips along my skin, Kai's dreads tickling my face, but when he whispered, "Baby," it wasn't Kasiem's voice. It was the wrong voice—it was Chino's.

"Not tonight, okay? I'm tired and I just want to sleep." When I felt Chino turn over and his breathing indicated sleep, a wash of relief came over me. Just for tonight I had avoided having sex with this stranger to my heart. I was left free—free to dream, free to be with Kasiem, just for tonight . . .   ✎

A letter from Luiza Callender to her mother

Olga,

Here I sit not ever thinking I'd bring pen to paper to write you. I don't even know where to begin. Do you ever think about me, your daughter? You probably don't put as much energy into thinking about me as I do about you, except every time I think about you I feel the pain stabbing me over and over like a knife. I have two children now, two girls. Lilia is 12. Glory is 6. Without knowing about you they know you through me, because I am the kind of mother to them you were to me, minus the physical abuse. I'm invisable.

I always told myself if I could ask you any question in the world it would be how come you just gave up? How come you had me if you were gonna just walk away? But the answer to that I realize won't fix the way you left me, damaged. I've gotten almost as good as my father at feeling numb by the sound of your name, a faded memory. I have adult A.D.D., Attention Deficit Disorder. I still look in the mirror and see an ugly duckling. I don't comprehend things as well as I should and I've spent a lot of years using my body to get what I want, maybe even need. I've left my children in the laps of my father and stepmother to raise. Aren't I just a chip off the old block, Huh? At the same time, I am smart to a degree. I have a good sense of humor. I'm compassionate. But I've aquired those traits from my father. Too bad I don't have the kind of relationship with him I need because I remind him too much of you. I never thought from a distance you could rob me of all those who I need love from. I hate you for not wanting me. I hate you for all the drugs you did and all the alcohol you drank that destroyed my mind. I hate you for taking the opportunity for me to know my little sister by taking her innocence and putting my face as the monster under her bed at night. I hate you for being too mentally sick not to get help and for me not to be enough of a reason to. I hate you for giving up on being my mother.

I love you for all that I didn't understand to once upon a time be your baby. I love you because at one point I'm sure you held me, told me you loved me and lullabyed me to sleep on your chest. To love you is to love myself, as I am a piece of you. But to hate you is so much easier. They say time heals all wounds, well it's been 33 years and I'm still waiting, waiting for the wounds to heal, waiting for my mother to come love me.

Your daughter,
Luiza

Excerpt from
The Book of Feelings

Rachel "Pinky" Lomini, age 17

"You need to read a little louder, Pinky . . . we can't hear you." That was our constant refrain for the first several weeks of her participation in the group as we would all lean towards her soft, almost-afraid-to-be-heard voice of the little girl, and still couldn't make out her words. Gradually, her voice grew louder and stronger, and when she was asked to read this short, stunning offering in one of our anniversary readings in front of a crowd of fifty, her voice rang loud and clear. Beautiful.

WHO AM I?? What am I?? What is my purpose for living on this earth? Inside I'm lost, running everyday away from the truth, away from the reality of my life! I find myself dreaming more than anything else. Life is so hard—dying seems the easiest thing to do in life! Living is hard! Finding myself is even harder. Where do I start looking? In the mirror seems the best place since the reflection of yourself is staring back at you wondering the same thing, asking the same questions! I don't have answers for my reflection and the person staring back at me has no answers for me! It seems like every time we meet the relationship gets more distant, like I know less about the girl in the mirror than I did the last time! I'm very unhappy with her, or is she just unhappy with me? Yesterday she asked me if I loved her, and in response I looked quietly, not saying anything. That was a hard question. She never asked me anything so deep before. Love between us two was never mentioned. I don't know how to love her. From experience, love hurts. When I love someone they always walk out of my life or don't love me back. I wasn't ready to

love her. I might not ever love her! Finally I answered her saying we
have to take things one day at a time. I can't love someone I don't
know.

PART TWO

THE JOURNEY TOWARD
JUSTICE, 2010-2012

Edited by Linda Coleman and Erika Duncan

INTRODUCTION

As THE NEW YORK STATE prison population shrinks, and continues to do so with recent reforms to the archaic sentence structure of the Rockefeller Drug Laws, which doled out lengthy sentences for low level drug offenses, the population of women in prison continues to grow. Although women still make up a small percentage of the total prison population, approximately 35,000 women and adolescent girls are under some form of correctional control statewide.[1] For women returning home from prison, the responsibilities are overwhelming and mountainous. About three-quarters of women in prison are mothers, for whom the return journey may involve the struggle to regain the rights to their children.

As we read through the stories shared in the final two sections of this anthology we find the challenges facing women in prison ever expanding: the need for housing upon release, mental health services, domestic violence support, issues of severe abuse, immigration challenges are just a few. We also learn about the victories, small and large found in these stories; a woman who discovers her true calling, another who pushes past the identity of a felony conviction, and yet another who challenges the cycle of domestic violence. What we find is women who are survivors, women who are courageous and brave beyond their years. For youth involved in the criminal justice system, we hear the insightful resonance of voices that refuse to be silenced by the systemic oppression intrinsic in our jails and prisons.

As readers we cheer the writers on, we want to know how the story ends, we hold our breath and root for a happy ending. For myself, I had

---

[1] Correctional Association of New York, http://www.correctionalassociation.org/issue/women.

never heard the word "reentry" before prison, a word I use often in my presentations and writings now. In what seems like a lifetime ago, almost fifteen years ago, I sat looking out of my barred prison cell window at Bedford Hills Correctional Facility. I was about to be released from prison without the slightest plan for my future. At the time I didn't have the perspective to realize that life as I had known it was forever changed by my incarceration and returning to some semblance of my old routine was not only ridiculous, but impossible. I wasn't just some young college girl who ended up in prison for a family related domestic violence issue . . . I was a convicted felon, barred from holding most jobs, very different from any other average 21-year-old I knew.

For most women returning from incarceration or confinement, the idea of leaving prison is a frightening one; we are filled with the excitement and anticipation of release, but also dread the day we go home. We know we leave behind the routine restriction of prison for the unpredictable, erratic world outside of prisons' electric fences. Incarcerated we are sheltered from emotional maturity, left without the ability to make our life's decisions. The smack of the real world is very hard to adjust to. This does not mean we can't move past our time in prison, we carry the lessons learned and the friendships forged with us always, although the transition home takes years sometimes to make peace with, to adjust to outside life.

For many of us a safe space to write and share our thoughts is a welcome reprieve from life after prison or jail. Having joined a wonderful support group, Prison Families Anonymous, they hosted a Herstory workshop where I began to write. I think back to a college class I took at Bedford Hills Correctional Facility. The question of resilience was being debated in the classroom, and I remember the professor telling us that researchers don't have a clear grasp on why some children are more resilient than others. When I think of the many women I've befriended along the way, women serving life in prison, political prisoners, and mothers mothering from behind bars, I see women who are resilient. Women who determine to get on with life, even if it is from within the walls of prison cells.

I would like to think a large part of my own resilience came from my own nurturing mother but I would be remiss if I didn't include another mother of sorts. Sister Elaine Roulet, an unconventional nun who worked in the prison, and pioneered programs to help children maintain ties to their incarcerated mothers. With the help of then Superintendent Elaine

Lord, Sr. Elaine created children's centers, with toys and books, reading circles and crafts in the visiting room of Bedford Hills Correctional Facility, a model program replicated throughout state correctional facilities. She also created parenting centers, where women were taught parenting skills, and among other things were able to record books on tape to send home to their children. When I met Sister she asked me to be her secretary, I worked with her in the RMU, regional medical unit, where we provided activities for the severely mentally ill and physically ill. I watched as she conducted prayer services that ended with singing and little trinkets for the women on the ward, she was always thinking of things to make life just a little easier for them. Sometimes she would hand out donations of soap and shampoo, the women were grateful. I sat with her while we created art work with women on suicide watch, some of their arms bandaged to the elbows from self-mutilation, cutting. She encouraged me to see past my own grief and pain, and challenged me to create ways to support those worse off than me in prison.

Since then I was fortunate to have worked on criminal justice issues and their impact on women at the Correctional Association of New York's Women in Prison Project before coming back to Long Island to start a family, where I began to think about ways in which I could support women in reentry here on the Island. During my time at the Correctional Association, I learned just how closely women's pathways to incarceration were related to domestic violence, childhood abuse, drug addiction and the slew of other factors that most of the women I was incarcerated with were coping with. I had seen the devastating results of these factors first-hand on my sisters in prison, but had not truly understood where the issues originated.

As a young person in prison, I hadn't really been able to understand that the oppression I saw was a direct and intentional result of our devastating system of incarceration in the United States. This system which intentionally targets and suppresses the poor, Black and Latino populations and women must be changed. In my opinion the challenges faced by prisoners returning to suburban and rural areas is often a much more difficult one than that of prisoners returning to urban life. With significantly less access to public transportation and with the mark of prison much harder to hide from employers unfamiliar with the plight of the formerly incarcerated person, life becomes much more difficult.

Now being afforded the opportunity to further develop Herstory's advocacy and justice initiatives, our intention is to begin to utilize the sto-

ries as vehicles to support those incarcerated and those facing reentry. These stories work to create paths of empowerment for our writers who are often marginalized by incarceration or immigration-related issues. Most importantly our Herstory writings develop a deep sense of purpose and importance for some of us who may for the first time be experiencing these sentiments. We will take these stories, lived experiences, just one step farther, passing them into the hands of legislators, daring them to create fair and just laws to ameliorate the plight of those in prison and those returning back to our communities.

We, as formerly incarcerated individuals, are the living examples those who choose to give back to the community, create ways to end the cycles of abuse, to improve our prison systems, to offer opportunities of hope for our brothers and sisters returning home from the oppression of prison and jail. In my former job, I remember taking a busload of women to Albany to advocate for a bill which would help give mothers in prison a fighting chance to keep their children after incarceration rather than losing them to the foster care system.

We sat with a senator, talked about the merits of the bill, stating that 75% of women in prison were mothers, etc., citing statistics, while he seemed to glaze over as we spoke. Then a formerly incarcerated mother told her story, how she longed to be given a second chance to raise her son, how when she got the chance she did indeed get to be his mother and watch him grow up. The senator began to listen more intently, something in his eye seemed to light up, he got it. And that was it, he was the swing vote we needed to get the bill passed, and it did. I can just imagine if this woman were to put her story into words, if the Herstory method were used it would have become memorialized in its power and ability to affect change. This unique tool is one that Herstory offers, one that sets it apart from others. I for one, am exhilarated by the thought of exploring ways in which we can affect community change through lived experiences.

For me, prison began as a debilitating silencing of my voice, and became in the end a vehicle for my metamorphosis. Herstory builds on the experiences I've had, offering a powerful vehicle to create ways in which people can learn from our stories. To find voice through writing and through the listening to others' stories, to change not only ourselves, but our communities and our world for the better is of great importance. I think of so many of the women I left behind at Bedford, and I hope they know that I take their stories with me on my journey. These brave wom-

en continue to have an immeasurable impact on my life and I hope that in some way I am giving back to them from the other side of prison walls.

Serena Alfieri–Liguori

Advocacy and Justice Program Director
Herstory Writers Workshop
September, 2012

TEENS WRITING FROM JAIL

SEVENTY THOUSAND *young people under the age of 18 woke up today behind bars in the United States. The vast majority of these young people are charged with non-violent crimes that posed no threat to public safety, but their futures will forever be complicated and marked by the effects of their arrests and incarceration. Most are youth of color and from low-income urban communities, whose offenses might well have been dismissed in more affluent white neighborhoods.[1] In spite of—or because of—their experiences behind bars, more than 70% of them will return to prison within a decade, often for more serious felonies, and to serve longer sentences.[2]*

---

[1] As of 2010, over 83% of young people in locked facilities were African-American or Hispanic. While we are working specifically in jails, where arts organizations rarely go—writing workshops in prisons are more common—the figures we have given here, in order to give a broader overview, include teens in prison and post-trial facilities. Our teen program serves between 50 and 75 young women ages 16-21 incarcerated in Long Island's three jails, while our women's program serves well over 100 a year.

[2] Thirty-eight states and the District of Columbia treat 17-year-olds as juveniles. Fewer than 10 states continue to treat 17-year-olds as adults. Illinois has recently amended its age of criminal responsibility to treat 17-year-olds who commit misdemeanors as juveniles. Connecticut raised its age of criminal responsibility to 17 effective January 2010. By 2012, Connecticut will raise its age of criminal responsibility to 18. (*OJJDP Statistical Briefing Book.* Available: http://ojjdp.ncjrs.gov/ojstatbb/structure_process/qa04101.asp?qa Date=2007. Released on October 31, 2009; Illinois Public Act 95-10310 effective January 1, 2010; Connecticut General Statutes section 46b-121.) By contrast, New York is one of only two states in the nation (the other is North Carolina) where all 16 and 17 year-olds in the justice system are automatically prosecuted as adults, without exception and regardless of crime severity. In a January 2011 report, *Advancing a Fair and Just Age of Criminal Responsibility for Youth in New York State*, the NYS Governor's Children's Cabinet Advisory Board states, "New York, a state longconsidered a leader in justice-related issues, is falling behind the vast majority of states on a critical issue—the age of criminal responsibility. While most states treat 16- and 17-year-olds as juveniles, New York treats all 16- and 17-year-olds as adults for criminal responsibility. If arrested after their 16th birthday, they are tak-

Almost all of the stories and faces of these young people—their bound-less energy, their already guarded hopes and dreams that lurk beneath the stories of what brought them to brush with the criminal justice sys-tem—will never be known to us, but a few of them are offered to you in this section of Voices. It has been our great gift to see these hopes and dreams emerge bit by bit, as girls who had been rival gang members in the streets, looking for the love, community and power so absent from the almost unbearable burdens that marked their young lives, found a safe space to express how their choices were made.

What emerges from the stories that we have included here is a poi-gnant picture of the search for attachment, power over circumstances, and a means of survival that has motivated the choices of these young women so far. As they share their fantasies—that enough love might make the men to whom they have attached themselves not only kind but "bullet-proof," that the babies they bear while incarcerated will be theirs to raise differently, that perhaps women will be able to love dif-ferently from men, or that mothers enslaved to addiction might return to a beauty only vaguely remembered—we cannot help but want to put our arms around the young selves they have lovingly, angrily—even at times playfully—brought back to life on these pages.

Like the women you meet elsewhere in this anthology, the majority of these girls have already been marked by the system. They are children of mothers who were too wounded themselves to have anything left to give, foster children passed along as pawns in unsavory money-making schemes, and victims of generations of addiction, violence and abuse. As each takes on the task of connecting the dots, to show how she navigated

---

en to adult court, spend time detained or do time in local adult jails and can be incar-cerated in state run adult correctional institutions if sentenced to longer than one year."

Moving into New York, where we are working with teen writers in jail, in 2009, a New York State Governors Task Force, along with a Federal Department of Justice investigation exposed system-wide abuse including brutal punishments for minor infractions, failure to provide mental health services, and dangerous restraint tactics that resulted in broken bones, concussions, and lost teeth.

Incarcerating one juvenile costs approximately $266,000 per year while Alternatives to De-tention programs cost as little as $15,000 per youth and have been shown to lower recidivism rates to between 17 and 36% (Correctional Association of New York, 2011). In spite of the very clear facts that youth employment strategies and community based programs geared to youth are the most cost-effective ways to increase public safety, to decrease incarceration rates, and to save taxpayer monies, federal funding for juvenile justice programs has been decreasing steadily since 2002, while more money each year is devoted to expanding the federal prison "industrial" complex.

life's circumstances, we gather more insight into what this dynamic tribe of incarcerated girls is up against, as we watch them struggle to find pleasure and mastery in the badly corrupted, broken places into which they have been thrown.

While for boys and men in many cultures, "doing time" can be seen as a rite of passage, women and girls who have brushed with the system are all too often shunned by the families and community members who celebrate this rite for their young men. We close this section with the story of another kind of violence and violation, without which the picture would not be complete, paying tribute to the many children whose sense of safety and justice was violated irreparably during dangerous border crossings, while their parents struggled to find them a new life.

For, it is only in connecting the dots that we start to see the whole picture—the disproportionate number of young people of color who end up in jail, the relationship between domestic violence and larger violence, and the unequal distribution of resources and opportunities—each story contributing to the creation of a just, equitable world, where no one will need to undergo what these young women have undergone.

The teen writing that we have encountered in Suffolk and Nassau County's three jails, is steeped in the mores of their peers and the popular culture of Rap and HipHop. Often these young women begin their journey into memoir by writing in rhyme, a medium that allows them to both express and hide at the same time, and to speak to their peers in the language of their "tribe." Only slowly, over time do they garner the trust in their writing community that allows them to break free of the rhyming that shields them, and to enter the particulars of their life experience.

While in Nassau County Correctional Facility, incarcerated girls are separated from their elders in almost all of their activities, in Suffolk County's two facilities, freer mixing has allowed us to create workshop formats where the teens benefit by working alongside older women who serve as mentors and guides.

These are the "mothers" who may have cared for or abandoned them, whose stories they can hear and tears they can see, as they bear witness to their maternal pain, remorse, and regrets for their actions, as well as their concerns and worries for their own teen daughters in trouble. These women are living examples of issues they are struggling with in their own relationships with their own mothers (and for the many incarcerated teen mothers who appear in our groups.) Side by side they work, cry, and laugh together, nurturing forgiveness and acceptance.

Herstory was born out of the notion that caring on the part of a read-ing or listening stranger isn't unconditional, but must be carefully earned. For much as we, as "Stranger/Readers," try to be open-minded, we are intrinsically judgmental. What makes Herstory workshops unique—both inside jail-based settings and out—is our work with each writer to chal-lenge the judgmental reader to enter so deeply that these barriers begin to dissolve. Never is this technique of daring the reader to care more im-portant than in working with our incarcerated teens, who take judgment to its very limit. What they learn in the process of listening to the gradual opening of each other's stories, just as they are encouraged to go deeply into their own, is how their willingness to be vulnerable turns fear and judgment into empathy, creating a new sort of strength and community.

Although the young women included in this section would have been thrilled to have their stories published under their own names, we have decided to create pseudonyms for those under the age of 18 still in custody of the state. As they come of age, in future editions or online publications, we will return those who remain in contact with us and continue with their justice work to their own identities and keep our readers up with what they have decided to do with their lives. For this reason too, we have decided to publish this teen section with only flowers instead of the photographs so many of the young women had friends and relatives on the outside forward to us.

I Can't Remember the Last Time

Cece Cleveland

Cece has a powerful quiet presence, a demeanor that belies her young age and can easily intimidate until you catch her smile—the smile of a 16-year-old—or are privy to a phrase or two of her dry, quick sense of humor. Once she embraced this writing process, she dropped her guard and her words poured forth and gripped all who heard them, touching the hearts of all who have loved a parent and been abandoned by them. Like other teens struggling with unreliable parents, Cece turned to a gang for family, and is serving state time in prison. While in our group, she shared the circle with another opposing gang member. Through their association in the writing group they moved beyond the dictates of gang protocol and became good friends.

Sometimes *I wish I could run away from the world. I wonder how can I ever gain peace when I run from my past? But I'm afraid of my future. I reflect on childhood memories when ignorance was bliss and around every corner was a new mystery waiting to be explored. In the essence of my innocence lie joy and content. But what happens when the innocence fades and ignorance becomes knowledge of the world's adversities and the coldness of society? You find an adolescent jaded by life, numb to pain and disappointment.*

I can't remember the last time I heard her voice and felt her warm embrace. Damn, is God punishing me? I don't understand why whenever I clench happiness it slowly slips away. In a state of denial I slowly walk toward my closet, never realizing my feet are meeting the ground. I remember this dress. I run my fingers across the fabric recollecting the pearlescent glow of her soft brown eyes. She feels so near to me, but where? She always leaves for a while, but she'll come back.

Every day I sit by the window, awaiting the handful of laughter and soul full of comfort she brings at her arrival. Days go by, weeks, months, and still no sign of her return. The reality of the situation subtly creeps into my circumference sending chills up my spine. I swallow my heart and come to terms with the fact that this time she has left, never to return.

Sometimes I imagine what it's like, death that is. Where do you go? Is it cold, dark and lonely? Is your spirit really at rest? In a drunken fit I pace to and fro contemplating whether or not I want to experience what the non-existence of life is. She was my best friend, my mother. How could I ever withstand the future without her presence? I long to find her, wherever that may be.

I fall into a drunken sleep that night and awake to a sick and twisted dream that seems impossible to break out of. I step off a couch onto the cold floor in a dark and damp room. My instincts know this is not the same place where I laid my head to rest the night before. I panic and scramble to find a light. When my eyes finally adjust to the darkness I realize my familiarity with this place. I realize I am standing in my old two-bedroom basement apartment which I had shared with what was left of my mother. The very place where we settled after my father drove us out of his life like a bad habit. And for what? I was only four. What was so horrible about me that I didn't deserve to be loved the same way every father loved his little girl?

I recline in my chair, break up some bud and twist it up. This is my escape, which soothes the pain and allows me to break free of the memories, break free of the things that clutch my heart like a wrench and haunt the deepest depths of my mind. With every toke I allow part of me to drift away from the darkness I call myself.

I can clearly remember the point in my life that I became cold and unremorseful from being let down and lied to my whole life. I was 12 years old. Like any normal 12-year-old I hated getting up and going to school, but it was made easier awakening to her angelic voice singing in my ear. *"When I look at you, then the world's alright with me."* Till this day I cling to that line of the song she sang to me until the day she died.

"Wake up, Mushy," she said pulling the blanket from over my head.

When I pulled the cover back she began to tickle me.

"Mommy, stop it," I yelled, as I squirmed and giggled. "Okay ma, I'm up!"

Even though I was old enough to pick my own clothes, she always ironed and laid them out for me. By the time I was showered and ready I heard the bus outside. I hugged her and yelled, "Bye, Carrot top!" then jumped over the stairs and out the door.

I always finished my homework before eighth period, so I made plans with my homies for after school. From sitting through a long day of doing more than enough shit I ain't wanna do, I was finally on the bus ride home. I hopped off, made sure there were no scuffs or creases in my Riccz, then pulled out my key and unlocked the door, praying that Mom-dukes made a nigga something to eat. I went upstairs and threw my books in my room.

I heard the TV on in the den, so I walked downstairs to let her know I was home. When I entered the den, to my surprise she wasn't there. So I turned the TV off and ascended the stairs and walked into the kitchen thinking she was there and I hadn't noticed before. Then again, what do you know, she wasn't there either. By now I was really starting to wonder, where the hell could this woman be? Still pondering my thoughts, I retrieved my dog's bowls, fed and gave him water. When I put the cans in the garbage, I noticed it was full. I walked out the back door and down the deck to dispose of the trash. I walked to the side of the house, only to find my mother in the gazebo, almost with her head in her lap, nodded out on pills.

In a pointless effort of trying to wake her, a furious streak of anger engulfed me as I thought to myself, *Why does bullshit like this always happen to me?* In a state of pure rage, I went back into the house and grabbed a Sharpie, a sheet of paper and tape. I returned to the backyard and taped a note to her chest which said, I'M LEAVING, NEVER TO RETURN. THANKS A LOT MOM FOR GETTING CLEAN, and stormed out of the gate, letting it slam behind me.

I've allowed these memories to strip me naked and cast me into a place in time when I look through the haze, and the reflection looking back does not have my name. I am stripped of what I own and what is free. I have nothing to look back at but the person who is not me. And my mother, she was the benevolent force that shackled me to the twisted evils of earth's depths, disallowing my soul passage as I now chase it to the land that is free.

Demons

Patricia McConnell

Patricia had to work hard to drop her guard, to drop what she thought she should write for her teen peers (Hip Hop lyrics), to drop her reticence for speaking her truth in front of an opposing gang member also in our group (they went on to become friends) and to let us into the vulnerable heart of the 11-year-old who'd been forced out onto the street to fend for herself. She spent several months working with us, working in fits and starts into the heart of the writing below. A difficult struggle for Patricia was even imagining breaking her allegiance to the gang that had "parented" her during her life on the streets. As she found the strength of her own voice, we also witnessed her rising confidence to follow her own path. She is still serving time for the actions that brought her to us.

Even *while I'm behind bars, even though I'm not able to do what I want when I want, I'm free behind these bars. I'm free in my heart, free of addiction, free of fear, free of my chains in the outside world. I'm free of the demons who walk, looking for trouble . . .*

Now I'ma go hard. It's time to face the demons inside me. My entire life, there isn't a day that goes by that I don't take at least five minutes from my life to look back to a moment in my past that without a doubt changed me. Whether physically or emotionally, abandonment continues to dwell within the walls of flesh that I call myself.

I really don't like to dwell on the past, but at this point that's where it's gotta go. My mom, she physically abandoned me, mentally fucked me, and emotionally scarred me. My dad, well he chose to cast out his own children for the sake of a woman who physically abused him and mentally got him to the point where he kicked me and my younger brother, his children of eleven and nine out on the streets.

Since I'm a toddler I've been around nothing more than addicts who center their lives around lust and the thrill of their next high and most of all the shiesty plots to get the money to get their fix. From the jump and the first five dollar bill my young seven-year-old hands held onto, I knew that makin' money and flippin' was gonna be one thing I was gonna be good at.

Now at 11, I'm kicked out on the streets due to a fight, like a beat down with my dad's new wife. I knew that I was much smarter than that. I called up my friend John and told him I needed a dub on the arm. Of course he had no problem with it 'cause most of his custies were sent to him by me.

I need to go home, I'm only 11 but I feel so damn grown. He said that he cared then showed me the door. I don't even feel bad I got her blood on the floor dumb whore. You said that "Daddy will always be there."

I feel so alone, you're away and I'm scared, I was so unprepared. I acted purely outta fear. Now I feel like I'm dreaming and you still not here.

Bein' here, it is now that I stand with my head held high, my soul no longer red-eyed and teary. Here I stand tall, towering over this demon after 15 years, with only a few words left to slide off my lips to lay him in his fiery grave. Here I stand strong and say *it's over*. Forever. I've gotta start living for me and not the past. But how, when the past is all I know?

My heart breaks in two when I think about what I put my family through. I think back to a time where there were no tears cried, even moments when tears fell they were easily dried. I see the pain in my grandma's eyes as she says coldly, "This mistake I can't let slide."

I swear I felt my heart stop as I wish I had died, but I held my head high, tried to swallow my pride. Damn, what a ride. How could I think to me the rules didn't apply, nothing to do but think why. I look through this clear Plexiglas wishin' for once that she would lie and say, "It'll be just fine." Tell me, "We'll get through this."

Mentally and physically I'm fit, but emotions are tellin' me "you can't do this." Every day I fight to push through the pain. Some days it's bearable, but other times it's insane. I was raised to never let 'em see you shed a tear. At one point my future felt mapped out. Now it's hazy and unclear.

Here I am at 19-years-old, sitting on a day bed in Riverhead Jail, in the middle of August—August 9th to be exact. It is only now that I realized 100% that the only way I'm gonna get over the past, to get through this is to leave everything, everybody that I've ever known behind.

Secrets, secrets are no fun, especially when they could potentially scar somebody for the rest of their lives. I sit here once again with my mind full of emotions . . . full of questions that I can't answer, questions that people are telling me half-assed answers to that I refuse to believe. Lies, Death, fear and sorrow go hand in hand. More so now, for me that is, that I'm behind bars. Only difference is, now not only am I locked in physically, but I'm locked in mentally. I'm a prisoner in my own mind, trapped in a whirlwind of emotions, of thoughts . . .

"I Thought I Could Bullet-proof You . . ."

Latrice Haywood

"I thought I could bullet-proof you," writes Latrice, who, like so many of the teen girls who end up in jail have given their trust to young men involved in gang life and violence. She joined our group with the encouragement of one of the older women, a surrogate "mother" who had "adopted" her. With little hesitation, Latrice dove into writing this layered love story, pouring out her trauma, grief and remorse in both words and tears. Since her discharge, she has continued to work on it in our Bridges group.

Sunday afternoon, I pull into the driveway, coming from the supermarket with Vonie's mom, niece and nephew. Get out and peep at Vonie sitting in the white jeep across the lot of the building with his cousins. I pick his nephew up and start towards the front door. I usually tell him to come, but he pissed me off earlier. I walk down the hall, past the fire exit and into his apartment, put the baby and the bags down, grab the broom and begin sweeping.

"Ring, ring," his mother's phone goes off.

"Eww," I say. "You need to change this ringtone, Big Ma." That's what we call his mom, Big Ma. Me thinking nothing of the phone call, I pick it up.

"Hello? . . . Helloo?"

"Babe is that you?" he asks nervously.

"Yeah, it's me, Vonie, what's wrong?"

"Call the cops," he yells.

I immediately call and run outside. First thing I see is little kids, little toddlers, no older than three, running towards the gate about

30 feet opposite the front door. I run out to the parking lot and see about 30 guys surround the jeep. Every single one has a bat, knife, steel pole or a stick, all but two. These two look different from them all. These two have big black hoodies on and have guns pointed towards the jeep. I know all 30 of them.

I begin to hear shots—four consistent ones and five after them like firecrackers. I run towards them. The tall dark-skinned male with big lips has a gun pointed to Vonie's head. I scream, the dark-skinned one flinches and lets off the last shot. I close my eyes as if I am seeing things. But it is as real as the stunned look on my face. Someone yells in a deep raspy voice, "There's Latrice, take flight." And they do. They all do. I take three more steps and the driver's side door where he was sitting, opens. He steps out and immediately falls to his knees.

White bright lights beeping and the buzzing of machines and the smell of Purell hand sanitizer in the air. I'm at Huntington Hospital. I'm looking around for familiar faces, but I see none. All I see are a bunch of women in blue and white scrubs. In the emergency department, distraught, out of breath, sweaty, teary-eyed and confused, running from room to room looking for him. A nurse approaches me with a concerned look on her face and asks if I need help. I can tell she is Dominican by her accent and dark skin tone.

"I'm looking for Davon. Davon White, he was shot, where is he, is he okay?"

"Ma'am, I need you to calm down," the nurse says.

But I can't. "He's allergic to Bacitracin, don't give him that . . . and bananas too, don't feed him that. Where is he?" The tears start to flow harder as she walks me over to the tan front desk, messy with papers.

"He's coming out of surgery now," she says handing me a blue tissue.

"No!" I scream. "You put him to sleep? You can't give him anesthetics he has asthma!"

What if he doesn't wake up? I think. There I go again, thinking of the worst-case scenario.

"There he is, being rolled into room three," she says, interrupting my jumbled thoughts

I dash towards the room. I walk into what looks like a white box with a whole bunch of machines beeping consistently. There he is . . . looks to be okay, lying flat on his back covered in what looks like thirty blankets. I walk over to his right side and grab his cold, dark, rough hand.

"Vonie . . . Vonie, look at me," I say sobbing already and the man didn't say two words yet.

He looks up, gripping my hand tighter and says faintly, "Babe."

"Yes, Vonie, I'm here."

His eyes begin to close, and his grip loosens.

"Hold my hand, Von!" I begin to panic.

"Hold my hand," I repeat. He looks up and holds my hand.

"I love you," he says.

"I love you too," I say, as tears fall on his white knitted blankets. He begins to drift back to sleep. I figure it's the morphine he's on. As he sleeps, I stare as I wipe the sweat off his brown dark forehead, touching his big lips and patting his rough black hair with the look of agony on my face.

I begin to hear heavy footsteps, getting closer and closer, reminding me of the Tims my father wore. I look towards the door and there is a white, blue-eyed, freckle-faced detective in a blue shirt, about 6′5″ with khakis standing on the threshold.

He looks at me. "You have to leave," he demands.

"What!" I snap at him. I hate when people tell me what I have to do.

"I'd like to speak with Davon alone," he says hesitantly.

I look back at Davon. We wake him. I tell him I love him once more.

As the DT walks closer towards me, he begins to nudge me.

"Don't touch me, and don't rush me," I say, cold and harsh as my face turns towards him. Davon grabs my hand tightly and says, "I love you too."

He releases my hand and I walk back out to the door. I pause and glance back at Von and say to myself, *I thought I could bulletproof you.* Walking back through the lobby out the sliding doors. At this point, all the tears have stopped, but my heart rate is still accelerating. Thinking back to that "suicide incident" last week . . .

November 23

After a day of tit for tats, unnecessary attitudes, smart comments and hurt feelings I remain silent. This argument has gotten old the third time around. *Yeah I cheated—three years ago—we're still on this—why?* But I never got up the guts to say this outside my thoughts. I'd just sit and stare as he roared like a wild beast.

Nostrils flaring—"Jennifer, you have a whore for a daughter-in-law!" he would yell.

"D.C. Stop talkin' to that girl that way."

He'd woken his mom once again at 2 A.M. with his B.S. I didn't want to deal with it—I hated myself for it—I didn't expect him to forgive me until I forgave myself. Damn, low self-esteem kickin' in so once again, I ran. As he was in the bathroom carrying on to his mom while she was try'na calm him down, I grabbed my cheetah print duffle bag and stuffed all my shit inside. I'd come back for the heavy shit, I figured. But all my clothes I took.

He opened the bedroom door with disgust in his eyes . . . I stepped up on the brown post at the far corner of the bed, hopped onto the ledge and out the window of his first floor apartment. Walked a mile home in the dark from First Avenue to Tenth Avenue. When I got to my tan two-story home, I didn't walk in. I sat on the blue cobblestone stoop, gazing at the stars trying to escape reality with the distractions of astronomy.

Five minutes later my phone vibrated consistently for 20 seconds straight. I knew who it was and definitely what it was—angry break-up texts.

"I hate you, don't ever want to see you again, I deserve better. Five years of you and I should've learned, I can't trust a bitch like you—I'ma find a new wife."

This was nothing new to me. I'd learned to deal with his temper tantrums and verbal abuse for a while. I felt I deserved it. I was wrong to hurt him the way I did.

I wrote back, "I'm coming home." Then turned my phone off—I knew he was opposed. It was late, cold and scary out. Dark and foggy, like a scene from a scary movie. All I heard was the sound of T.V. on the inside and faint crickets. I got up and walked inside . . . up six steps to the hallway, Jayden's room dead ahead and on the right my mom's room . . . a little farther down-mine . . . I threw the bag down the hall—it landed in my room.

Walked back down to the front door and took the keys to my mom's midnight blue Honda off the key hook and headed out, locking the door behind me. Got in the car and headed back to First Avenue doin' 80 through the dark quiet streets of the South Side. Pulled into the parking lot of the apartment building anxious and dizzy. As I parked the car I felt so lightheaded, my mind going 100 mph but focused on the one thing. Von. I got out and started towards the door. When I got to the front door I called his 14-year-old niece, Jada.

"Hello?" Push the button to open the front door.

"What's wrong?"

"Please, Jada."

"It's open."

I hung up and walked to the end of the hall and there he was— not surprised to see me but not happy either. I followed him into the house. He was on the phone talking to Quae, my cousin. Not really payin' me any mind. He hung up with Quae and walked back out into the building's hallway, me two steps behind.

Walking close as he made his way back to the front door, he stopped and turned to face me. "What do you want?" he said.

I stared into his bloodshot red eyes as he waited for a response clenching his jaw though I froze silent and still as a statue. He turned to leave and I blurted out, "Where are you going?"

"To the store, why?"

"What, what, what do you want from me?" he yelled.

"Lemme drive you."

"No, I'll walk."

"Either way, I'm coming."

"You're a nuisance!"

"And you're stubborn!" Am I complaining?"

"Leave."

"No!"

"I don't want you!"

"We go through this constantly . . . you don't mean, watch what you say this time. I'm so close to the edge, I'ma snap."

He stepped closer to me, face to face—well, chest to face—and he said "I'm done."

"The day you leave is the day I die—remember that?"

"Man fuck that, I wish you would."

"You don't care remember, so lemme grant your wish."

I ran out the front door and back into the car. He followed and sat in the passenger seat.

"Leave me alone, I'm gone. Just like you wanted, word to it all you won't see me again and you're not invited to my funeral bitch . . . fuck out of my car."

"I wasn't planning on coming!" he laughed.

"Let me go or close the door—shit, nigga, you wanna come too?" I yelled. "I'm tired of you—of you treating me this way, I deserve so much more, my father be so disappointed to see what I'm putting up with."

"Yeah, he'd also be disappointed to know that nigga was between your . . . " He stopped as I stared and shook my head. I'm sayin'—if looks could kill.

Right then he took the keys out my hand.

"I'm getting off this earth one way or another," I said staring at the house keys sticking out his sweat pants pocket. I opened the car door in preparation for what I was about to do. I quickly snatched the house keys and ran. I got through the front door of the house and headed for the stairs (the elevator would take too long) running up three flights, hearing his close footsteps behind me, his pace picking up as he realized my goal.

The staircase got narrow. It led to the roof access door, cautioned with red signs reading "Do not enter" and "Restricted."

Vonie yelled, "Stop!" but I kept going. He yanked the hood of my grey Abercrombie sweatshirt to restrain me. It didn't work. I ran faster and faster—I'm now sweating, legs are cramping and tears are flowing. I got to the door and pushed it open. It was now raining, the roof was slippery. I ran and found a metal chair I threw behind me to place in his way. Step after step closer to the edge, splashing in puddles on the dirty white rooftop I began to see the green of the grass more and more. I reached the edge and pivoted staring at Davon still struggling with the metal chair that got caught on his sweatpants. I screamed out, "I love you," trying to pierce through the loud raring of the sky's thunder. My face soaking, not able to differentiate between tears or raindrops all in the matter of three seconds I stretched my arms out and leaned back, closing my eyes waiting for the moment my pain would vanish.

Unexpectedly I felt him grab me right after most of my body weight was shifted backwards, pulling me from the edge back to the middle of the roof. He just hugged me apologizing repetitively,

"I do love you, I do, I can't live without you—why would you try to do this?" he asked.

"You told me to leave! You told me you didn't want me, I'd rather die a thousand deaths than deal with the pain I caused you, I'm sorry—I'm so sorry."

Then it started to pour as we sat in the middle of a rooftop puddle. I was never one used to admitting mistakes—I would run away from them, thinking they'd disappear. But this was the moment I'd realized that this conflict was internal and I had been trying to escape my own mind.

If he would've let go—he would've never got shot.

Pain

Deidre Jackson

When women come into Herstory, whether they are behind bars or living outside, we ask them to imagine that they are writing a book in which gradually their lives will unfold. The exercise of finding the "Page One Moment" becomes a trigger for beginning to tell a story, leading to chapter after chapter and page after page. Jackson, as Deidre preferred to call herself, presented a tough and guarded picture when she came into our group, but the person who emerges on the page is quite different. Intermingling prose poems and prayers through these short chapters that trace her journey away from her first foster home into a life of her own choice, she gives us a vivid picture of a 14-year-old coming of age in the tragically uncaring atmosphere of "the hood," looking for power, mastery of the world that she has been thrown into, and ultimately for a relief and tenderness not to be easily found. The magic of this story is the vulnerability she displays, even while we watch her harden and toughen into being able to cope with the life she is given. It is in her spirit and her search that we begin to contemplate what healing might be possible when our stories begin to connect the dots.

If you looked into my life you'll see what I have seen, go where I have gone and feel what I have felt. My eyes have hurt me more than my ears, but my heart is the one that has been hurt the most.

You see me then you think you know me but have no idea. You hear what people say then you judge me, which I don't care.

Who am I, why I act the way I act, all I know, what I been through, what I see, how I feel, why I don't trust and why I hate with passion is because of the pain.

I am angry, I hate, I curse, I don't love, I punch, I spit and I will kill because I hurt and am in so much pain. All I know, all my life, don't want you to care, don't wanna see no shed tears. Just want you to know who I am.

Abandoned, beaten, betrayed, hurt, hit, judged, molested, picked on, raped, lied to, lied on is mostly what I battle with from day in and day out. With all of this on my brain I then have to cope with people which I can't, 'cause I don't want to. People/humans are made to hurt and cause pain so when I can I turn to nature. Nature—the trees, green grass and water—soothes me. I feel more at peace when alone. Do I trust myself? Yes, only when I'm alone.

(1)

I think I'm making the right decision, I know I'm making the right decision. These are the things that are going through my head as I am walking down the block, a bag full of clothes, freezing my ass off. I really don't wanna leave Ms. Best, because she is my mother, the only woman I call Ma, or Mommy. Over the past 11½ years she has been good to me. Yes I've had my ass whooped, but I deserved it.

Mommy is on dialysis and is very weak. She is dying soon so I refuse to be living under the roof of the rest of these abusive people! I hate them. All they do is beat on me, embarrass me, talk shit to me and make me cry . . . I mean Ms. Best could discipline me, 'cause she is the one who took me in, the only one who really loves me and the one who is my foster parent. But now Ms. Best is getting too sick and she can't even speak up for me and when she does they be hating . . . So I don't know why they are always trying to be my mothers.

These are the things that are going through my head as I am going to this new home. I really don't want to go, but I'm 14-years-old now and when she is dead and gone I will not be left with them, they will not treat me the same . . .

So here I am freezing, rolling my valuables down a street in the ice cold October weather saying bye to my old neighborhood, "Bed Stuy," and hello to the new foster home, Ms. Inez Lindsay.

(2)

"Hello Ms. Lindsay this is Deidra. Did the agency notify you to let you know I was coming? Okay, well I'm not sure of where you live could you let me know the address? Okay, I'll call you if I get lost. Thanks, good-bye."

I just got finished talking to the new foster mother with the directions to the new foster home. I hope this home is better. I hope she allows me to shop with my own money. I hope I get new sneakers. Thank God it's still in Brooklyn. That way I could still visit Ms. Best and my friends. Hopefully I could have a little bit of freedom to do any of these things.

I arrived at the house.

"Hello, Ms. Lindsay, I'm Deidra."

"Well, come in and you make me seem old by calling me Ms. Lindsay. Just call me Shoogi."

Shoogi lived across the tracks, which is Crown Heights in Brooklyn, in a house. I came from a house, so I was familiar with house duties and chores. I just hoped I wouldn't be a slave. Shoogi escorted me to my room, which was big. It had a sink in it and I had the front window. I was hype 'cause I had a room before, but it was never this big, and this even had an extra bed—not to share, but for company if I made friends. The best part of this room was that I had a door for privacy and I could play music. Shoogi told me to unpack and when I'm done if I'm hungry I could get something to eat and meet the rest of the family.

As I unpacked I was thinking of so many things and how my life would change dramatically just by all this freedom. What I wondered most was, *Will this be the end of my journey—Will she treat me right? Will she love me like Ms. Best?*—and if she was abusive, 'cause that was the rap! *No one will put their hands on me again.*

As I went out to go downstairs, I turned back to close the door. I looked out the window and noticed how cloudy it was. Is it a dark cloud like this all the time? Well I don't care cause this is the life right now! Freedom, what every teenager should have. As I went out the door and thanked God for this home, I was thinking about Ms. Best, missing her already, but pushed it to the side 'cause I had a decision that had to be made and I believe it was a good one—so I thought.

(3)

I left Boys & Girls H.S. and started going to Sarah J. Hale. I could have stayed at the High but I just wanted to be in a whole new environment, period. Ms. Lindsay turned out to be different, real different. I was able to do whatever I wanted, could stay out to 12 A.M., if not stay where I'm at—*Don't come in the house high*—so basically for a 14-year-old it was the life for me. I was hanging outside more and met the neighborhood. I was a pleasant kid. Instead of being popular I was "popping." I guess people liked me 'cause I was eager to learn about the streets and my surroundings. I was never scared, I was in fights, a go-getter, and my friend and I were loyal to each other. We never let anything happen to each other. My life was wild and crazy. It was headed in the wrong direction right before my eyes and I didn't even realize it 'cause I was so young, plus I was having fun.

Well anyway, one day while in the house I met Nicole. Nicole was Shoogi's daughter-in-law. Shoogi loved Nicole and I could see why. They were cut from the same cloth. Anyway, Shoogi had a son who was in jail and couldn't come home until he at least did 15 years. He had a lot of street cred and everybody knew this nigga.

Well, Nicole was cool, she was 12 years older than me at 26, and chose to be around me. She tried to get me in clubs, which worked sometimes. She made her runs in the hood with me riding shotgun, she brung me to her house and let me chill with her smoking and drinking what I wanted and doing what I wanted. Nicole always had money, always smelled good, was fresh and always wore a lot of jewelry.

One day I was sitting on the stoop and Nicole said, "Deidra I'll be back."

"Where you going?" I asked.

She said, "Out. I'm going out shopping."

I said, "I wanna go," thinking to myself, *Who wouldn't wanna go shopping and why she acting funny for?* So then Shoogi came in front of the door from the inside and Nicole looked at Shoogi like getting permission through eye contact and I believe Shoogi gave it to her and I was happy because Nicole said, "Let's go."

That day—I believe it was winter and almost spring around March—when I was 14, was the beginning of my life being changed. To Nicole and Shoogi I was a pawn, a money-maker, young and crazy with drive and something to prove. To me during that time I was the happiest person on earth to be going shopping.

That day, when I think about it, it was the day shopping would become a drug, far worse than dope. The clothes was cool and money gave me a rush. So basically I was hooked/an addict to the fast life at an early age and got hooked in a foster home.

That day my life changed for the worst and it was the beginning of my life being ruined.

(4)

"Deidra, we going to Staten Island Mall and you must listen."

Of course I was gonna listen, I wanted new clothes. I never had anyone who ever wanted to take me shopping, let alone take me all the way to Staten Island to do it.

Well, when I got there to the mall it was amazing. I went shopping before but not to a mall and not to get anything I wanted, especially if it was name brand. I was told to hold two Gap bags. The bags were empty and I looked at Nicole. She must have read my mind 'cause she said she will fill them up and I was to leave the store and wait for her at the same exit we came in.

I did that and made it in and out of every store w/o being detected about ten times. By the time we finished we had two black garbage bags filled with merchandise on the Staten Island ferry. Nicole was impressed with me. She didn't have to tell me much. I was smooth when it came to getting in and getting out of the stores, and I had a baby face, which worked in my favor. If anything happened, all I had to do was call Shoogi or Nicole and they would come to the precinct and get me. Nicole was creating a monster and was excited 'cause of the money she was about to make.

When Myquan appeared, he and Nicole started busting down the items two ways. My things were in Nicole's pile. They were asking me my size in jeans, shirts and coats. I was so shocked and happy at the same time, but I kept it to myself and acted nonchalant about the whole situation.

Everyday was a good day for me and every boosting team was trying to cut Nicole's throat to have me on their team. It was like

I was already seasoned and I didn't talk much, plus the fact I didn't ask for much. They gave me new clothes, extra to sell, plus $200 for pocket money, but at the end of the day whatever they gave me they had double. I was just for once happy. I was fresh to death cute with paper in my pocket. I was doing better than any 14-year-old around. In school I was getting attention but I even stopped going 'cause I started chasing money and kept up to date with the latest wears. I was like a walking mannequin in the hood 'cause the way people used to window shop and gawk at the latest fashions in the store windows that they could never afford was the same way they used to look at me. Little did I know I was being used. I started to get a name around the hood. Every time I would see older hustlers, they would ask what I got or just give me their numbers. All the teens wanted to be my friend and in that way I was being used to recruit others. They would see how fresh I was and want to be down. Others just used to be hating on me and wanted to fight me and I would. I made a couple of examples and wasn't fucked with, or the one to be fucked with.

After that I just started chilling with the older people. I never cliqued with the younger people my age anyway 'cause they weren't on my level and they weren't about nothing—at least nothing I was into and I was into money. I was able to be a teenager but very little. When nobody was around that was the only time I had to myself so I started hanging out with this girl Sandra. I was attracted to her at first because she looked just like Foxy Brown but better. She was gorgeous.

Now that I am older I can understand what I was going through. I first met her at my corner store and I asked her was she related to Foxy and she said, "No."

I said, "You look just like her" and we introduced ourselves and that was the beginning of our friendship.

(5)

Back at Shoogi's house, shit was kinda getting crazy. First of all Shoogi was a drunk. She used to go to church every Sunday and her brother was even a pastor at the church, but after service was over she used to send me to the store to get her Bud—a 40-ounce and a six-pack—and yes, they used to sell it to me. Well anyway Shoogi used to be in the house getting twisted, and once I came in the house all hell broke loose. Every time I came in at the wrong time, trying to satisfy my hunger from the chocolate weed I just smoked. She used to sit me in the living room questioning me for two to three hours, asking me have I smoked, over and over again, thinking my answer would change from no. Truth is, if I was high, she just blew it and she knew she did.

So I just started going to my friend Sandra's crib and her grand-mom's used to always have some shit cooking on the stove. Sandra's grandmoms lived in the projects, Albany Projects, and it was always something going on there, but once you got on the inside of Sandra's grandmom's house it was a different story. It was peaceful and I just felt like I belonged.

Sandra turned into my best friend and we started doing every-thing together. I was in love with her and used to give her half of whatever I had. Not only 'cause she didn't have it, but because I se-cretly treated her like a girl I was seeing. At the time, I really didn't know about the life, but I knew I was feeling something for her and she was feeling something for me. But I didn't wanna speak on it, 'cause I didn't know how to, plus I didn't know what I was to say. I learned about my feelings years later. I didn't even know what I was going through until I learned about it in the streets where I learned everything.

Sandra stuck to me like glue, but I didn't want her doing what I was doing like stealing, smoking, and not going to school 'cause her family was feeding me and I didn't want them to believe I was influ-encing her in a bad way. Sandra really liked me and she always had my back and would curse and beat up anybody for me, but I would never want her to be in a war with me and her family. I would never put her in that predicament to have to choose, and that is why I told her, "Don't let me start you doing anything, do it 'cause you want to. Be your own person."

From that day on she respected me and put me onto liquor and told me that's how she got high and not to tell her brothers or sis-ters. Everywhere I was, Sandra wasn't far, and one day Myquan saw her and wanted to know who she was, and I told him as well as the brothers she had that I would fuck him up if he even thought about it. We were 14 and 15 and he was 26 and that was old to us because we were virgins. So Myquan I guess thought about it and left it alone for now.

Trust U? Why should I? U R a snake in nice clothes, U smile in my face and plot behind my back. U R not a friend of mine and could never be. I know people like U, all my life I've dealt with people like U and all my life I've seen people just like you. U act like my friend but I see through U. U R not my friend. I put my guard down around U but U just R plotting to hurt me. I despise U. U think I don't know what's going on? Well I do, I know everything and it's best I stay away from u, that is why I keep my grass cut short so I can see people like u a mile away even with my bad eye sight and all. U R no different from the others that is why I recognized who u were from when I first looked into your eyes.

Back to the streets things started to get crazy. I was officially on Myquan's team 'cause I wanted more and Myquan gave it to me. Nicole was hating on me. She got three 19- and 20-year-olds to pour bleach in my eyes and jump me. I guess she was hurt because I screamed on her and offered her to fight and she backed down.

I guess Nicole was embarrassed 'cause my little self wasn't scared of her, so she did what any project chick would have done. Shoogi was riding with Nicole, because she didn't like Myquan anyway from the beef her son had with him, so I left Shoogi. I had a couple of choices which were to go to a group home upstate, be with my crackhead mom, go back to the Best family or stay with Sandra and be in the hood still getting fly and getting money. Which one do you think I chose?

(6)

I chose the fast life. The money, the clothes and the cars would come later. I stayed with Sandra and her family. I had no rules to follow and I could do whatever I wanted. My life became a routine. Get up, smoke me some weed, which would relax me, shower, pop tags, get dressed and get ready to get money. When I came back from getting money it was usually the same: Sell my items stash my money, then bullshit around the hood. I became addicted to popping tags and if I wanted to pop tags every day I would have to go out to get it every day.

The more I went out hustling, the more I became better as a professional thief. Myquan was slick. He taught me everything I knew. I didn't say much—all I had to do was watch him. If I saw something that I wanted, he would get it, no matter if it was chained down, locked down, high up in the ceiling, in the managers' faces or even in their hands. Whatever it was he was able to get it. He was 27, but he looked much older than his years. He was a nice dressing man with a big ass head covered with long braids. He had some big ass hands like the hulk, so if he grabbed anything he was able to grab enough of it. He had been doing this since 15, so he knew a lot that I needed to learn and I did learn it. That's why as of today I could smell an undercover officer and sense trouble.

I was a good listener, so I knew a little something about him, at least the things he didn't tell me like not knowing the time unless it was digital, and I soon learned he couldn't count money as fast as I could, so with a little fast talking I was able to beat him out of a $100 here and there, but in all actuality I was taking my money back.

(7)

Back to the living conditions with Sandra was cool. I came and went as I pleased and didn't have to answer to no one. Like I said before, I was raised in a house so I had manners. All Sandra grandmoms was concerned about was: she don't want no one poppin' up pregnant under her roof or else you got to go! She did not have to worry about that, 'cause that was the furthest thing away from my mind. A dude couldn't do anything that I couldn't do for myself. Besides these dudes were broke, and only wanted one thing, and from me they weren't getting it.

Everywhere me and Sandra went guys would chase behind us. Sandra was 5'4", wore a size 27 in female's jeans, small to petite, dark brown smooth complexion, naturally arched eyebrows, pretty teeth, nice smile and long hair that she wore in a dubie. Me, on the other hand, I wore size 30 in female jeans, medium top, with long hair that I also wore in a dubie. So dudes would always ask or mistake us for sisters, thinking in their heads it would be some sort of double dating going on. I would immediately shut them down letting them know I got a man and his name is B.F. I just laughed in their face 'cause me and Sandra knew my B.F stood for that dead president, Benjamin Franklin.

After a while I just started wearing looser clothes 'cause guys got on my nerves at the way they just stared at your backside. So I just started the Aaliyah look, wearing loose pants and tight shirts with shades over my eyes. Still that didn't stop the attention—guys actually thought that was sexy. I figured they must have had a real crush on the singer Aaliyah. So I just started wearing men's clothes period. Not too big, not too small, just men fitted clothes that kept the men at bay. Now instead of saying, "Shawty what's ur name?" they would say, "Sandra who dat?" Scared to even say anything to me thinking I would bite their neck off. Sandra would wonder what was up with the transformation, but would never ask. Her sisters and brothers did, but I ignored them. I just despised men—they think with their dicks only. They rape, molest and disrespect women all day, everyday, then expect you to be like pudding in their hands. I just didn't and still don't have the patience for them.

(8)

With Myquan things started to change and so did I. Not only did I start to dress like a man, but I also thought like one. Myquan started to feel threatened so he did the ultimate. We were in this store and he was tryna put some coats in my bag while the sales lady was staring right at us. Not only was she staring at us, but the manager came upstairs from the basement. So as soon as he and Myquan locked eyes, they had a race and Myquan got out. So I was left in the store and they kept me there and called the cops. I was scared to death. I didn't know what was gonna happen because I didn't even know about nobody in jail.

Remember, I came from Ms. Best house where I never knew about anything ('cause we never went outside) about being exposed to the world. I was naïve to a lot of this but like I said before, I caught on quick. The cops arrived and one officer stood near me asking me questions while the other officer was with the store manager and the saleswoman.

"How old are you?"

I said, "14."

So he then asked, "Where do you live? Do you have any I.D.?"

I said I lived in Brooklyn and the only I.D. I had was my school I.D. They took a look at my I.D. and held it until they finished with the manager. After they finished with the manager they escorted me to the cop car. When I got there I was crying like a baby. I started saying things like, "Please don't take me to jail, if my mother finds out she is gonna beat me. Please, Mr. Officer, please, God help me, I'm gonna be in trouble. I swear I am not gonna be in that store or no other store again."

A few minutes later the officer stopped the car. When I looked around we were on a public block. His partner got out of the car opened the back door and said, "Get out of here, kid." He passed me my I.D. and said, "Stay out of trouble. Today is your lucky day. Next time it won't be like this."

I hurried up and got out the car and went to the train station that they dropped me off in front of. I got on the train, thinking of a story to tell them, 'cause if I told them the real story they would not have believed me.

When I got back to the hood my anger surfaced when I saw Myquan. He was chilling, hanging out, joking and laughing, while I could have lost my freedom. I got so upset 'cause I felt I was not that important and while my life could have been put on hold, his just went on. As soon as I got up on him, I asked, "Why the fuck you leave me for dead in that store?"

He couldn't say nothing but, "How did you make it out?"

All I knew was I blacked out and 2pc'd him. One fist to the mouth and the left hook in his jawbone. I knew he could beat me, but he had to know just like everyone else who was standing around that I was no slouch. With that 2pc he didn't stagger, but I drew blood so after that we locked ass. He got the best of me, but I stood my ground. After what seemed like a long five minutes some dudes broke it up, yelling at him once they saw he was fighting a little girl. When we were finally separated I told him, "It's not over," and headed towards the projects to Sandra's grandmom's.

On my way to Sandra's all the dudes who knew me and of me were asking me, "Are you okay?"

I said, "Yeah, why you ask?"

Then they pointed at my shirt. I had Myquam's blood on me from when I punched him in the mouth. I told them I was good and if I needed them I'd holla. No sooner when I got inside the crib the phone was ringing. Sandra answered it while asking me was I okay. I told her, 'Yeah, why?" then remembered the blood that was on my clothes.

"Yeah, who is it? " Sandra said into the phone. It must have been for me, 'cause Sandra looked my way. I said, "Who is it?" And she said, "Myquan." I told her to give me the phone.

"Yo, what the fuck do you want, 'cause I'm on my way back down there for round two."

"You, Deidra, you need to calm down."

"Don't tell me what to do! I do as I please now. What the fuck u call up here for?"

"Yo, I'm sorry . . . my bad."

"Yeah, you sorry alright." Then I hung up the phone. I was pissed off. That punk motherfucker wasn't sorry, not the least bit. There he goes only thinking about himself. He was not sorry, back at that store when he purposely left me for dead. He didn't care about no one but himself, and since I was young, liked clothes and money, for him it was like a kid at Toys R Us.

I walked in the back, into me and Sandra's room and got undressed. When I was naked with nothing but my 34B bra and my medium underwear Sandra began to giggle. I stopped my train of thought and brung my attention to Sandra giggling.

I said, "What's so funny?"

She said, "You."

"And what's so funny about me?"

"You act and dress like a straight dude, but now you look like a straight bitch in your Vicki Secrets."

I looked at myself in the mirror and we both began to laugh.

"I see I have to make some changes then."

"Nah, not really, I love who you are and you are very beautiful . . . I mean as a girl."

I left it at that and began to run the hot water so I could soak. I got into the water, but not before locking and stuffing the bottom of the door with a towel. Then I began to roll up some weed. As I took a pull of it, I contemplated on my life and how in less than a year it had changed. I thought about Ms. Best and how she was doing. I thought of why she kept me in the house. I thought about how I would never in a million years would have been able to enjoy my life like this if I would have stayed there, but I also thought about how I would have been going to school and I thought about family. I was on my own, there would be no more family get-togethers for me, no more Thanksgivings with family I was raised by, no more Christmases or cookouts, no more nothing. Was it worth giving all that up just to rip and run the streets, wear the most expensive clothes and the latest sneakers, and smoke the best weed? Yes . . . Yes, it was to a 14-year-old who never had nothing.

(9)

It was midway through October 1996 and I created a buzz in the streets. My summer was spectacular and my winter was gonna be the same. Me and my new crew of four 16- and 17-year-olds tore up the stores. People started to put in orders and we used to fill them. We were almost on the same level as the old heads, but not quite. I didn't want too much attention on me anyway, 'cause then the stuck-up kids would have guns in our faces in a millisecond. I was still 14-years-old and doing my thing. I had Auirex leather coats, Guess jeans, suits, Ralph Lauren knitted sweaters, Tommy Hilfiger everything, Gortex boots, Polo boots, a pocket full of cash and a draw full as a stash. I was getting taller so I was slimmer than before wearing a 31/32 in men's jeans rather than a 33/34.

I still wore a men's medium sweater but could pull off a men's small, depending on the maker. I smoked weed . . . a lot of it so that kept my weight down plus running the streets helped out. I still wore my hair in a ponytail blow-dried out by the Dominicans, but now it was covered by a baseball cap from whatever designer outfit I wore. So if I wore a Diesel outfit, I had on a Diesel hat, Armani Exchange w/Armani Exchange, Polo with Polo so forth so on, but on my off days I rocked Nautica sweatsuit, some Air Max and a Yankee fitted cap. I had four top teeth covered by gold caps, but mine were frames with diamonds around each of them, gold balls in my ears and a 16″ herringbone chain on my neck. I was doing quite alright for myself.

I woke up on this particular day and I was hungrier than a hostage. I jumped up, took a quick shower, got dressed in a grey Nautica Competition sweat suit, red Nautica Competition vest, a white nautical T-shirt, some grey, red and white Air Max and an Angel red and white fitted cap, rolled me up some weed, put it into my pocket as well as the money that I had in my other pants pocket. I called our neighborhood cab, 'cause that's the only cabbie that allows us to smoke or drink while we ride for a tip. When cabbie arrived, I told him to take me to the best Spanish restaurant Brooklyn has. After 20 minutes, I reached this Spanish restaurant. It was in East New York, a rough part in Brooklyn. Thank God I left my jewelry, because these niggas looked thirsty out here and I didn't have my bitch cutter on me.

I told cabbie I was gonna call him when I was done and gave him

$20. I went into the restaurant and ordered my favorite Spanish dish and sat down. The lady brung my food to me, and no sooner than she left I started pigging out.

"Can I take this seat?" A chick voice I heard. I just stared at her.

She said, "the chair, table seat . . . Can I sit here with you? There is no other table available."

I said, "Sure, let me just get this out of your way."

She started giggling.

I said, "What's funny?"

And she said, "You seem to be dropping and spilling everything except for that piece of pork on your fork."

I gave her a half smile, knowing she was right.

I said, "I'm getting my money's worth," and smiled.

I asked her what she was ordering and she said, "Chicken soup."

I said, "Chicken soup."

She said, "Yeah, did I say it right?"

I said, "Yeah, but you could of got Campbell's, if you wanted some chicken soup."

She gave me the evil eye, explaining the difference between Spanish and Campbell's chicken soup. She even let me taste a little, once it came. It was awesome.

She said, "By the looks of things, you like what you just tasted, so don't be judging things you didn't give a try."

I said, "Thanks for the info."

I asked, "What is your name?" and she said "Nubushe." She asked me mine and I told her. We started talking and I started to enjoy the conversation. Then she asked me, was I a lesbian?

I said, "Lesbian? What is that?"

She looked at me like I was playing, then I said, "Nah, I'm for real. What is that?"

Then she went on to explain how a lesbian is a female who likes other females.

I said, "No, what makes you think that?

She said, "Well first of all you are dressed in men clothes, and with that baseball cap on, you look like a dude from the back." We started to talk more, and then after an hour she left. I didn't know how fast time could go by, but it did. After she left I got my things ready and got on the phone to call cabbie. I had plans for today as I waited for cabbie.

I cleaned up my mess and I stopped when I saw an unusual napkin. It wasn't unusual, but it wasn't the ones the restaurant gave us—it was from Dunkin Donuts. I knew I didn't have Dunkin Donuts so what was it doing on the table, 'cause it wasn't there before? I looked at it, and it was the girl Nubushe's number on it. And it said, "Call me if you want to be friends." She must have wrote it when I got a refill on my iced tea, but why couldn't she just hand me her number instead of being secretive? That will just have to wait 'til I speak to her. A horn honking brought me back to reality. It was cabbie.

The ride back, I finished the rest of my weed and thought about Nubushe. She was fine and by the way she talked I could tell she was smart. I had to check myself, 'cause I caught myself fantasizing about her. What was going on? Maybe it was the weed playing tricks on me . . . or maybe it wasn't.

I love you so much, but don't know how to show it. Sometimes I show it in crazy ways. Sometimes I neglect you, maybe I don't love you, I'm just learning. I take away from you, just to give to others. I put others before you, only to see others happy, even if I'm suffering. I let my guard down, only to get hurt. Every time that happens, it is a hard time to get back on my feet. I should take the time out to get to know you, but where would I start? You are a decent person that someone could easily love, but you are so angry that you don't allow no one in, afraid to get hurt. I love you, but I'm loving you from a distance, which is not okay ' cause you are all I got.

(10)

I went back to Sandra's and put on some decent clothes. A Diesel sweater, some Diesel jeans, some Zara sneakers, a Zara leather jacket, put my hair in a ponytail and put a Zara hat over my ponytail. I went to go get some more money out my stash and went outside. The first thing I had to do was get a $10 roll of quarters to call Nubushe. I chose the pay phone 'cause I didn't want Sandra or no one hustling in my conversation with her. I wanted to talk to her and let her know how I felt or how I've been feeling about my sexuality. I got my quarters from the Laundromat and headed to a phone. On my way to the phone, I saw Myquan and he blocked my path from walking. Every time I would walk, he'd get in the way.

"Come on, Deidra. You gonna stay mad at me forever?"

"I might, I haven't thought about it yet. Now get out of my way."

"So you not fucking with me no more? You not my friend no more? You don't know how to appreciate a friend. Yo, Deidra I'm sorry, please just call me, I wanna get some money with you. "

"I'll think about it. Now just move out my way, so I can do more important things."

After I finished talking to Myquan, I went to call Nubushe.

"Hello, can I speak to Nubushe? "

"This is she."

"Well, this is Deidra . . . "

Nubushe and I talked for a while—through five dollars worth of quarters—before she asked me to come over to her house. I asked her where she lived, wrote the address down, then hung up the phone. I was thinking of the things I had to do on that day and figured, I'll just chill with Nubushe. I had a couple of thousands in the stash and a couple of hundreds in my pockets, so to me that was good. Plus I had four garbage bags filled with clothes in Sandra's closet and a closet rack filled with leathers of every color, plus goose down vests. Good thing Sandra had two closets in her room or else I didn't know where all that shit would go.

I called the houses of my other crew members and told them, "Don't wait on me, because I can't make it." They were shocked but happy cause they wanted to chill out that day also—only to show off their clothes and spend up their money. My next call went out to cabbie, I needed him to take me cause I wasn't too familiar with Canarsie and didn't want to get beat in the head. Then I bumped into Sandra.

"Where were you this morning? I was sleeping and when I woke up you were gone."

"I know. I was starving, I left you an order of roast pork and white rice in the fridge."

"You did? I thought that was Grandma shit. Where you about to head with all them Dutches, Smokey?"

"I'm about to go to my people's crib, then we going to make it happen."

She then asked me for twenty dollars. I told her to take it out of my stash and I'll see her later. I saw cabbie, and we walked away from each other. I got in the cab and told cabbie the address and to put the music on.

Cabbie was at the green light, but it turned yellow, then red, so we were stuck at the light. Myquan was lookin' out his window, staring at Sandra and Sandra was staring back at him.

Look at these two motherfuckers!!! I can't believe it! They are creeping. Myquan is a snake and a molester. Sandra ain't but one year older than me. He is crazy. He is 27-years-old. If her family knew about this, Myquan would get fucked up. Especially her brother Pook—he would knock Myquan the fuck out. He is mad, sneaky, and when the shit hits the fan I don't wanna have anything to do with that.

Myquan must have been in her car to get Sandra's attentions, 'cause she don't even be around like that. That's crazy, 'cause Trina, his girlfriend, lives next door and she and her cousins are my home girls. I fucks with them hard body and they brother Ninja and they cousin Hasan. Matter of fact, Ninja got a bad crush on Sandra and be beating and extorting Myquan every chance he gets, 'cause Myquan be fighting with his sister . . .

I was madder than a motherfucker and didn't know why. I had some type of feelings for Sandra but didn't understand them, and now I had a hate streak for Myquan for stealing what was mine from me.

What is wrong with Sandra? Do she not know I have a thing for her? How could she know? That's a secret I keep to myself, but how could she mess with people I get money with and messing with girls' men that I am cool with? How do I look smiling and eating and smoking in Trina and Em' crib when my home girl is fucking her man? When shit comes to a head I could see now that I'm gonna be in the middle of a hot mess and gonna have to smooth things out. Anyway, until the dark comes to light I'm just gonna play stupid. I got my own issues to deal with.

"Yo cabbie how much longer?"

(11)

I arrived at Nubush's house and she was waiting outside of it for me. I got out the cab and told cabbie the same thing I always tell him, "I'll call you when I'm ready to leave." Damn! This girl was good looking. Her skin was a caramel complexion, almond shaped eyes, a pretty smile, a nice curvaceous body that stood on bowed legs. Uhm! She was bad.

"You look nice, Deidra, you changed your clothes."

"Yeah, didn't want you to think I was a Hoodlum."

"Don't worry, when I saw you that was the last thing I thought," she said while I walked into her house.

"What's all that in the bag?"

"My meditation medicine, you smoke?"

"Nah, and you gonna have to smoke that outside. I got a way to smoke and it doesn't go through the house."

The Birth

Denise Irby

Denise wrote this story at a time when almost all of the girls who attended her workshop each week were incarcerated mothers like herself. During her incarceration, the story was shared among juvenile justice reform advocates, first in Harlem at a reading organized by New York State's Coalition for Women Prisoners, and later at the 14th Annual Conference: Prepared and Proactive—Laws, Policies and Practices in Youth Violence and Gang Prevention, *which took place on November 17, 2011 at Hofstra University. Denise grew up in Manhasset, NY and currently resides in West Hempstead, where she is now raising her daughter. She enjoys reading and writing and playing sports. Her goals for life are to raise her daughter, giving her the life she never had, and going back to school to become the veterinarian she's always wanted to be. Poignantly, she illuminates the conditions of incarcerated teens forced to give birth in conditions that most of us cannot even imagine.*

"**W**hat time is it?"
"6:35."
"What time is it?"
"6:40."
"What time is it?"
"6:45."

It's Thursday, June 9, 2011. Here I am at Nassau County correctional facility, nine months pregnant, 2 cm dilated and four days away from my due date.

"Why do you keep asking the time?" Kera asks me.

"Because I think I'm having contractions."

"What do you mean you THINK?!" She says with emphasis on the "think."

"I'm feeling pressure and tightness, it goes away and then comes back, I'm tryna time it."

"Well you keep asking the time every 5 minutes, yes its contractions."

"Oh," I say.

Next thing I know the whole dorm starts going crazy.

"She's going into labor! The baby's coming. Officer! Officer! It's time!" the inmates are screaming.

"I gotta go to the bathroom," I say nonchalantly as if nothing's going on.

"No, no, no, you have to sit; you're not suppose to use the bathroom."

"I gotta get in the shower," I say heading for my cell.

"No, you have to sit."

"Well I gotta get my shirt and ID," I say getting up from the chair.

"No, I will get it," Mrs. Pat says.

"Can you grab me a bag of chips while you're at it?"

"No! You can't eat anything."

Great! I think to myself. I have to pee, I'm hungry as hell, I want to shower, and apparently I'm not allowed to do anything but sit and wait, wait and sit.

"I'ma call your mom and Justin and let them know you're going into labor."

Unfortunately, neither of them will be allowed to see me or be in the delivery room for the birth. In fact, I won't be allowed to contact anyone till after the baby is born.

"Irby, don't have the baby yet, medical is on the way," the officer says over the loud speaker. The entire dorm starts laughing.

"The baby gonna be here before medical," Mrs. Pat jokes.

"Fuck a bullshit medical. I need an ambulance," I say.

15 minutes passes by before medical comes running into the dorm, asking stupid questions such as "What's going on, how are you feeling, and are you okay?" I'm wanting to slap the living shit outta them.

I remain calm, answering "I'm going into labor, and yes, I'm okay."

Duh is the only thing I can think.

After repeatedly telling the nurses that the contractions are five minutes apart and having my vitals taken, I am wheeled down to medical. There I am faced with the stupidest questions I have ever been asked.

"How far along are you?"

It takes all my might not to yell back, "Obviously if I'm going into labor I'm full term!"

I just simply say, "I'm nine months, I'm due June 13th."

"Oh my God! Are you sure you're that far along?"

Obviously, you dumb ass, I think to myself. This new medical shit is pathetic.

I didn't get to the hospital until after eight dealing with these simple motherfuckers. By then my contractions were three minutes apart. After being rushed through the hospital hallways, handcuffed, escorted by two officers and the public looking on, I was hooked up to some machine that monitored my contractions as well as the baby's heartbeat. I was bum-rushed with more questions and papers needing my signature.

After answering the questions, signing the papers, and two hours later the doctor approaches me.

"Ms. Irby we are gonna need you to walk around for a while to induce your labor."

"Um, okay," I reply. At the moment I feel something wet.

"Um, excuse me," I say. "I'm leaking and I don't know what it is."

The doctor comes over to me, sticks two fingers inside, then says to the nurse, "Her membrane has been ruptured. She's about 30% . . . wait . . . yea, 30 over 100." She pulls out and I see the blood-covered glove.

"What does that mean?" I ask nervously, scared to hear the answer.

"It means that your water broke and you're about 3 cm dilated."

"What about the blood, is that normal?" I ask immediately.

"Yes, everything is just fine," she assures me. "I guess you really didn't want to walk!" she says jokingly.

I laugh. Truth is she was right. I wasn't looking forward to walking around the maternity ward handcuffed and shackled, I guess

Kylie wasn't either. They move me to my own room where they continued to monitor me.

"Would you like an epidural?" the nurse asks.

"No, not right now. I'm not feeling any pain," I say with my eyes glued to the TV. I was watching the Heat vs. Mavericks finals game four, of course going for Miami. In the middle of the third quarter, with Miami in the lead, it hit me. The excruciating pain was unbearable.

"Oh nurse, I would like the epidural now," I say, holding onto the bedrail, ready to tear it off.

"She's 50 over 100," the doctor says sticking her fingers inside me.

After another 20 minutes and four pain-filled contractions, I finally get the epidural. I slowly start to nod off, only to be awakened by loud beeping noises. Nurses start running into the room, checking the monitor. I'm startled.

"What's going on?" I ask.

"The baby's heart rate is dropping."

Now I'm intent. Looking at the monitor I see the numbers slowly dropping down from 100 to 90 to 80.

"Lay on your right side," the nurses tell me, so I comply.

"Switch to your left," she says again, so I do so,

"Is she okay?"

"Yes," she replies, as she watches the numbers on the monitor start to go back up. I drift off to sleep, only to be awakened by loud beeping noises. I'm alert, immediately fearing for my baby girl. The nurses come pouring back into the room. I see the numbers on the screen dropping again.

"Is she OK?" I ask nervously.

The doctor sticks her fingers inside, wiggles them and then tells me to lay on my left side. The numbers slowly start to increase again. The nurses leave and I'm off to sleep, only to be awakened by the loud beeping noises once again. The nurses return.

"It's happening again?" I say to the nurse.

"Yes," she says back to me.

"That's bad, isn't it?" I say commenting and asking at the same time.

"It's not healthy for the baby," she says. "This is the third time this has happened, a baby's heart rate isn't supposed to drop no lower than 100. It could be very critical for the baby if it does."

I look at the monitor—it displays 76. I start to panic.

"We have one more option, but if this happens again we would have to prepare you for a C-section," she tells me, and then tells another nurse to please bring her amniotic fluid. At that point I start to beg God and my baby girl.

"What is that for?" I ask curiously.

"It's amniotic fluids. It's gonna help the baby feel more comfortable being that there's no more fluid inside you. She's being squished by the contacting muscles, which is causing her a little stress . . . this should help."

"Is that why her heart rate keeps dropping?" I ask.

"Yes, that, and mostly because she won't move, she's very lazy, it seems as if she's going to sleep."

"I see you're taking after your momma already," I say to my stomach.

I laugh, so does the officer. The officer. I almost forgot she was here. A silence comes over me. I closed my eyes and lay quietly in the bed, as if I was sleeping, but I wasn't. All I could think about was how my boyfriend wasn't here. I won't be holding his hand during the delivery. He won't be here for the birth of our princess, his first child—no cutting the umbilical cord, no holding her. How could I hurt him this way? Because of me he couldn't take part in the birth of his first child, because of me he couldn't cut the umbilical cord of his baby girl, because of me he couldn't hold her, he couldn't be there the way he wanted to, everything he was looking forward to doing he couldn't, because of me. It was my fault. I felt like shit. It wasn't fair to him, he didn't have a say in it. I felt like dying.

The doctor walks in and snaps me outta my thoughts.

"Push" she says. I give it my all. "Push" she says. I go at it again.

"You have to push!" she says again.

"I am."

"No you're not," she says.

"I'm not? I thought I was."

We all laugh as I try again.

"There you go," she says, "now you're pushing."

They start to push me to the delivery room with the officer following.

I push. She counts to ten. I stop.

"She's coming!" I hear her yell, "keep pushing." I do. She counts to ten. I shop.

"Ok, one more time."

I push. Out comes the baby.

"6:43 A.M., it's a girl," the doctor announces. I hear her cry. My eyes tear up.

"You did a good job, she's beautiful," I hear a voice say. I look up and all I see is blue and gray. It's the officer.

"Thanks," I say softly, wishing to myself that it was Justin's voice I was hearing.

I hold her for the first time, my child, my baby girl, my daughter and then it hits me; I'm a mother now. I glance down at her, "Kylie Nicole-Lynn Thurmond," I whisper to her. She smiles. I thank God for such a beautiful gift. They take me back to my room, shortly after Kylie returns. I hold her. I feed her. I burp her. I can't put her down or take my eyes off her. I'm amazed by her beauty. She's precious. Delicate like a flower or an angel. My flower. My angel.

I whisper sweet nothings in her ear. "Mommy loves you, your Daddy loves you, sorry Daddy couldn't be here; you're so beautiful, so precious."

I see her smile, I smile. She opens her eyes, it's like I'm staring back at my own. She's so innocent.

Her father arrives, but he's not allowed to see me. Being that I'm still in the custody of the jail, he must follow the jail's visiting hours and has to check in with the jail first. He spends time at the nursery with Kylie and tells me he will be back later because he left his ID at home, rushing out the door to get to the hospital. The officers tell him the last visit is at 7 P.M.

My parents make it to the hospital around 6:30.

"Whose little Chinese baby is that?" my mom jokes immediately taking the baby out of my arms.

"You sure you wasn't with a Chinese man?" my dad continues.

"I'm sure," I say laughing.

I look at my parents taking turns kissing and holding their grandchild. For my dad it's his fifth, for my mom, her first. I can see the excitement in her eyes. Kylie is quiet. They stay for an hour and then leave.

My boyfriend comes back—it's ten after seven. He tells me that he can't stay.

"Why?" I ask him.

"They say I got back too late."

"What time did you get here?"

"Five to seven, but they said I had to be here before 6:45 to make the last visit." He kisses me and then Kylie.

"I love you both," he says and then disappears.

I call him later and he tells me that he will visit me on Monday since there's no visits for the jail on weekends, but he is definitely coming to see his daughter first thing tomorrow. We sit on the phone for hours.

"I can't wait to have both of my girls at home and in my arms."

"I know . . . I can't either."

"Let me speak to the babz."

I put the phone to her ear. I think back to how he used to talk to my stomach, and how I used to put the phone to my stomach so he could talk to her when we was apart. I can't wait until all three of us is together as a family.

I continued to talk to Justin, watch TV, feed, change, and hold Kylie. The next three days were the exact same.

Sunday comes around, and now I must do the hardest thing I've ever had to do. Today is the day that me and Kylie have to go our separate ways.

"Normally we discharge at 9 A.M., but because of your circumstances you will be discharged at a later time," the nurse informs me. I'm thankful for the extra hours. I spend the whole day apologizing to her.

"I'm sorry, Babz. Mommy loves you. You mean the world to me. You're my everything. Don't you ever forget that, don't forget about me," I say repeatedly into her ear.

For the remainder of the day I talk on the phone with Justin, watching Kylie. Watching her smile, watching her open her eyes, watching her sleep. She looks like him. Cheeks, nose and ears—they're all his.

"You're my heart," I say to her. The time is drawing near and reality is starting to hit me. It's 6 P.M. I call Justin crying.

"Mama, what's wrong?"

"It's almost time."

"Don't worry, baby. Everything is okay. She's gonna be fine. Just try to stay strong for her."

"I'm trying but I can't, I need you, Daddy."

"Babe, just stay calm. Talk to me."

We continue to talk until 6:45.

"Babe, I gotta go now."

"No, please don't hang up!" I beg him

"I have to so I can meet your mom at her house when she gets back with Babz."

"Okay," I sniffle. Two minutes later the nurse comes into the room.

"I have to get the baby ready to go. Your mother is here," she says.

I look at the clock. It's 6:50. I have ten minutes. It's just like my mother to be early. The tears start to fall from my eyes and onto Kylie as I say my final goodbyes. When she takes Kylie from my arms I break down. My tears fall down like rain. There's nothing in the world that's more painful than a child being taken from its mother's arms. That's just another dagger in my heart. I'm crying uncontrollably. After about ten minutes of crying nonstop the officer walks in.

"I'ma allow your mother to come in, two minutes and no touching." I don't respond, just keep crying.

"Niecy . . ." I hear a shaky voice say my name. I turn around to see my mother. She's crying too. My tears fall even harder.

"Don't worry, honey, you know she's in good hands," I hear her say.

"I know but it's too hard, I don't wanna let her go." I cry back. I think to myself if this is how my mother felt when she had to give me up. I wonder if this reminds her of that day. I look at her; I can tell in her eyes that it does.

"Thank you," I say.

"Anytime," she replies.

I never imagined I would be like my mother. I always told myself I never would. First, my mother having to give me up and go to a drug program, and then me having to give my daughter up to return to jail.

"I'm a bad mother," I whisper to myself and continue to cry.

"You Were Such a Beautiful Woman . . ."

Taylor Nolte

As with many women who come to our workshop in the jail, Taylor came to her writing with the question, "How did I get here?" Certainly she had been doing her very best, shouldering responsibilities that would have been daunting to most adults. Shouldering way too much for a 17-year-old until, in the blink of an eye, in a moment of bad choice to drive while drinking, her entire life changed. In spite of this serious interruption of her life plan to join the Marines, in a circumstance where many others of her age would have caved in to bitterness, Taylor always presented herself with a calm abiding maturity and acceptance, taking responsibility for her mistakes, and intent on making the best of her "time." (While serving her sentence in prison she is a full-time straight-A college student).

In sharing this writing, her one concern was that her anger towards her mother at the time we meet her on the page would be misinterpreted as a lack of love and respect, when in fact it came out of the fearful and desperate heart of a young and very devoted, struggling daughter. Though shy to share this piece, it is her hope that it might comfort others in the same, all too common predicament of living with an addicted parent.

I pulled into my driveway and laid my head back on the seat with a sigh. This was the seventh day in a row working at the pizza place. *Sixty hours this week,* I thought, *more days, more hours, more money. Whatever pays the bills . . .* I realized I had only ten minutes to get ready for night school. Damn, I had to hurry. I walked to the door thinking, I hope Mommy cleaned up. I walked through the sliding doors into the living room, immediately disgusted as usual.

Cigarette smoke filled the air. My mom's bed, the couch, was a mess as she sat there in the same clothes she'd had on for the last three days—her boyfriend's sweat pants and a shirt. She used a kitchen chair in the living room as a table with a filled ashtray, her drink and more junk on it.

On the floor lay more cigarette butts and the half-gallon of vodka, half empty, with her Diet Pepsi next to it. I knew her back-up was in the freezer. What a hot mess. Her drink in her hand was almost done . . . soon she'd refill. I took all this in in an instant as soon as I walked in. Certainly not the mother I used to come home to. That mother had burgundy big 80s hair, green eyes and red lipstick. That mother made me breakfast in bed and put a scoop of ice cream in my hot cocoa. She taught me how to do my make-up and tease my hair. This woman in my living room—her hair was brittle and frizzy, her lips were bare and chapped, and freckles covered her face.

"Poo-poo head, bring me to the store."

Ugg, I hated when she called me that.

"Wait till I get ready for school and I'll see if I have time." I looked at the clock . . . damn, five minutes left. I poked my head in Grandma's room.

"Hey, Grandma, are you hungry?"

"No thanks, baby girl, I just ate some oatmeal."

"Are you sure? I'm leaving for school soon."

My Grandma was my world. She was an overweight eighty-year-old woman who always wore dresses. Her eyes were hazel and she smelled like Elizabeth Taylor's White Diamonds. I noticed her hair was growing—I had to cut it soon. She too was changing in front of my eyes, becoming weaker in the knees. She used her walker to get up from her desk and transfer to her hover-round wheelchair. Me and Mommy called it her motorcycle. She started it up and zoomed right past me.

I got dressed for school, still smelling like bread from work. No time to shower . . . damn.

"Okay, I'm ready."

"Let's go," my mom said.

"Um . . . I don't have time. I can't be late for school. Take Grandma's car."

"I don't like driving that car. Plus, you know I had a drink."

Yeah . . . a drink, I thought. I closed out the rest of the argument. I'd become very good at practicing selective hearing and tuning out the slur in her words.

Coming home from school was no better than coming home from work. As I walked in the door, I heard Mommy screaming at Grandma. Oh Jesus, not again!

"You're a horrible mother . . . you always were! That's why Daddy died. You know, he cheated on you!" my mom yelled viciously at my Grandma.

"Just leave me alone!" Grandma cried back.

I could see her getting upset and hearing my mother talk to her like that stabbed me like a dull knife. I had to break in.

"You're the horrible mother! You're always drunk while I bust my ass for the both of you!"

I had to defend Grandma because I know she didn't start it.

"Grandma, go relax and listen to music."

I turned to my mother, "What are you doing? How dare you speak to Grandma like that! Who do you think you are? Clean this living room . . . it's a fucking mess!"

I knew their fight was about my mother stealing Grandma's money, like always. I opened the freezer and took her vodka and ran to the toilet.

"I hate this shit . . . it's the fucking Devil!" I yelled.

"Taylor don't!"

I poured it out before she got to me. She pushed me.

"That costs money! What do you think you're doing you little bitch!"

"Yeah . . . Grandma's money!"

She would do anything to get her alcohol . . . lie, steal money, or even ask my friends to take her to the liquor store since I refused to enable her. It was so embarrassing.

I had to get out of there. I had to get away. I left to go meet my friends outside. Hanging out with them was my escape. With them

I could act my age, have conversations like what we'd do with a million dollars, or what would happen if the world really did come to an end in 2012. I met up with my homies and we played badminton in my yard for a couple of hours. As the night came to an end, we said our goodbyes and I watched them pull out of my driveway. I sat on a patio chair and smoked a cigarette, drinking the rest of my drink and watching the television flicker through the blinds.

I knew my mother was in there holding her drink in her hand. It was the same as holding a knife in her hand, because she was killing herself with that poison. She was moving less and less from the couch each day. Something in my gut had me frightened. This time, instead of worrying about the bills, or school, or her getting a job, I feared for her life. I'd seen my uncle die from alcoholism. When you drink like she was drinking there was no happy ending. Maybe she didn't help with anything in my life or Grandma's, but she was still my mother, regardless of what this disease had turned her into.

I finished the rest of my drink and debated whether to sleep in my car or pop a DVD in my TV. Guilt and sorrow were pumping through my veins. I hated seeing her in her own filth, looking like hell, drinking around the clock. This was not the life of a happy woman. How did she get to this rock-bottom level of depression and loneliness? I needed to do something even though I always ended up feeling helpless. I was sick and tired of making plans with her to go job hunting, buying her an outfit, just to get turned down the next day because she was "sick." She's always sick. But who the hell prescribed her vodka? I tried to hold the tears back and decided I was going to go inside.

I walked in and she was sitting on the couch with her cigarette and her drink. I tried to walk past her and say goodnight, but I couldn't. No matter how hard I tried the sobbing came out and I couldn't stop. I gave her a hug and she hugged me back. I let go and sat on the chair across from her. I had to do something and this time I wasn't taking no for an answer. I couldn't let her die like this.

"Mommy, why do you keep doing this? Can't you see you're killing yourself? I know you're not happy and I'm sorry, Mommy, but you can't do this to me and Grandma. Stop being selfish!"

She couldn't understand my blubbering cries, so I tried to calm down and repeated what I had just said.

"This is what not working has done to me," she said.

"So, let's get you a job. I'll take you shopping and buy you a new wardrobe."

I stared at my mother, knowing she couldn't work in the condition she was in. Bartending was out because she was way too slow, she moved like a turtle and acted like she was eighty but she was only forty.

"You were such a beautiful woman . . . You still are, but you don't care about anything anymore. Listen, if Chris doesn't treat you right, let's go and get you a new man. Once you work and get out and have your own money, you'll be back to the same cocky woman you were."

She played with the straw in her drink, swirling it in a circular motion around the melting ice.

"I just need to work. I'm a social person . . . I need to be around people. That's why I loved my job . . . Bartending, it's what I do. You like to do what you love for work."

I got a glimpse of how she felt inside . . . a scared, lonely little girl who felt incompetent in doing something new.

"Mommy, sometimes you have to do what you have to do. Almost any job you socialize with people. You'll feel so much better getting out there again, looking beautiful, and breaking necks . . ." I said trying to boost her confidence.

"Mom, you're killing yourself with this alcohol. It's not making anything better. Didn't you learn from Uncle Kevin? You can't go that route, Mommy. You have to stop! You wake up and drink 24/7 . . . that's not normal."

"Don't you notice I've calmed down? I told Chris I want to check out an AA meeting . . ."

Denial! I felt like I was running in circles with her.

"You keep putting me down," she whined, "and I don't want to get up. I have to want to do it. You can't make me!" She paused and looked into her glass. "Honey, go get me some ice, would you?"

I ignored her and walked into my room. How could she just brush this off? I felt robbed of my mother and robbed of my childhood. She didn't care anymore. Coming home to argue with her and to clean up her mess was becoming overwhelming.

Another night of crying myself to sleep.

"Beep . . . beep . . . beep!" I hated the noise of my alarm clock. I had an appointment to check out this studio apartment that I'd been thinking about moving to, but I called and cancelled. How am I going to leave these two people who need me so much? My mother would eat Grandma alive and spit her out. I had a feeling that once I did move out I wouldn't see them again . . . especially my mother. These would be my last moments with them and I wasn't ready for that. I needed them like they needed me.

My mother surprised me by coming into my room with breakfast. She made me an egg-in-a-nest and a chocolate milk shake with some soda. She sat on my bed and handed me the plate. Breakfast in bed? Today really was going to be a good day! I loved when she did these things. My mother was still here, but seldom seen—like an eclipse.

I told her I wasn't leaving, that we'd stay together.

Heading westbound on the LIE wasn't as exciting as eastbound. The sky was getting darker, reflecting my mood. Exit 51, the one I took for work, came faster than I wanted . . . back into the routine. School was getting more intense as the year came to an end.

At home, it was like me and Mommy hardly talked. Grandma told me she wasn't eating very much. I tried to call a few of my mom's friends and family members to try to arrange an intervention but no one seemed to care. I didn't know what to do but keep my life movin'. I felt like she'd started getting worse quick.

Monday came and I presented my mother with flowers and one of those jumbo cards. She actually looked happy. It felt good to put a smile on her face.

The due date for my Health Project was about a week later. It was a serious percentage of my grade and included a seven-page essay, a presentation with a visual. I had to do a good job to maintain my good streak of 90s. That night, I got home from school and the lights were off as usual and Mom was asleep on the couch. I hopped onto the computer to get busy. A few hours later I heard my mom scream from the living room, "Madeline! Madeline!"

What the hell? I thought. It's nearly 4 A.M. She's probably having a crazy dream.

"She's been actin' real strange tonight, Taylor," I heard my Grandma mutter.

"What do you mean?" I became really scared and stood up from my desk when I heard my mother call for Madeline again.

"Mom??" I was surprised to see her eyes open. She had crazy eyes, like there was nobody behind them.

"Where'd Madeline go? Tell her I forgot something!"

"What the hell are you talking about!? Madeline was never here! Are you dreaming?" I suddenly grew very angry, feeling like why is she doing this shit now?

Earlier in the day I'd hidden her vodka from her. I'm surprised she ain't fiending.

Curtains separating desperate families. Doctors and nurses running frantic. The smell of anesthetic and the sound of shoes clicking on the linoleum floors. The beeping of the machines. I stood next to my mother holding her hand. She looked even worse under the fluorescent lighting. She was so yellow, so weak. She asked me to take a picture so she could see what she looked like. "I'll never drink again!" she managed to blurt out.

It was only me and her, with the occasional nurse poking in. "She's dehydrated," I said to the nurse. "She needs water!"

"I'm sorry, she can't drink. The IVs are hydrating her."

My mother's tongue looked like the tongue of a cat. Finally the nurse gave me wet Q-tips.

"What the hell am I supposed to do with these? Where's the fucking doctor? She needs attention now!"

The nurse demonstrated how to wet the inside of her mouth with the Q-tip to keep it from drying out and then left.

Where was anybody to help? I thought. I couldn't believe Grandma was home alone and I wondered what she must be feeling, waiting to hear from us. But it was just me and Mommy in our little cubicle of hell. It felt like everything around me was in slow motion. People screaming, bleeding, clipboards being passed around everywhere. A social worker came to speak to me, but I blew her off and went outside. Walking past each curtain, seeing the patients with their families. I turned around. Mommy was alone, but sleeping now.

Outside, the weather was beautiful but my mood remained the same. I reached into my purse for my cigarettes. Shit! I didn't have any. Everything had happened so quickly, I'd left them at home when the ambulance came. I leaned against the wall of the building and slid to the ground. My legs couldn't hold me up anymore. I felt like I couldn't handle this anymore by myself. I kept screaming, "It's over! It's over!" and cried harder than I'd ever cried in my life. I knew this day was coming and now my mother was here in Good Sam and she was going to die!

I kept hiccupping, gasping for air, my whole body shaking. I rocked aback and forth. It was hard to be optimistic when it's the truth. Just the other day we were watching *Desperate Housewives* together. Just the other week we were at each other's throats with vicious words. How did this happen? How did this happen so fast? She's not getting out! She's not getting out!

My phone rang but I didn't want to talk to anyone right now. My emotions had me by my throat and I was suffocating. This is my mother—the person who gave birth to me and has been there for me for most of my life! She's in trouble and pain . . . internal bleeding and dehydration, liver and kidney failure and getting a blood transfusion. How could her body just fall apart so quickly? Why didn't I notice this? I should have been home more! It's my fault! She was my responsibility! What did I do wrong?

I Just Wanted a New Gift . . .

Jodie Biondo

While on the surface, Jodie's background is very different from that of the other young women in this anthology—adoption at the age of five by a female couple who provide her a rich, caring childhood in London and become her two mothers—once she started to write, gathering strength from the stories of the other young women whose back-grounds more closely echoed her own early memories, she was able to call onto the page those first ghosts of her past.

So often the process of writing together, whether in jail or on the outside, creates commonalities across those barriers of race, class and culture that keep us apart, as our ghosts "talk to one another" through the words that bubble to the surface, and we discover that we are not all that different.

The numbness, the relief, the high. It had all faded. A flash of lightning—there one minute, then gone forever. I saw black with a slight light in the distance. My body so numb—nothing I had ever felt before. It was peace at last and no one could take it away. I couldn't reach the distance, the numbness was fading, and the pain was reoccurring. It was worse than living, it was survival.

I strained to open my eyes. I saw blurred figures running around me, muffled sounds repeating the same five words I didn't want to hear. My mind was racing. I couldn't connect with any physical pain. I felt paralyzed. The mental pain was excruciating, knowing that I was still alive. The silence, the relief, the peace flashed before me and in a matter of seconds it was all gone.

Growing up, our parents give us many gifts, but the best gift we are given is the gift of life. Without that one sperm, which traveled and raced hundreds of others in order to reach that one egg and fertilize it to create me, I wouldn't be alive today. It seemed like such a long and tiring process. Was it really worth it? All the time and energy put in when it could be taken away in the blink of an eye.

The first three years growing up I didn't connect to my mother. Yes, she gave birth to me, but every time she looked at me she had this blank look on her face, like she didn't care. I had spent nine long months connected inside her womb. I was a piece of her and it was like she was angry with me for being here. She gave me the best gift but didn't care to build me up and teach me how to use it.

I lay there with wires and tubes all over my body—that annoying beeping sound, its repetition running concurrent with my heart beat. I opened my eyes to see the same walls, hear the same noises, and feel the same feeling. It was like I was born again, except this time I knew what life was. Yes, it's a gift, but if it's given at the wrong time, then there is no point in giving it at all. As I lay there and observed my surroundings, I realized that I hated this gift. It wasn't fun. It wasn't like anyone else's. It sucked. My thoughts were racing and even though I felt nothing, I knew the feeling was there. Why did I pull through? Why was I still alive? I just wanted a new gift, one that wasn't broken and torn and so difficult to put back together. I felt the tears trickling down my face, my body tensing. I closed my eyes and drifted away.

It was April 4, 1998. I was six years old. I was so excited I could hardly stay still. Today was the day my new family was coming to pick me up. It was a brisk spring morning. I had put on my favorite flowered dress. It was white with a lace trim and had pink and purple flowers all over. I slid into my new white tights and snapped the buckles to my best white shoes. I was rushing all around my room, gathering every last thing before they arrived. As the time of their arrival drew closer, I sat on the couch staring out the window. I couldn't believe today was the day.

I had met these two women many times. They had taken me to see movies, we ate at beautiful restaurants, and we played together in the park. They were perfect for me. They also had a piece of me— my sister. She was four years older than me and had been adopted one year prior. I felt safe and close with her. She was my source of love during my first years of development. I felt a deep connection to her and I knew that if she was happy with these new "moms" I would be too.

I was so ecstatic words couldn't begin to describe the butterflies in my stomach and the warmth in my heart. There was no more waiting and disappointment. Today I was no longer a little blond-haired blue-eyed orphan. Today I received the best gift. Not only did I get one new mommy, I got two! Today was my fairytale dream come true.

A black Ford Fiesta pulled up. My stomach was in a knot and I felt tingling sensations throughout my body. I wanted someone to pinch me and tell me it was really happening. I couldn't believe it. I jumped up as I saw my new moms and my sister walking up the path to the front door. I opened the door before they could even knock and greeted them. My sister was wearing black Adidas track suit bottoms, a green Nike T-shirt and brand new Nike sneakers.

She was smiling at me and said, "Hey Sis, are you all ready to come and live with us in London?"

I answered so quickly, "Yes."

My new mothers came into my foster home and met with my caretakers and social worker, whilst I showed my sister where all my things were packed and ready. We put all my things in the boot of the little Fiesta and came inside. My moms were standing in the hallway. They asked me if I was ready. My face lit up like a Christmas tree and I grabbed my little purse and said, "Yes, let's go!"

The constant beeping awoke me and I opened my eyes. I had to open and close them a few times before I could see clearly. I felt a warm hand enclosed in my cold shaky hand and I looked over to see both my moms staring back at me, with tears in their eyes, their faces pale and eyelids drooping from lack of sleep. They smiled at me and told me they weren't going to leave me. One of my mothers kissed my forehead and wrapped her arms around me and just held me. I felt her warmth running through my veins, her smell overpowering my senses. I felt so safe, like nothing could harm me, she just gave me protection and I knew it was going to be okay.

I looked up and saw the women who chose me, who did nothing but love and cherish me, gave me everything I needed, wanted and desired. But as I looked up at them, they were tired, worn and sad. They did everything in their power to make me happy and I showed no thanks. I didn't listen, I drank, I smoked and I disrespected them.

Why were they still here sitting at the edge of my bed, nurturing me and caring for me when I had hurt them deeply? I felt the pain weighing me down, my thoughts circling my brain. I couldn't live with it, I'd be better off alone, they would be better off without me. I couldn't bear to look up any longer.   ✎

The Dad That I Love and Honor

Daytona Goodwin

Daytona joined the Voices writing workshop in September of 2011 and worked with the group until her move upstate in June of this year. From the onset, Day-Day, as she preferred to be called, said she wrote because she was angry. In her natural poet's voice, she wrote furiously about her anger and missteps, her recurring dreams and longing for genuine understanding and caring. Perhaps Day-Day's greatest challenge was moving from her innate verses and spoken word style to fuller scenes and storylines, to weaving more concrete images and moments of being along with the metaphors running through her unique rhythm and rhyme. This brave and honest letter in particular—a letter to her father—was the last piece she shared in the workshop, and captures this growth as a writer. What distinguishes this letter as more than just a trite "letter to your parent" exercise is the layering of story that emerges in reaching out to her father to say how she truly feels about him. As a literary device, the letter captures Day-Day not only writing it, but her father also receiving her words in jail, the letter itself a living piece of her story.

Dear Dad,

I made it. I hope you're very proud, I'm sure you will be. I'm not losin' n-e sleep. I eat every day now. Fightin', I slowed down a lot. I show everyone respect, and honestly, it sucks to say, but I also think of you. I wonder, do you miss me or even think of me? Do you wonder what I have become in life? Wait, how 'bout how many kids I have? Do you wonder did me and my mom receive your gift? I doubt it.

Why did you leave? Was it because you were scared? If so, what the fuck were you scared of? If you could do it all over again, would you make up for lost time or would you repeat this fucked-up episode. What about my brothers and sisters? Did you ever think that I would like to meet them? How about your funeral? Do you want me to show up? Do you even think, what if I was your killer one day?

Well, let me tell you about my moms. She's so sorry that she even met you. She hates when I ask about your no-good-tired-ass. If you wanted to, she wouldn't give you the time and the day to apologize. By the way, she made it all on her own. She didn't need you and neither did I. She raised three boys and one girl. My birthday passed. I'm grown now. Now she's raisin' another girl. She just turned one in July. Sometime I wonder what she thinks about her mom and dad. But at least her dad and mom do come around time to time.

N-E-ways, like I said, she raised us well. So well you couldn't even tell we didn't have our father in our life. So to this day she is our mother and father and she's more of a father then you will ever be. Oh, by the way, she's legally blind. Her eyes cocked out on her when I was 13, and she still made it. Just thought I'd tell you that.

Well, me, like I said, I made it and I'm not talking 'bout successfully. I made it in your footsteps—started smokin' weed at nine, poppin' pills since 14 and started jailin' since 15. Caught my first five and a half year bid like you. Date bitches just like you. I never had a boyfriend, but I don't know 'bout you. I don't have kids like you. Oh, and I was born negative. Me or my mom didn't receive your little gift called AIDS, so I can say we Guccii. Sucks to be you. I wanted to come find your pussy ass to see if you had answers to my questions but that's out, 'cause now I'm facin' ten years in prison. When I come home, I'll be 32. You'll probably be gone. Maybe not. Who knows? Well, just know I hate you. Well, not hate, but dislike you for the dead beat you turned out to be. But I love and honor you for giving me life, 'cause I turned out to be the best thing you never had.

Always with feelings,
Daytona Goodwin

110 Degrees

Esperanza Caminante

While from our earliest school years we study and cele-brate the stories of children who endured great hardship and showed great bravery as they crossed over to a new land or blazed new frontiers, with current attitudes to border crossings we do not listen enough to the voices of the immigrant children of today who were asked to rise to heroic acts beyond their young years. From the moment Esperaza was given the tools she would need to craft a compelling "Page One Moment," she held her writing group spellbound as she added scene upon scene every week. Because we never ask the women in our writing groups what brought them to jail, we have no idea what transpired between the end of this story and the time of Esperanza's arrest, nor what sentence snatched her from the jail where she was starting to open up as the details you will read here came back to her. We can only admire the fortitude and spirit of this young girl, as we ask our readers to think more deeply about what it means to create such fences, barriers, and obstacles that children, separated from their families, never choosing the journeys they are sent on, must struggle to surmount.

It's around 110 degrees; it is so hot, so humid, I'm sweating, the air is dry and it's hard to breathe. I know I'm not in the desert, but it almost feels like it. I can't stand the heat and the sun.

This is Mexico D.F. (Mexico City) and I'm waiting on the streets.

I really don't know who is coming for us. I know my destination, but I have no idea what's going to happen from this point on. In a way I'm excited. I get to see new places. It's a new adventure and I feel free like an adult.

I hear a car and the noisy sound of the brakes against the rotor.

I can smell the burning brakes in the air. I notice a black SUV with tinted windows. The street is empty. The doors open, the driver remains inside, and every other man gets out— around five men. They are all wearing black T-shirts, black cargo pants, black boots, and their faces are covered with a black bandana all the way from their noses to their chins. I notice how two of them have golden chains with crosses around their necks.

A man is screaming. As soon as he steps out of the SUV, he gives us the order to get inside, "Get in. Hurry up—NOW!"

I've never seen them before in my life. I don't know any of them. What is going on?

As soon as I step inside the SUV, I feel the air conditioning hit my skin. It feels cold and nice inside the SUV. I am able to smell a mix of antifreeze, cologne and cigarettes.

Everything has turned dark. I cannot see anything. My hearing becomes twice as acute. As I'm touching and feeling the texture of the fabric covering my face, the voice of a man is saying, "Don't try to take it off. It is for your own protection."

They put hoods on our heads to avoid our seeing where we are or where we are going. I brush my arm against somebody else by my side. I know this person very well. I know the way she smells. I know every single thing about her. A relief invades my body. My heartbeat gets back to normal. I'm okay now, my sister still by my side. She is still with me.

I don't know what time it is. I can't tell where we are. The only thing I know is I'm still inside the SUV and its engine keeps on going.

I fell asleep. I guess I was tired. My sister—I recognize her voice—she is talking to me, trying to wake me up. My hood is off.

As the doors open, I clearly see the blue sky, the white fluffy clouds, and the nice sunny day. Outside men are waiting for us. They quickly say to us to hurry up and get inside the house.

I'm very good at observing my surroundings. It does not look like a nice neighborhood, a lot of movement going on in the streets, lots of people. It's loud and hot. The house looks like a cute little and colorful cottage, Mexican style. It's painted with white and green paint.

I'm entering the house and I see an old wooden table, an electric stove, a microwave, and a big old white refrigerator. It's not cute looking. It looks deserted.

At my right side there is a big open space and this is when I find out we are not alone anymore.

Around 12 to 13 people are all over the place, on the floor, everywhere. It's too crowded and hot and smelly.

There is only one old couch and lots of old mattresses on the floor. There is only one fan blowing air for all of us in the room. It's not even enough. I'm sweating already and it's getting difficult to breathe, it is so hot.

I'm hungry, I'm starving. I haven't eaten all day. I don't want to complain. I'm okay. It's alright. Nothing else matters. I'm alive and my sister Jenny, a 25-year-old woman, is still by my side every second that passes.

That night we sleep on the floor on top of the old, ugly looking mattresses. It is very uncomfortable because of the hardness of the surface.

I open my eyes after a long night. I look for my sister. She is right there, drinking a cup of coffee. I smell the coffee in the air. I see the sunshine through the window glass, some people still sleeping.

My stomach is growling, asking for food, letting me know it is empty. I'm hungry.

"Jenny, *tengo hambre*," I say to my sister. She hands me a hard, long Mexican bread and pours black coffee into a plastic cup. The bread is really hard—so hard that when I try to bite on it, it will crumble. So I dip the bread into my coffee and eat it like that.

All my life I've been doing this. I dip whatever I'm eating, cookies or bread, into my juice, milk or soda. It's just something I do all the time. It's just me.

I don't recall eating anything else that day but bread, coffee and lots of tap water.

There is nothing good to watch on TV. All day long all they play is Cantinflas, which is a famous comedy sequel of this poor man with his pants down his ass with suspenders and a little hat.

The TV is very small and it works with an antenna. It is also black and white.

We are told the rules:

- Listen to them.
- Do as they say.
- Stay together, keep the same pace.
- Don't turn back, no buts.

We are divided into three groups. Me and my sister are in the same one.

He is talking to us. He is the coyote, the person in charge of bringing us to the other side of the border. Group #1 is already on its way. They were on the move early in the morning. Each minute that passes is full of tension. The clock keeps ticking and soon it will be my turn.

A couple of hours later, a telephone is ringing. The coyote grabs the telephone. Then he says a code and his nickname. This phone is no ordinary phone. It is black, big, with a long antenna.

The coyote keeps talking on the phone. I'm just so amazed with this object. I've never seen one like that before.

He presses a button and puts it back into his pocket. He says, "Group #1 just arrived at the other side of the border. We have the green light."

It is our turn now.

We all get into a circle, hold hands and pray to the Lady of Guadalupe.

For an instant I feel like she is there, present, watching us, protecting us.

It's getting late and we should be going to sleep. Tomorrow it will be a very long day, and we need to rest. I go to sleep on an empty stomach.

I remember having this dream of being in space, while I'm floating and looking at the rings of Saturn, the gas storms on Jupiter, the Milky Way and the stars. It is just me alone, surrounded by the darkness and the glints of light from the stars that look so much like glitter as I am trying to reach for one.

"*Despiértate*, Esperanza, *levántate*." Time to wake up. My sister looks ready. I don't know what time it is.

"Everybody, you are just allowed to bring one pair of clothes and one pair of shoes, nothing else." The coyote speaks.

I have to get ready. I brush my teeth. No time for a shower. I'm looking into my luggage, trying to find something to put on as I discover in a corner lots of old backpacks and suitcases with clothes in them. They were left behind by people a long, long time ago, which is the same thing we are about to do. We are leaving our stuff behind. Maybe it'll help somebody else after us.

My sister Jenny is rolling the dollar money and important papers like her ID, phone numbers, and directions to addresses in case of an emergency. She bags it and saves it in her bra, just like mom and grandma used to do when going to the market. As she is doing this, avoiding anyone in the room seeing her, my stomach makes a loud noise. I'm really hungry. I think my sister hears it. She might be hungry as well. I haven't seen her eating. We haven't eaten anything.

She approaches the coyote. She is taking money out of her jeans pocket and handing it to him.

"Can you please get us something to eat? Please."

He says he will as soon as his partner comes back, because he can't leave us in the house by ourselves.

A while later they switch, and then he comes back with two big white shopping bags. There are two two-liter bottles of Jarritos—Mexican soda, pineapple flavor—and inside the bags are tacos—Mexican tacos—he bought from the lady across the street. We have enough tacos to share with everybody. We share them with these poor and worried people and the coyotes. We all ate, I remember. Eating like six tacos by myself, they tasted so delicious.

We asked what they were made of because it didn't look like chicken or steak. The coyote said in a very suspicious way, "You really don't want to know. If I tell, you might stop eating them. All you need to know is that they are made of different parts of pork."

Oh well. It is not really a big deal. It tasted good and I'm not hungry anymore. That's what really matters.

Some time around noon he got a phone call. It's our turn. We've got to be ready, we are going NOW.

After two days of being inside the house with no communication with the outside world, the big wooden door opens and the light is bothering my sight. I step out. The sky is bright blue, sunny with big fluffy white clouds.

I started thinking of my mom, wherever she might be. She is looking at the same sky I'm looking at this exact moment. I feel she is with me, she is watching me. I picture her face in the sky looking down at me.

"I'm getting closer and closer to be with you Mami," I say to myself.

Outside on my left side there is the SUV in the driveway. I don't know if it's the same, but it looks so much like it.

"Get low, stay low, hurry, hurry get in!"

The door is open. I get into the SUV. This time they throw us the black hoods to put them on by ourselves. This has become so familiar to me, I am so used to it, I'm not scared of it anymore.

The doors close. Everyone is inside. I feel the air conditioner on my skin. I can hear the air exiting from the vents. I smell air freshener mixed with body odor all compress inside this packed space.

The car is on the move. I can't see where we are going. All I hear is the motor running.

Sometime later a man says we can take the hoods off our faces. The car keeps moving. I'm confused. He says there is no more need to use them anymore.

The first thing I notice is the big and high steel fence to my right. That's the border. My eyes cannot believe this, so big and close. The street is deserted, no other cars present or people at this time. I keep staring at the wall all the time. The SUV keeps on moving. Some parts of the wall made of steel have graffiti painted on them, plastic flowers and crosses, missing people and wanted posters, and of course, warning signs in both Spanish and English.

The SUV keeps on moving, the driver changing gears, turning the steering wheel, until he stops and meets with a man inside a blue pickup truck. The engine never stops. The man in the pickup waves his hand and the driver keeps on going. Nobody ever got out of the SUV, it was more like everything was well planned, so well organized to avoid any kind of problem.

The SUV stops, no buildings or houses around. I see through the windshield a very deserted area. The prominent color is brown.

The doors get unlocked and they open. We all start to get out. In the air, I smell erosion, dust, rust. The heat is so uncomfortable. I look around. It kind of looks like a junkyard, scrap metal everywhere, cars parted out with just the frame itself.

There is a trailer house with no glass in the windows, no doors. It looks very old and uninhabited.

We are told to follow the coyote inside. While we are on the move a second man is sorting us.

We get inside. It is very dusty and dirty. Picture a big long rectangle, that's what it looks like. It is unfurnished. There is nothing inside.

The coyote hands us black plastic bags like the ones used for construction work, the heavy duty ones.

"Get naked. Everybody now undress!" The coyote has given us an order and we are supposed to follow it.

What does he mean "get naked," is he being for real? Right here, right NOW? His facial expression seems very serious.

He yells again and in a blink of an eye everybody starts to get naked.

I'm trying to focus on myself. I don't want anybody to see me naked. I was told my body is God's sacred tool, and so as I am getting undressed at the same time I am trying to cover myself from others. It isn't an easy task.

I don't remember being curious and trying to see others. I was so concentrated on myself. It was very awkward because we were all strangers with the same dream and situation.

Of course it all happened really fast.

The coyote gives each and every one of us wet suits to put on. They have a very strong smell like rubber. They are black and very difficult to put on. They cover us from our feet all the way to our necks. The zipper is on the back and it has a long string to help us unzip it by ourselves. It is uncomfortable to put it on, trying to fit in and stretch it at the same time. It feels very tight and makes me hotter than before.

Remember the bags we were given. We are to put the clothes we had on inside them, make a knot and double bag them. As I am doing this, the loud sound of a helicopter appears.

"*¡Al suelo, todos al suelo rápido!*" We all get on the floor without thinking of it twice.

Adrenaline starts pumping in my veins. I don't know what's going on. My instinct is to cover my head with my hands. As I'm doing this, I get a flashback from when I was little, living in Nicaragua and being so scared when earthquakes happened. Mami and Daddy would always be present to rescue me, pick me up, and I would feel safe with their arms around me.

The sound stops. The helicopter disappears. We are told everything is fine. We can get back up.

This time Mami and Daddy are not present, just my sister is with me. I say to myself, *I'm okay, you've got this, you can do this,* and somehow courage flows through my body.

The coyote is giving us instructions. Once we exit this trailer, we are told to follow his commands.

We should keep together. No one is to stay behind. If someone does so, we shouldn't go back and play hero. We should keep our bags close to our heads, watch very carefully where we are walking and listen.

The time has come. It's time to leave the trailer and start our quest. Everything seems to be under control.

The sun is bright. This wetsuit is making me sweat so much. It is too hot.

We start walking out, leaving the trailer behind us. We have a man guiding us up front and one behind us, making sure everything goes well.

At my left there is a huge concrete wall and straight ahead all I see is scrap metal, pipes, and these huge square-looking metal frames.

There is no way around it. We can only go through there, avoiding trying to get hurt, being careful. I am ahead, just behind our guide, because I am young, more active and flexible, and I can move faster.

All the time I am on the move, climbing the bars and going under the squares and below. I am always turning back and keeping an eye on my sister. She is pretty far back, and also she is kind of heavy. She manages to do well and never falls behind.

After a while we finally get to the other side and there is an opening in the wall. It isn't very big and it is made in a triangle shape. Nobody is missing. We are all together.

One by one we go through the hole in the wall and get to the other side.

There is water, a pond, a canal, kind of like a river, I can't tell exactly.

No grass, no trees. The hill on the other side of the river is mostly soil. Grass I guess is hard to grow in this unsuitable and brilliant weather.

With my bag in my right hand, and looking around me, I approach the edge of the pond. The coyote is already in.

"Do we have to get into the water?"

"Get in. Hurry up. Get into the water. Jump," he says.

"I don't know how to swim."

"Don't worry. I'm here. It is not deep."

No time to think about it or negotiate. It is out of the question.

I jump into the water. I don't know how it happens. I think I bend my knees, because the water gets into my nostrils. My reflexes quickly kick in. I straighten my legs, get up and cough. There was no way I am going to let this water into my mouth. This water is not clean or treated. The water color is black! Black, can you believe such a thing, how dirty and unhealthy could it be?

"This is bad, this is really bad," I say to myself.

It even smells funky.

I keep spitting because I have this nasty, horrible taste in my mouth. Yuk . . . I think I didn't swallow. I spat and coughed just in time.

We need to walk to the hill, climb it and get to the other side of the metal fence—the border—we can't keep going through the water. It's blocked.

The coyote is the first one on the hill. The next is me. There is a thorny shrub on the way. My suit almost gets caught on it. It scratches my face. I don't notice it at the time until my sister pointed it out.

"What happened to you, Esperanza?" I touched my face and noticed blood on my hand. The salt from my sweat was burning into my scratched face.

Face to face with the famous fence, so high and impenetrable-looking.

At the bottom of the fence there is a hole dug into the ground. Just like the one dogs dig in the backyard.

We get on all fours, and slide through the hole. My hair, my nails, my face are all dirty.

My sister does pretty well. She isn't so huge after all. We laugh, it's so funny! I'm so proud of her. She's keeping up with me. She is doing all this for me.

We jump back into the water. Ahhh, I can't stand the funky smell. It is a combination of motor oil and sulfur.

Time to keep on moving.

Every step I take, I keep on feeling metal objects and pipes on the bottom of my feet. I'm trying to be as careful as I can be because I don't want to trip and fall and repeat the same mistake from before—no, no, no way!

A while later, the coyote shouts, "Slow! Wait! You two go first. Keep your head out and keep the bags close to your heads. Next the three of you. Do the same and follow the current."

What's going on? What's happening? Something is wrong.

Curiosity is killing me, so I turn around and take a look, trying to see around me.

Surprise. I'm in shock.

"OH MY GOD—OH MY GOD! Did he see me? Can he see me? OH MY GOD—OH MY GOD!"

All these questions running in my head. I'm freaking out.

I've seen an officer up on the hill, standing in his brown, greenish uniform with a rifle around his shoulder and binoculars in his left hand.

For some inexplicable reason we didn't get in trouble. The bags were supposed to hide our heads and give the illusion of garbage bags floating on the black and dirty water. Apparently there is no danger anymore.

The coyote tells us to keep moving faster.

What just happened? Impossible! I'm sure he saw me back up there. Why didn't he do anything? We are so lucky! God is on our side.

We keep on walking in this black, dirty stinky water. Ahead of us there is a tunnel. As soon as I start walking into it, I notice plastic crosses, flowers, names written on the walls. The tunnel is kind of dark and I'm getting goose bumps.

"Do people die in here?" I ask myself.

At the other side of the tunnel, at the end, I see far away the end of this water. I can't wait to get there. I'm getting closer and closer . . . to where I really want to be, with my Mommy.

What's that foam on top of the water, white foam with brown stuff on top?

"What is this?"

At my right there's a three to four-foot high hill. It's pretty high. The coyote gives us the order to climb it.

One of the coyotes is up there. The other one is still in the water.

"You go first," he says.

I'm the youngest, the lightest, so I go first. I'm trying and trying to get up there. I'm digging my nails into the ground, digging and digging till I get a grip and try to push myself up. I feel hands holding me. The coyote is helping me and it's being so difficult, I'm feeling so, so heavy. I finally get up the hill . . .

I turn around. Now the only people in the water are my sister, the coyote, and another tall skinny man. They're trying to help my sister to get up. We are running out of time. A lot is going through my mind. These two men are trying to push my sister up the hill. What can I do? I lie down on the ground and start cheering for her, "Vamos, Jenny, tu puedes!" Come on, Jenny come on, you can do it!

I grab her arms and try and try. She is so heavy. Or maybe that was the moment that made it feel so crazily impossible. Between the two guys in the water pushing her up and me, she finally gets up the hill.

"Ahh," I gasp. We are still together.

"*Rápido, desnúdense. Cámbiense la ropa.*" What? Here? Right now? They want us to get naked and get our clothes out of our bags and get dressed? If I did it once, I can do it again. It shouldn't be a problem. My sister is naked already. I'm trying to stay behind this little bush, which doesn't help a lot, because it doesn't even have leaves in it. I open my bag. OH MY GOD!

"What happened?" someone asks me. *My clothes are wet, my clothes are wet.* How did this happen? Now I remember that spiky tree back there when I was crossing the fence.

"You go last," the coyote says. I'm scared, I'm last. We all have to jump this little four-foot wall. On the other side there is a big parking lot and a supermarket, with not a lot of cars around. I'm trying to rinse out my clothes as much as I can.

"Dios mío, Dios mío, Dios mío," I keep saying to myself, just asking for a miracle. My clothes are still wet, but that's not the worst of it, my sneakers are soaked and wet too. I'm in big trouble. They are not stupid—they are leaving me for last, just in case I get in trouble they—the ICE people (immigration)—will take me while all the other ones will be safe. Right now all I'm doing is praying and praying.

Finally after everybody goes into the supermarket it is my turn. Every step I take my shoes go squishy, squishy and leave a trail behind, which evaporates from the hot asphalt. I look behind. I look up front and I see the heat waves. That's how hot it is. All I'm asking is, *Please God, dry my clothes.*

I walk into the supermarket, my shoes squeaking, everyone looking at me. I'm leaving the floor behind me wet. These people are looking at me. I don't know what to do. I don't know what to say. I keep my head up and just act like I'm buying some cookies. This American old couple looks at me like I'm an animal. I will never forget their looks and their heads shaking in disapproval.

One by one, two by two, we will start getting into a truck outside waiting for us. Again I'm the last one. Am I going to get in trouble at some point? I'm just waiting. It can happen, I know it is possible.

There is a gray pickup with a camper in the back where soon we will get in. We all are stacked, yeah, one on top of the other one. It is so hot. We're all sweating. We're all stinking, and on top of us they throw a heavy blanket.

OH MY GOD. It's getting worse. I'm about to get a heat stroke. I'm just trying to keep my breathing in sync.

"Concéntrate, Esperanza. *Concéntrate."* My sister is in the front passenger seat, while I'm burning from inside out. The pickup keeps on moving. I can't wait to get to wherever they are bringing us. My breathing becomes slower, and slower . . .   ✎

VOICES BEYOND INCARCERATION

T HE PLAYWRIGHT, Karen Malpede once referred to caring as a muscle, which, if it wasn't exercised would wither and die. The stories in this anthology give heartbreaking and deeply disturbing testimony about what happens when the people who make up our worlds forget how to care. They speak to the heart in a way no statistics or abstracted case histories can. Can they wake what has died?

Herstory began with a series of dares, intended to wake up the caring buried inside an imaginary "Stranger/Reader." Working with women coming out of backgrounds of family and political violence, poverty and abuse, novelist and essayist Erika Duncan began to develop a technique for playacting—and then writing—scenes that would force the most hard-hearted imaginary listener or reader to care. Never did she imagine that over the next couple of years a whole network of workshops—based on daring the community to care—would come into being up and down the hundred-mile length of Long Island. Nor did she imagine that the words "Stranger/Reader" and "Page One Moment" would be echoing in Spanish and behind jail walls.

What she didn't take into account when she first devised this exercise, was the profound effect that asking the stranger to care would have on women with lives riddled with trauma, who hadn't yet developed much caring for themselves. Long before these women were ready to feel much compassion for the wounded selves that they had set out to write about, they were energized by the "task" of inventing forms to evoke the concern of the ever-shifting crowd of strangers who came to listen to what they had written every week.

What resulted was an amazing body of work, by women whose voices hadn't been heard before, carefully shaped with the idea of creating empathy.

With the coming of our workshops to Long Island's correctional facilities and to neighborhoods divided by violence and hatred, Herstory was already *well on its way to evolving from a direct service model focused on individual empowerment for women, to a social change model, identifying areas of injustice and inequity and then working with members of the affected populations by providing the tools to those most often silenced so that their voices become part of the public discourse.*

What then does it mean to the unheard writers behind jail and prison walls to begin to have their voices heard? So many of the women with whom Herstory has been working over the years have been incarcerated for the sorts of crimes that do not involve specific victims, but rather a larger community of people affected by drug sales or children born to mothers unable to keep them from danger, so that the more traditional ways of looking at reparation and guilt in the movement for restorative justice must be redefined. Would there be another way to restore themselves and their communities to wholeness, through reassembling the broken shards and deeper meanings of their stories, one by one? What would happen if they found a way to give back to their communities by using their stories to break cycles and patterns, and to reach current and future decision makers, changing lives and laws? Was this possibly a more inclusive way of looking at reparation and restoration, moving beyond the traditional ways of looking at forgiveness and guilt?[1]

The final section of this volume focuses on the stories that grew out of our "Education and Activism" project, supported by the Women's Fund of Long Island (2009 through early 2010) and our "Youth Writing for Restorative Justice and Racial Equity" project, supported by the MS. Foundation for Women (late 2010 through early 2012) and Ben and Jerry's Foundation (2011).

Some of these stories were written in the jails, and then read to large audiences in programs organized to bring to reach students of criminology, sociology, psychology and law. They were read in large auditoriums and in small classroom settings, opening dialogue around specific issues and initiatives extending into juvenile justice, violence against women, the targeting of minorities and immigrants, with different themes and ideas for action emerging at each reading, leading the majority of the institutions engaged

---

[1]   The research of Dr. Natalie Byfield is exploring these questions, using the Herstory method and its results as the centerpiece of this investigation.

to design their own follow-up programs or ways of incorporating the women's stories into their curriculum. They were read to advocates in forums addressing second chance legislation, legislation around raising the age for the prosecution and incarceration of juveniles, alternatives to incarceration and workplace rights.

As the project grew, formal bridge groups were established in which formerly incarcerated women began to write alongside influential women in the larger community, and in which students who themselves had brushed with the justice system or had parents in prison, gang-involved and homeless teen mothers, and other young people caught in the "school to prison pipeline" raised their voices together.

This section includes two short selections by Captain Helen Geslak from Yaphank Correctional Facility, who stepped forward at a reading engaging over 100 criminology students at Suffolk Community College to announce that she had come up with her own "Page One Moment." As you read the poem by the captain, which ends with the lines, "It could be you or me," we ask you to try to imagine what it meant to the formerly incarcerated readers on the college stage to hear their captain reading the words that showed how deeply their stories had reached her.

Shortly before this, in April of 2010, the rehabilitation department of Riverhead Correctional Facility had purchased 250 copies of VOICES to be used for the training of incoming corrections officers in Suffolk County's correctional facilities. In November of 2010, the first group of 50 corrections officers (42 men and 8 women) were trained using the women's stories in a special class taught by Lieutenant Darlene McClurken and Sergeant Noreen Fisher, to resoundingly positive evaluations. These readings were made a requirement for graduation from the academy that year, a major breakthrough, which we hope, moving forward, will be adopted by other counties and states, so that every person, man or woman, assigned to guard women and girls in jail or prison, will be able to give the people in their charge a face.

Together these writings will take you through thinking about a number of issues which are on the verge of change or have changed through action in the New York State Legislature during the years when the stories were written: An anti-shackling bill which ended the barbaric act of shackling incarcerated mothers during labor, posing harm to their babies and their own health; A domestic violence survivors justice act which, if passed, would create more fair and just sentencing instead of the now harsh sentences given to victims of domestic violence who have defended themselves against their abuser; A second chance act, which would allow for second chances for cer-

tain crimes where the conviction would be expunged; and most promising, the Rockefeller Drug Law reform, which did not end mass incarceration of low level offenders for drug related crimes, but offered some relief to its unusually harsh sentences. They will give you a firsthand look into what happens to children who are placed in foster care through no fault of their own, and what happens to children whose parents are incarcerated, how the ghosts of the conditions that caused incarceration continue during reentry. As those coping with reentry and those fighting for restorative justice join their voices, they will give you a sense of the relationship of issues and root causes.

Whether you are reading this book in your prison cell or in a classroom, whether you are a corrections officer or someone just beginning to look at the impact of the criminal justice system, we hope that these stories will inspire you to add you own voice to whatever most needs to be said.

We invite you to join us, as our voices for restorative justice extend over and beyond the prison walls.

A "Page One Moment" and a Poem

Captain Helen Geslak

 When we think of the trajectory of our workshops for women in Long Island's three county jails, we realize that our project could not have come to fruition without the support we received from four Suffolk County corrections officers who immediately saw the purpose and potential impact of what we were trying to do. With great care Captain Helen Geslak and Lieutenant Darlene Mc-Clurken, and later Sergeant Noreen Fisher, selected the women whom they felt would be able to benefit the most from our workshops, spreading the word, until there were long waiting lists on the tiers, helping to create a model—first in Riverhead Correctional Facility and then gradually expanding to Long Island's two other jails. When we moved into Yaphank Correctional Facility, Jonathan Scherr, who was in charge of the women's trailer, felt the program was so important that he mandated it for every woman, along with other compulsory rehabilitation activities. He was later to write:

> At first it was uncomfortable to listen to these women share their lives, fears and needs. But I have come to understand that all need to hear the words of these women; they are our mothers, sisters, wives and friends. The women who raised us, loved us and supported us, even now deserve no less.

As these officers helped us break the stereotypes that so often exist around women in jail, by providing opportunities for the women—and later teen girls—to write with us, so our experiences with them also broke our own stereotypes of the corrections officers hidden behind the dark blue uniforms shining with badges and stars.

Still we cannot adequately convey how moved and surprised we all were when, at a reading at Suffolk Community College, Captain Helen Geslak *came forward with her own "Page One Moment," which we are sharing here. In the time leading up to that moment, the officers closest to our project had participated in many of our readings and events for the public. They had raised their voices about the issues that afflicted women in jail, and had called for the teaching of the women's stories in Suffolk County's Correctional Academy. But each time Captain Geslak read her own story—whether to women still incarcerated or to audiences of students—a deeper, more compassionate dialogue across the roles that would normally divide the players took place.*

We are ever so grateful for the opportunity to share this story and the poem that follows with the captain's permission, as we continue to break down those stereotypes and barriers.

Pause Button

WHEN A WOMAN comes into jail, the "PAUSE" button is pushed on her **TIVO** of life. She will enter her new home of concrete, steel, fluorescent lights and piercingly loud slamming steel doors. Her soul is surrendered upon entry, as are her dreams and aspirations. Her dignity and self worth are stuffed inside a small brown bag, stapled shut, marked with only numbers, and then stuffed inside a foul smelling metal box crammed with identical small brown bags. Her given or married name is erased and substituted with a series of numbers and letters; the numbers for identification, the letters to denote her legal status. Personal clothing is confiscated and replaced with a drab green—a stiff and poor-fitting pajama-like outfit, not flattering to any female shape or size.

She will not be cleansing her face with cold cream tonight, but with her molting, no frills, jail issued bar of soap. She'll be washing her scarred and tired body without a washcloth, shampoo, body lotion, or baby powder. She will be using the one jail-issued 16″ × 30″ towel with the drying power of a cheap paper towel. There will be no nightgowns or bathrobes, no slippers or warm fuzzy socks. There will be no cozy comforters or big fluffy pillow to nestle into. She'll be assigned to a cold metal bed with a 4″-thick plastic used mattress, two sheets (possibly intact) and one recycled polyester-blend twin size blanket. Surely, not the Ritz-Carlton or even Motel-6. A cardboard cereal box will be her dresser, and an overturned bucket, if she's lucky enough to score one, will be her chair. All that is comforting and soft is no longer an option. All that is warm and soothing has become unattainable and forbidden.

At 11 P.M., as the lights are dimmed (but never off), and before the reverberating clang of that massive steel door slams shut for the first time, she sits cold and alone, wishing it was yesterday, because today she has lost what was left of herself.

Why Is She Here?

Why is she here? Doesn't anybody know?
Did she drive her car while drunk?
Did she get busted with blow?

Why is she here? Did she come here all alone?
Does she maybe have a husband?
Or some children left at home?

Why is she here? Did she rob someone for crack?
Did she steal to feed that monkey
that hangs tightly on her back?

Why is she here? Did she hurt someone or kill them?
Did she plan to do this crime?
Was it sparked by rage and passion?

Does her mama know she's here?
Does her mama even care?
Was she there for her when little
or was it just too much to bear?

Does anybody love her?
Does her heart beat just like ours?
Is it capable of feeling
or just cold and numb and scarred?

Why is she here? Was she beaten as a child
abused by ones she trusted
who then laughed at her and smiled?

Why is she here? Is it safer than the street?
Does she need somewhere to go
to hide and sleep and eat?

Did she ever have a chance to live and grow and thrive?
Did someone care enough
to teach her to survive?

I don't know why she's here, and it saddens me to see
this woman without freedom.
It could be you or me!

Roll Up

Melody Roker Sims

Melody left Riverhead Correctional Facility in time to be a reader at Herstory's tenth anniversary celebration in 2007, where she expressed the wish to live as a writer and to train someday to be a facilitator. This led her to join our bridge workshops, where she worked for well over a year. Although Melody, like so many other women facing the struggles of reentry, has had her hands full with the challenges of daily life, she periodically returns either to the bridge group or to join other formerly incarcerated writers at our public readings.

This piece has remained as her contribution to the study of what happens to women who are victims of domestic violence who fight back. She has read it in a number of Long Island venues, including the Islip Museum of Art, the Islip Public Library, St. Joseph's College, Suffolk Community College and Queensborough College, and in Harlem at a meeting of the Coalition for Women Prisoners in support of a bill to revoke or lighten the sentences for victims of domestic violence who fought back in self defense. At a classroom presentation at St. Joseph's College she told students of criminology that Patricia, the young woman in this story, had been freed through the new bill.

"*R*oker. Roker. Roll up! Bedford Hills has come for you." Excited but scared and disoriented as I begin to focus, I look to see what time it is on the clock outside the bars on the walkway—4:30 A.M. People I've gotten to know and became close with are waking up, as the guards begin to wake up another female on the opposite housing unit that will be my partner going upstate, I guess. Bedford Hills wants her too.

As I begin to file away my clothes and a pair of sneakers, with the exception of my outfit I put aside for this day, I pray silently: *Dear Lord, thank you for waking me up, and Dear Lord, please do not let no harm or danger come to me in this unknown place, what I'll soon have to call my home, and please, Lord, protect me. Don't let me get raped or beat up. Lord, thank you for relieving me from myself. In Jesus' name, amen . . .*

Before starting on the ride to Betty's house (Bedford Hills) in a sheriff's car, a woman and male deputy are my escorts. While holding my mug shot, the female deputy asks me my name, date of birth, home address and Social Security number. After giving the information she requested of me, her partner handcuffs me and then he puts the front shackle on my ankles, which makes it very hard for me to move, so he helps me into the back seat of their squad car, and while they do the same thing to my partner, while listening, I learn her name is Patricia. I wonder: *Is she just as scared as me? Is she an addict like me? What's her charges? She looks like a baby.*

As the officer helps her into the car, I notice that the tears are pouring down her face. Instantly my heart goes out to her and I don't feel my fear.

I can't help but to say to her, "It's going to be okay, don't cry."

She says, "I'm trying not to."

While sobbing she asks me have I been upstate before.

I tell her, "No, but I hear it's better up there than here—the air, the food . . . and although you're locked up you're allowed more freedom."

She says, "Promise me that you won't leave me."

"Well, I don't know if I can make that promise, but I will promise to be with you for as long as I can. But since this is our first time upstate, maybe we will be sent to the same facility".

She asks me, what am I in for? I tell her for selling drugs to an undercover cop and for possession. She asks me, how long do I got to be locked up for? I tell her three to six years, but my lawyer got the judge to give me the Shock program.

I asked her how old was she? She replied, 17. I asked her, was those her sisters and brothers in the picture she held in her hand? She said, "No, they are my three children." I thought to myself, *17 with three children. UNBELIEVABLE.*

I asked her what she was in for. She said "Manslaughter." I couldn't believe what she just said. She then explained to me that her children's father was 20 years her senior and used to beat her every day—started when she was four months pregnant with their first born and when he started beating her kids, which in the end she lost custody of them, she made a vow that the next time he raised his hands to beat her she would kill him, and she did just that.

I wondered: *Would or could I ever commit a crime like that?* I asked her how much time did she get? She said 25 years to life. I almost fainted but instead I shed tears for the innocence lost and stolen from this child and for the childhood she never had.

I would learn later that she was one of thousands that I would meet on my journey to finding myself again while at Betty's house. Patricia and I sat there silent, lost in our own worlds as the deputies were talking and driving.

To break the silence I said, "Well hi, I'm Melody."

The first smile I see when she says, "Pleased to meet you. Hi, I'm Patricia."

Somehow I knew I made of my first friend on this journey, but I also knew life would never be the same again for either one of us.

I Dance in Spring Wind

Nancy Rich

 *Unlike the other pieces in this section, this ode to free-dom was written while Nancy was still in jail. However, we believe it was only when it was read out loud in free-dom that it was fully realized. By the time Nancy accom-panied us to our various public readings she was studying the healing processes of recovery, yoga and writing. Her career path includes a duel Bachelor of Arts degree in Psychology and Wom-en's Studies with a focus on domestic violence, activism, policy, reproductive rights, substance abuse, and women's empowerment. She has read with Her-story Writers Workshop at St. Joseph's College, Stony Brook University, Suffolk Community College, Queensborough Community College and the East Islip Public Library, and was featured in a special bilingual interview on Radio Fiesta, WBON where her words reached 120,000 listeners in three states. She hopes to use her personal experience to empower people to promote change by the use of consciousness and spirituality and service to others.*

As I am gazing through my six-inch-wide window, I can hear in my mind the imagined sounds of Robbie Kreeger playing Spanish guitar, which leads into a wild Gypsy/Flamenco piece. The spring winds blow frantically through the trees and they begin to dance for an audience of clouds.

I press my face close to the bars for a better view, but I cannot spot the yellow buttercups anymore. I just know that those little fuckers can dance. I imagine that they would be cutting up a rug if they were here. I like to pretend that they had escaped, making it past the twelve-inch chain link fence with the barbed wire on top, through the wire in the middle and beyond the next fence with the barbed wire on top. Although the harsh reality is that the butter-cups were most likely innocent victims of the mower, I like to pretend that they found freedom dancing their way off the grounds of the correctional facility. I resent that they were cut. I mean, really, can't I even be allowed to enjoy the beauty of the yellow weeds dancing in spring winds? Why can't I just sit back in my chair, sip my drink and watch them dance for me? We would be two consenting adults enjoying the sensual freedom of the dance. Tiny buttercups have been born within the past few days but they are not yet mature enough to dance.

I used to have buttercups by the truckloads on the lawn at my cottage. It was a tiny three-room cottage, built in 1860. Just over an acre, it still had the original outhouse. I was absolutely fascinated by wildflowers that grew around my home. When I found out that the buttercup was really just a weed, I didn't care. To me they were beautiful. I mixed them with lily of the valley, which would bloom for only a few weeks every year in the early summer months, provided that the rains had not fallen too heavily during the spring. Their gorgeous fragrance would breathe life into my tiny home.

I used to love to pick flowers. I was taught to ask permission of the Mother Spirit before plucking them from the ground. Although my roommate told me that by picking flowers I was disrespecting Mother Earth, instinctively I felt that it was all right. Looking back and knowing that I suffered from an "appalling lack of perspective" I do indeed hope that it was all right. My intensions felt pure and loving. I loved that sweet and sacred piece of land. My selective memory tells me that it was a magical time. I don't live there anymore.

Today, I live here at the Suffolk County Correctional Facility, in Riverhead, New York in a tiny cell. I have a six-inch-wide window. I wonder if the bar running vertically down the center of the six-inch glass gap serves some kind of purpose. It's not as if someone could fit their body through. There are also six-inch horizontal bars that lie across every two and a half feet. My thinking is that the bars are not really serving a purpose. Maybe it is just décor. Or maybe it's to obstruct my view of the landscape, ever reminding me of my lack of physical freedom. You know, when I used to work here at the courts I would gaze through the same two fences—same barbed wire—at the same skinny window and wonder what it was like inside here. Today I am inside here dreaming of what it is like out there.

When I worked here, I could never get here on time. I would leave early and lie to my boss about my whereabouts. It seems almost comical that today I can't leave because I live here, locked up. I worked as an advocate for women who were abused at the hands of their men. It is never okay to beat a woman. Inside here women beat women while other women watch, chanting barbarically. Women outside these walls fight for us and in here we fight each other. I can't help to wonder what we're doing to our daughters. Although I hold it close to keep it protected, it feels as if my spirit is breaking. Hopefully it's just a bruise.

"I will break your fucking wrist if you touch that bread again." You see, up on the fifth floor we were just supposed to help ourselves to our bread. Down here in the pods it seems that we need to wait to have it handed to us. Of this I was not aware. It was an innocent mistake. To have another woman tell me that she wants to break my "fucking" wrists over wheat bread? It hurts my soul. Had her daughter or sister sought help to escape an abusive partner, I would have helped her in any way that I could. I swear . . . I would. I feel like it's my purpose and my duty to Creator and just the right thing to do. We need to take care of each other. I could not fathom ever intimidating another woman with violence. It is not my way. I go by way of love and I will not be afraid of women.

My sisters are destroying each other here in the snake pit. But as my beautiful friend Katie reminds me in her letters, I am standing in the snake pit with the antidote.

That officer can go ahead and break my wrist over a piece of wheat bread, but my spirit is not hers and it will not be broken. Today my body may be locked up, but my spirit is free to dance like a wildflower in spring winds.

Two Stories

Anjelique Wadlington

Anjelique began writing in 2004 with Herstory's first work-shop in Suffolk County's correctional facilities, so that her journey to give voice to incarcerated women begins with our own. From that moment on, she has never stopped writing. Nor has she stopped working to help others through her words, so that even when she was sent up-state to complete her sentence she stayed in close touch. In 2008, when she was released she became part of our first group of speakers, reading to students of criminology, sociology and law all over Long Island, and took part in the organization of a "bridges" workshop to allow women coming out of jail to write with women from the larger community. In response to the problems that re-entry poses for so many who dream about changing their directions while writing in jail, she developed a "Herstory Inside Out" Facebook page to help women who wrote together to find one another upon their release and to raise awareness of political issues affecting the for-merly incarcerated upon re-entry. While working full-time, she attends Suffolk County Community College, through a scholarship that will cover her expenses through graduate school, wherever she decides to study next, allowing her to work toward her dream of becoming a social worker.

The first story that we have reproduced here—"How do you see me?"—was commissioned by the Women on the Job Project of the Long Island Fund for Women and Girls, to illuminate what happens when women with felony convictions seek employment, and has been read by various task forces work-ing on Second Chance legislation which would allow for the expunging of criminal records for perpetrators of nonviolent crimes who have stayed within the confines of the law for a five-year period following their release.

The second piece—"You, Me, Them, and Us Equals We . . ."—addresses not only the question of how outsiders see women in jail, but how incarcerat-

ed women are taught to see themselves, as it rises out of its prose to become a poetic invocation that turns from the violence against oneself, with which it begins, to a new cry for freedom, daily coping, and grace.

"How Do You See Me?"

I did my last check in my rearview mirror, my make up was perfect. Nice and simple, I had left it natural with a light lipgloss. My hair was straightened with a little flip in the front. I wanted to make a great impression. Mommy had always told me, "Your first impression is the only and most important impression you can make." So I always made sure of it. The sun was shining bright and at its peak, so I knew everything was going to go without a hitch.

Change wasn't anything I was fond of; I hate having to jump into things or rearranging my daily schedule. I was perfectly fine until I noticed I had to get out of my car and hit the alarm. I wasn't in my skin, because I had to enter another. I felt grown and professional when I dressed up. Like the people do in the City. They looked important, which made me feel important, *I want a cigarette, I need to calm my nerves, I just don't want to smell like I just came from a bar, walking into the building.* The building wasn't too far from where I had parked, so I just had to tough it out.

I decided to wear black slacks creased to perfection by my own hands. Like I had learned when I wore my uniforms. It's been a few years since then. I haven't really needed to use an iron recently, but some skills you never forget. I had decided to go with a nice simple button-down blouse with a bright tank top underneath. "Never show any of your secret body parts, you don't want to portray something you aren't," Mommy had said to me over the phone as I got dressed earlier.

It seemed to be a longer walk than I thought it would be, or my feet were just dragging and digging into the concrete. *What will they ask? Will they like me? Or am I just like everyone else? Will I get a chance to explain my answer?*

I don't know really know what to expect. I just hope they give me the chance. Picking my head high and hands to my side, I knew

I was out of place. *What am I doing here?* Another thought crossed my mind, as I seemed to walk slower.

I felt the slacks hit my legs in each step I took—one was green and one black. My shoes decided to feel flat. I was no longer wearing my heels. My feet started to hurt. My boots were tight, hot, and sweaty. My shirt seemed to get tighter at the neck, as the bowtie got more uncomfortable.

I gave myself a quick glance down to see that I was no longer in my semi suit, but I was in full uniform of forest green and white. My pants were no longer black. They had become inmate green. I felt the goose bumps run across my arms and a feeling of embarrassment as everyone pointed and laughed. The number read across my shirt 05g0418. I realized that I had jumped out of my professional skin into a skin I didn't want to be in anymore, but lived with for years and recognized well, one that I had left years ago to die.

I walked to the building. *Ready Anj? Take a deep breath,* I told myself getting closer and closer to the office building. I placed my hand on the door and jumped into my white girl skin, just still black. It had worked a lot over the years when I had to speak to clients over the phone or complaining customers when I used to work at Bagel Boss. I entered the quiet fully carpeted office.

"Hello, may I help you?" a tall man had asked.

"Yes, my name is Anjelique. I am here to speak with Joe Lepton," as I extended my right hand out to shake his pale cold hand. My dad used to tell me you can tell a lot in a person by their handshake. If it was firm, weak. It gives them character without having to say a word.

"Yes, that's me," as he firmly shook my hand back. *Strong willed,* I thought to myself.

"I had called you yesterday morning for the job that the company had listed on the internet," I said as I looked him in his eyes.

"Yes, it is nice to meet you. Come, come in."

He seemed to be uneasy after I had told him that I was the woman who had called him. The dumb found look on his face, as I have seen many times over the years. When the voice doesn't match the other person's body, or color.

We walked to a smaller office around the corner where it looked like they have their business meetings. It's real, a REAL office, where real things are discussed. I was so amazed to actually be invited in. He directed me to sit across from him.

"So did you fill out the application?" he asked.

"No, Sir, I haven't."

"Okay," as he shuffled in the bottom draw of the desk we sat at. He pulled out a book . . . well, it seemed to be. I looked wide-eyed and shook my head before he started to raise his body up. "Okay, fill this out and we will talk after you are done," he directed me.

"Yes." I had responded back with a light smile. He got up and excused himself and headed toward the office door.

"Do you have a pen?" he asked trying to test my preparation skills.

One thing I had learned on my own throughout the years. Always be prepared for the unknown. You never know when you need a pen and paper. I nodded yes. And he exited the office and closed the door lightly.

Breezing through the first few basic knowledge questions of myself and morality questions I had stumbled and ignored one. If I didn't know, I skipped. Finish the rest and go back to it later on towards the end of the test. I hear all my exam teachers' voices over the years of test taking. Maybe I just didn't want to face these questions. Or maybe I didn't want them to know my weakness and what I feared.

Have you ever been convicted of a felony? If yes, for what and when?

The question was there. In plain sight! It wasn't going to go anywhere. I went around the question. I tried to even act like it didn't even exist. I really just wanted to get up and walk out. Maybe even lie. How will they find out? I thought I had dealt with it, but I was not ready to face it. Yes . . .

I just stared at the completed application. Incomplete thoughts and "what if's" and "I just hope so." Until a light knock on the door and his head popped in.

"Everything okay?" he asked cheerfully.

"Yes," and I turned my head looking back and smiled.

He came in and sat back into his chair and looked over the application. He nodded his head as if he was impressed. I just made sure I always looked at him and smiled.

"Okay. I have two questions. First, why should I hire you?"

I really wanted to say, *Because I need a job. And I am broke and I am parole mandated.* But I didn't, I couldn't sound desperate. So I was logical about it. And he just nodded and smiled while I answered his question.

"Good, I like that. Question Two, I see you checked yes for being convicted of a felony and that you will explain in interview. Well, here is your chance." And he sat there and made it so easy.

"I was young . . . 17; I sold drugs to an undercover for my boyfriend. He told to save his own ass, but I had refused to talk or to have knowledge of anyone else in the drug game." He just actually sat there and listened, the last stranger to ever listen to me was no one.

"I learned my lesson, but that doesn't define who I am. And what I can be. I am a very loyal and dependable person. I complete what I start," I commented before he spoke.

"I will hire you, I think this is a great opportunity for you, and you will be a huge asset to this company. Call me on Monday for your schedule so we can set you up with a patient," he said extending his hand to shake mine.

I was part of something! The cocoons hatched and the wings spread wide. They were beautiful and ready to continue their journey. I wanted to scream for joy and excitement, but it had to wait.

"Thank you, thank you so much," as I shook his hand back and exited the small office, around the corner to the door, to exit my past and enter a promising future doing what I loved.

The weekend seemed to not matter. I was working Monday, and nothing made me change my mood, or steal my shine.

Monday came and I was up at 6 A.M. I got myself together and waited until the office opened at 8. "Good morning, Senior Care. How may I direct your call?" the receptionist had answered on the other end.

"Yes I would like to speak to Joe Lepton. My name is Anjelique Wadlington."

"Hold, please." The music came on to keep me entertained.

"Anjelique, Hi how are you?" Joe had answered on the line.

"I am doing well, and yourself?" being polite.

"Well, thank you. I looked over your application and I spoke to my brother who is my partner. And I am sorry, but it isn't going to work out," he informed me. I just stood in my bedroom in silence. I was heartbroken. And the tears flooded my eyes.

"Okay. Thank you. Have a good day." And I hung up quickly. I felt my final sentencing. The judge has spoken once again, and my fate was in his hand . . .

You, Me, Them, and Us Equals We . . .

*L*ow *lives, dirty, worthless females.* To summarize what I feel about women that go to jail . . . *selfish, selfless, cowards* . . . to add a few more. I only see them in their dirty greens, and mopped hair-dos. *Shame, pity, and weakness* to throw into my pile of names. *Caged dogs, sloppy pigs* to top off my list of painful words of hate and opinions. *Killers, liars, thieves, drug dealers, addicts and crimi-nals. . . Your mother, and his sister, but this is my life. Bitch, whore, trick,* just so I can add on more gasoline to this UN-lit fire pit. *Strong, hurt, beauties* as I peel each little girl off each other. *Raped by her father, killed by her abuser, fought to have food and shelter for her sick child . . .* are who we turned out to be. *No mother, father has left, born with drugs to survive . . .* are the reasons why we were brought here. Fighters for all of our lives. From the handmade pipe with plastic bottles, straws, and foil, that they are introduced to, to the fist of his balled up hand across her face. This is all ME! We learn from what we see . . . Flying or swinging objects are more beautiful than hateful words . . . Physical is more desirable then verbal . . . *I hate you,* so much easier and glamorous than *I love you.* Because, we have watched our mothers, sisters, grandparents and friends. Fear of commitment . . . with loving too hard, is why she is so confused . . . scared not to love you. Honesty and fear of the truth is why she is forced to stay. Why we sit there and ask why do these same doors slam shut behind us and we smile that we are home?

Beyond Control

So today I'm exactly four years, four months, and 14 days from my big three-zero. Crazy because if you were to ask me ten years ago, "Where would you be in ten years?" I would have told you a dream, a fairytale Disney love movie—Jasmine & Aladdin, Ariel & Eric, Belle & Beast—I would have loved to have lived, or died like the person I have seen shot before my very own eyes hanging out in my Bronx days. But today I'm a collection of varieties . . . a mother, but not by blood . . . an aunt to four outstanding nephews and one outspoken outrageous niece . . . a wife but not from New York State papers quite yet . . . a friend to many that aren't to me . . . an ad-

vocate for silent voices that haven't been heard or want to be heard
by people who care not to see . . . a person of importance to ME,
MYSELF, & I like the Beyoncé song. I didn't have say-so in this path,
I fought kicking screaming, yelling, having a temper tantrum the
entire way here, but I can say that one thing is for sure is that I love
the experience of walking it. Hell of a rollercoaster ride without
having to be afraid of gravity. But getting here wasn't a walk in the
park. Like Mommy said to me, "It's a jungle out there, so be ready."

Yes, it would be better to write a full-length story, but eventually
it will end up that way, weaving in and out, tying the knots up, I
guess. But as of this moment let's just talk truth, the rare reality of
what's on Anjelique's mind. I've been home six and a half years. It's
not the hardest six years like the lost two years. But it's only as hard
as I would or have made it for me. Like my moments when . . .
    . . . I fall off the mental wagon and fall into a day or so of depres-
sion. I just lay on anything in my reach . . . the couch, or the bed,
maybe even the rough carpet on my living room floor, wherever the
place I lay my head on as long as I'm accompanied by my extra-large
king-sized blanket to wrap up in and my phone and charger, in case
I need a helping voice to connect my brain to reality. Also a cup,
can, or bottle of liquid, a snack like chips or popcorn, and finally
the remote control. I just lay there tossing and turning, bunching
up in the blanket, a pillow between my legs, then not. Some movies
or music, do I want funny or sad? *American Teenager* or a repeat
episode I've seen over a million times of *Grey's Anatomy*, my new
excitement in life to draw my attention in drama and fantasy land.
TV land, the late night shows that played *I Love Lucy*. I love this
show *Grey's Anatomy*, I daze into it. Place myself in anyone or all
of the characters . . . the love between Meredith and Derek. The
confusion of my sexuality if I love men or just enjoy the grace of a
women's touch like Torres. Wishing I had the intellect like Lexi and
her affection for Mark but had interest for another man. The bad
boy of Corez and his troubled marriage and using sex as an escape
goat. Makes me smile when I want to cry. Laugh when I need to
scream. Just enough of full satisfaction into blank stares falls into
nothing of what so ever . . . evers and evers . . . I feel like that, like
I'LL NEVER EVER get out of this "MISERY" I call all my mood swings.

Then again, have I truly, honestly tried? I'll close my eyes and try to think of the worst things I've been through like going to jail, and getting jumped several times, losing my grandma, my parents split. Just so I can tell myself I have had worse days. Like the whole two years I lost . . . my education that didn't get any further, my family being very broken, my relationship with the man I thought was the real love of my life at one point, my brothers growing up being tiny little ants to jolly giants, my sister's loss of her friends the month after of my incarceration. Lost time, that I can't get back . . . not even if I tried.

"Jus Another Day"

A blank page, I stare at this blank, college-ruled, loose leaf page always. But it's still just a blank page. The skinny blue lines and the two red ones are all starting to blend together and have become one big blur. No thoughts of anything, no feelings or emotions, memories of colors or even a picture or single caption. Not sure what's beyond it, and honestly I'm not too sure if I really want to know. If I daydream, if I let myself wonder what it could be about? . . . the once-upon-a-time loves of my life, men, women, death, my broken family, of drugs, money and betrayal, my life of complete confusion, my past of hurt and betrayal and loneliness, a melting of a crush's scent as he walks by or something not real at all, just a fairytale out of a Disney princess story. Could I just make up a dream or relive a moment of just pure satisfaction of truth? What kind of satisfaction from him, from her, or from them . . . some hidden feeling I hold onto for some type of false hope . . . or more for a backup plan? Where does this all come from? Why does it continue at times longer than others? I flip over to another blank page . . . no new images, but some small bit of relief. What may it be? It's still cloudy. I'm starting to feel tight and guarded . . . just closed off in this huge space of nothing. Every time I sit and all I do is pull out my binder and stare at the blank page. And just another incomplete thought and incomplete feelings, unanswered questions of everything . . .

Torn between Two Worlds

Angelita Peete

Few have surmounted the obstacles that Angel has experienced in her short life of 28 years, and she has used this process in every way possible to do so. She has been working with Herstory without a break since March of 2009, when she began a very difficult and honest memoir at the Riverhead Correctional Facility. Immediately upon her release she joined our Huntington Station bridge group, where she quickly became a mentor for other women coming out of jail, and also an inspiration for the retired school principal and other community leaders who make up the group. Another survivor of savage childhood sexual abuse at the hands of the men in her mother's life, she uses this group not only to tell her own story, but for the support of a "family" she never had and the unconditional love it offers. Before she plows into another chapter of the trauma in her early years, she often says, "I really need to write about this!"

As more of her story emerges, we have watched Angel grow into one of Herstory's most charismatic speakers, as her evolving understanding of the roots of her struggle has deeply moved others to both tears and action. She has brought her powerful voice to audiences in colleges and in the community including St. Joseph's College, Suffolk County Community College, SUNY Old Westbury and Queensborough Community College.

We have watched her develop the strength to divorce herself from her former lucrative drug dealing "career" and take on in its place a fierce dedication to helping others who have been assaulted by domestic violence, drugs, and abuse. In doing so, she obtained a full scholarship towards a degree in drug and alcohol counseling, and loves being a student again. The piece that we are publishing here looks with unflinching honesty at the temptations that come to former drug dealers coming out of jail who are ousted from the legitimate job market, much as they wish to change their ways, telling a vital part of the story of what happens when formerly incarcerated people are not given second chances.

"**Y**o, A, I got a new connect and this one is the best one yet! My brother's baby's mama has a new man and he said $50 for three grams."

As soon as the words escaped his lips, I felt the regret radiating from him.

Today of all days! NIGGA DAMN!!! Of course today has to be the day you say some shit like that. And now the room is silent. Not a comfortable silence but a painful tension-filled silence that grips your throat.

After the day I had, that was really the last thing I needed to hear. I had another interview earlier and once again, as politely as possible, they told me to go fuck myself! Not in those words, of course, but they reinforced what I've heard too many times before: *It doesn't really matter who I'm trying to become or how neat my résumé is or even how extensive my credentials are, the only thing that matters is that I checked that little box.*

Well, at least today I got the answer as to why I keep getting denied. The Department of Health put a hold on my CNA license because of my felony and until I get a Relief of Disability, I can't work. Who knows how long that'll take! Oh well, another sad story for me, right?

Wrong! I'm hurt, depressed, frustrated, and just plain pissed off! The tears just won't stop falling but I barely even notice. I haven't had a job in almost two years. I'm sick and tired of sitting at home, bored with the current state of my life, and sick to death of being broke.

Why am I broke? Because I'm trying to live a positive and productive life and unfortunately, no one will give me a chance. Maybe it's because I feel guilty about my mom's suicide and the part I played in her demise, or maybe I just turned into a pussy and punked out on life!

But I'm not a pussy and I'm far from a punk. And now I can feel my emotions superseding my intelligence. The wheels in my brain are turning rapidly and the thoughts are coming faster than I can even process them. If I can just get my hands on $50, I can reclaim my financial freedom. $50 can turn into $300 in an instant. I can turn those three grams into seven and keep it moving!

Is that really what I want to do? Well, yes and no! Yes, I want to be able to support myself, and yes I would love to not have to ask him for $$ for the simplest things. And sure it would be great to feel like my old self again. But no, I do NOT want to poison the people of my community. No I don't want to disappoint the people who care for me, and no I don't want to be a slave to my phone anymore.

But really, what am I left to do? I'm tired of getting my hopes up to only be disappointed. Tired of people turning up their noses when they see my check mark in the little box. Tired of wanting and needing SO MUCH and yet having so little! Tired of having my hand out, asking for charity. And I'm sick and fucking tired of listening to people throw in my face the little that they do for me. So sick and tired of being sick and tired!

You see, I no longer fear jail. I know exactly what to expect and at this point I would almost welcome its return. No bills, no responsibilities, no worrying about where my next meal is coming from or how to afford the most basic necessities. And now I'm torn in two completely different directions. On the one hand, I really want to be a productive member of society. I just want to go to work, go back to school, and have a career and a family. But on the other hand, I miss the power and control that the money brings. I miss being able to do what I want, when I want, but most of all, I miss the rush! I miss having so many things to do, people waiting on me, money constantly touching my hands. That rush that you get when you're doing something that you know is wrong but you do it anyway.

The pressure in my chest is building and there's only one way to shake it. If not today or tomorrow, I know one thing's for sure. The inevitable, being inevitable, is bound to happen. One way or the other!!!!!

You see, even though it is wrong, I'm good at the game! I'm a damn good hustla and at my peak I was getting more money than I knew what to do with. I may have lived in my car for eight months, but every day I made enough money to rent a room or a studio apartment.

The biggest problem is: it's not just a hustle, it's a lifestyle! It sucks you in, chews you up and spits you out! When you are making money all day, constantly, you develop a certain attitude towards it. If you aren't careful, you start to spend it just as quickly as you make it, simply because you know you will make it back.

I stashed a nice piece of change first, and then I got comfortable in my hustle. That's when I started spending $300 a night at the bar and sniffing almost the same amount of cocaine as the crack that I sold!!

After a while, this game becomes your whole life and only a few are lucky enough to walk away. Some get addicted and can't get out because they don't know anything else. Others end up strung out on the same drugs they sell and fall from the top, hard. Some lose their life to the system, addiction, or death! Others just lose their minds and themselves and spend the rest of their lives telling stories about what they used to do and how they used to be! And the lucky ones, like me, are fortunate enough to have my sanity, my health, and my freedom. And because of that, my resolve has grown strong and I refuse to go back and allow "The Game" to get the best of me.

I want more, I am worth more and I know I can do better!! They say that the players change, but the game remains the same. Well, I don't wanna play anymore, so game over!!!

Living with the Warden

Lisa Biggica

When a man comes out of jail, he is often greeted by his community as a hero who has completed an important rite of passage. When a woman returns, she is too often seen as a pariah and object of shame. Lisa's piece about needing to return to living with her mother at the age of 46 puts a magnifying glass on the day-to-day struggles of existing in a world where dreaming and moving forward is nearly impossible, letting us know how much work we have yet to do to make reentry a viable path.

Lisa has been a dedicated member of the Herstory Inside Out group in Huntington Station ever since her release almost two years ago and has participated in our program readings at various colleges and universities. She has relied heavily on her Huntington group members as a primary support for her sobriety and in dealing with the frustrations of her living situation and probation.

Often people have stereotypes in mind when they think of who lands in jail. A middle-class suburban mom, devoted to her children, Lisa reminds us that anyone can get stuck in the traps of addiction and land in jail as a result. Now that she has reestablished her relationships with her children, they have become a primary impetus for her sobriety. In spite of an accomplished background as a recreational therapist however, and multiple applications, she has not been able to secure work since her release.

Trapped. Caged in. Isolated. Restless. Although I am out of jail, the confinement and restraints are with me every single day. I am hopeless, thinking that if I have to go through life as it is now, I don't want it. Sometimes I think jail was better. I didn't have to think. I was told when to eat, when to watch television, when to go to sleep. Even when to get my mail. No responsibilities or life changing decisions whatsoever.

Every single day . . . every single moment . . . every waking second, I have twenty million things going on in my head, and yet not a single thought gets expressed. I want to scream, but no one will hear me. No one will care. This pity-party only has one guest. It reminds me of jail, looking out, separated by those iron bars.

Nothing's funny. I'm in a tunnel and it's dark. There's no one helping me navigate. I'm walking blind. My hands reach out, but I don't feel anything or anyone. I can't sit still. I'm desperate to "break out" of here, knowing that I could just make one phone call, literally letting everything "go up in smoke." I cannot escape. Even in my sleep. I am helpless. I am haunted. Bizarre flashes of my former life, mere glances of my future self. I am chained and cannot figure out how to set myself free. Flashbacks of being on the side of the road, hood popped up, making it look like car trouble. All the while, just waiting on someone to sell them drugs.

My short-term memory is shot. I walk into a room and forget why. I have a conversation with my son Peter and forget my point mid-sentence. My equilibrium is off, as I bump into furniture that is in plain-sight. What is wrong with me? How have I turned into an absent-minded mess? I am still confined. I live with my mother, the "Warden."

"Are you still on that computer? When are you gonna get ready? Don't you have to take lunch? What's that on the floor? Did you eat all the crackers? Must you smoke so much? Where are you going? When will you be back? I don't want turkey for Thanksgiving, I want ham." She is relentless. I am 46 years old, yet she treats me like I'm 12.

I feel like a tennis ball, stuck in the net. Depressed, disgusted, resistant, impatient, and most of all hopeless. I haven't figured out how to bounce back. I can listen to everyone until I'm Smurf-blue in the face. I wish this part of my life was over. I want to break free of this net. I want to stop struggling everyday for things that come so naturally for others. I don't want to be the "invisible child" anymore. I'm tired of getting pushed aside. I want to matter to someone.

Intensive Outpatient Services, mandatory on probation: "Your behaviors are not normal. You lacked something in your childhood. You were looking for an exit. There's a deep-rooted reason for your drug abuse. It all comes down to your core-belief system . . ." Blah, blah, blah. How about this? I liked the feeling of getting high, and don't need to be analyzed! Just push me on through and give me my completion certificate. Probation will be very happy; I, on the other hand, am undecided.

The other side of the net is within reach. If only I could stretch out and grab it. But I am too weak. The motivation is somewhere inside, but it's found the ultimate hiding spot. I think I see glimpses of it at times, only to find out it's a figment of my imagination, for reality right now is distorted. I think harping on what I don't have is why I'm stuck in this mindset. The caged-in feeling of being trapped comes too easily. I can't sit still. Sitting ducks get caught. It's a known fact.

All day long, I dream and I wish. My thoughts bounce as I walk towards the shabby, brick building. In the parking lot are Crown Vics all lined in a row. The sight of law enforcement. Knowing that these probation officers have the power to send me back. Although I know I'm clean, my heart still races as I enter the building. There is an old metal desk sitting by the door. It has seen better days, as the graffiti and the smudges of grime fill the sides. The designated sign-in sheets are on top, pencils on the side. I sign the sheet and take a seat. The benches are worn, and half of them are broken. There is a payphone in the corner, but the receiver wire is cut. The wallpaper has been peeled back in certain spots. The glass in the windows is in dire need of a cleaning. Suffolk County tax dollars at work! As I sit there, looking around the room, I am thinking that I only have one more time to be in this building. I cannot wait to be done with all of this!

After a while my name is called. A tall, older gentleman, with big hollow eyes leads me to the back. He is silent as we walk down the hall. I know it's nothing personal, but he looks annoyed to be there. I figure he's just about done with his time here and wants to retire. I take my seat, but can't sit still. I rock in place, I shake my leg. I push my cuticles back. I pick the dirt out of my nails.

"Miss Biggica, September eighth brings you to your eighteenth month, not August."

A ton of bricks just crashed down upon me. My spirit crushed.

Hope, only a distant memory. My heart aches as he continues talking, knowing I have to endure more time with my mother, "The Warden." Wondering how long the jail time would have been if I'd maxed out so I wouldn't have had to do any probation.

At 10:30 A.M. I walk through the door, and the first thing I hear is the Warden. "Oh, you're back already? I guess I can never be alone."

I roll my eyes as I lock the door, surprised that she's even up at this hour. Normally it's quiet until about noon. I figure that my computer time is shot for the day since it's her machine.

"How'd you get home?" she asks.

"I took a cab."

"Oh, my aren't we extravagant," she hisses.

"No, not extravagant, just didn't want to spend two hours and three buses to get back. Why? Did I spend your money?" I snap.

"You don't have to be a smart-ass," she replies.

"No, I don't, but you don't have to watch how I spend my money."

She starts to say something, but I ignore her and pour myself a cup of coffee. I head out, straight for the patio, coffee and book in hand. If I could live out here for the rest of "my sentence," it would be fine with me. I pull out a chair and take a deep breath. It is so peaceful out here. My cluttered mind gets to relax as the sun is shining bright. There is a cool breeze that brushes by, blowing my bookmark from the table.

"What are you cooking? Do you have the gas on?"

"I just lit the oven Mom"

"Well, I smell gas, is it lit?"

"No, Mom, I just want to blow us sky-high," I chuckle.

"But I why do I smell gas?" she pushes on.

Maybe it's the bloodhound in you, I think to myself.

"I can't stand your coughing, and the smell of that smoke is all in my throat! " she barks.

I drum out my usual response. "At least I'm not smoking crack." It usually stops her in her tracks. I don't really care if it's mean or not. As long as she stops, I'm good.

Thank God it's Wednesday. She'll be gone from noon until about four P.M. My hours of peace.

The television is finally shut off. I put the radio on, blasting Metallica. I walk over to the thermostat. It reads 75 degrees. It's the middle of March. I sigh heavily, not believing that she keeps it so high. I drop it down to 66 and turn my attention to the computer. I can get lost here, plus it helps keep me out of trouble.

At exactly 4 o'clock the Warden comes through the door. She shuffles in with her walker. Her gait is slow, but steady. I don't see any family resemblance, and at one point in my life I actually thought I might have been adopted. She is about 5'1" in contrast to my 5'7". She reminds me of one of the old-fashioned Italian grandmas you see in the movies. She is bundled in many sweatered layers.

"Why is it so cold in here?"

"Are you kidding me?" I ask, shaking my head.

"No, it's cold in here!" she snaps.

I get myself up, go to the patio door, pick up the screen and slam the glass down. I turn and give a great sarcastic smile.

"Would you like me to raise the heat back to seventy-five?" I ask.

"Don't be smart! What is it on now?"

I don't even answer, as I get up once again and walk to the thermostat. The heat immediately kicks on.

"We'll be boiling in a minute," I snarl.

I feel my body tense up as I my grip tightens around the pack of cigarettes I'm holding. My pace to the patio quickens, as I just want to get the hell out of there. I sigh heavily as I walk through the door and plop down trying to get my mind off of her. As I look around, I can see the start of the crocuses, poking their tips out beyond the soil. They're so close I can just reach down and touch them. And then it hits me . . . Sometimes, I let her get me so crazy. I let myself get so frustrated and so focused on what I don't have that I fail to see what's right in front of me . . . freedom! I can just reach out and touch the crocuses! I have the freedom to come and go, even if it's walking the garbage to the dumpster. The freedom to sit on the patio, to breathe fresh air, read my book, have a cup of coffee, pet the cat that passes by daily for her dose of loving. Freedom to use the telephone to call someone, without them having to accept collect calls from a correctional facility. No more visits with my loved ones through a Plexiglas partition, wearing the "big-bird" jumpsuit. I now have normal people visits, hugging and kissing as much or as little as I want. And I have choices. It's no longer green or white, thermal or sweats, V-neck or round. I can wear a pink tank top with yellow shorts if I really wanted to. Polka-dots with stripes! Not that I would, just saying, I COULD! I can even stay in my pajamas all day if I want to.

I now own a coat that is not stamped with Suffolk County Property, shared by inmates, from a bin by the door. I can go to the grocery store and buy whatever I want. No more commissary lists and trading stuff for more coffee packets because there is a limit. I can cook whatever I want and eat with a knife and fork and just have a quiet meal by myself. No more strip-searches after a family member leaves or having to ask them if they left me a package or if they put money on my books. No more worrying about someone else taking care of me. I now have an opportunity for a "do-over." It seems pointless at times, but how often do you hear the phrase, "If only I had a second chance." Well, I've been given that chance. And I plan to take advantage of every opportunity that comes my way.

I have fewer friends on this side of the net, but they accept me for who I am, not how much Crack I have. I am grateful to have them in my life. Their friendship gives me a different perspective on things. It gives me hope to know that I can be like them: drug free.

Although I express my loathing and my desire to get out of the Warden's house, I am truly grateful to my mother. I have a roof over my head and I have a small spot to myself. I have a family that truly loves me, with all my faults. They have forgiven me for my past mistakes. I need to not let my mother get to me. I will not change who she is or how she feels. I can only accept her as she is, as I hope one day she will accept me as I am. I tell myself it's not her fault. That's the way she was raised. Her era was shaped differently from mine. It makes us individuals. And I know, just like me, she only wants to see her kids healthy and happy.

Ironically, the other day I was watching this football movie. The coach made a statement that I strongly identified with, " I see two men standing here before me. The one that you are, and the one you're to become." I can't wait to see who I'm to become!

The Dark Side

Stephanie Harrison-Mason

As we look back at an introduction to a piece Stephanie contributed to our first VOICES journal, which came out in 2007—bravely sharing her childhood experiences of sexual abuse by a close family friend, so that others might draw comfort and heal—it is hard to believe that this woman who would only put her pen to paper in the safety of our writing circle in Riverhead jail, is now the dynamic public speaker and respected deaconess of her church, whose voice resounds with so much power and pride wherever there is the need to speak up.

Linda Coleman and Lonnie Mathis, the facilitators of Stephanie's first writing workshop described how, when she finally allowed herself to write, "her tears flowed as fast as the words hit the page. But write she would, without backing down for a minute. When it came time for her to read, her voice emerged in the tone and cadence of the six-year-old girl who she was when these incidents began.

"Gradually, week after week, as others raptly attended her story, Stephanie's voice grew stronger, older, and eventually, she made an effortless shift from writing and reading in the present-tense voice of the six-year-old, to the past tense perspective of the adult looking back. Her voice deepened as she read, the adult woman claiming the events. While she remained tearful, her crying was now interspersed with a conviction that telling her story might one day help, or even prevent, similar occurrences in another's life. By the end of her five-month tenure of working with us, Stephanie chose to be one of our readers in our anniversary celebration.[1]

---

[1] Twice a year—for the anniversary celebration of "Herstory Inside" each spring and for the December holiday season—women from our Yaphank workshop are bused in to join theRiverhead workshop members, a service that is usually reserved for medical emergencies. Readers are allowed to invite guests from the tiers, so that audiences can number 50 or more, including male guards, prison officials, photographers, and press.

When her sentence was completed, she not only continued to write with Herstory, but attended every reading where another voice was needed to help people understand the devastating effects that violence against women and girls can have on health, happiness and the desire to live in dignity and freedom.

This more recent piece—written after she had safely left the world of which she writes—brings to light the ways in which girls who were victims of violence become helpless in its face as adults, as it charts the struggle of women everywhere, struggling to find love relationships free of the old repetitions. Stephanie married her current husband while they both were in jail, and together they have built a new life.

(Phone rings)

"Hello."

"Hey, girl. What's up?" asked Michelle.

"Hey. What you up to?"

"Trying to figure out what I am going to wear tonight. You still going, right?"

"I don't know, girl—I have bills to pay and my money is tight this week."

"Come on, girl. This is the night to be in attendance. They are giving away free V.I.P. passes to the All White Affair Boat Ride to a selected few and I have all intensions of being one of the selected few!!"

(Laughing)

"Girl, you crazy," I said.

"I'm just keeping it real. Those brothers got a lot of money."

"Yeah. And a lot of women too!!"

"So?"

"So, nothing. I am not getting ready to go to that club acting thirsty."

"Even if I told you that Mr. Fine was one of the sponsors?"

"Who?"

"Tony, that's who, wit' his fine ass. You know he's after you."

"Child, he got too many women for me."

"Yeah, but he always send you a bottle of champagne on the house."

"True. But like I said, my funds are tight and my hair and nails are a mess. You go and call me later with the 411."

"Better yet, can you take a ride with me somewhere?"

"Where?"

"I need you to go to the mall with me to pick out an outfit."

"I guess so. I'll see you when . . ."

(Phone hangs up)

"Hello . . . hello. Ugggh. I hate when people hang up while I'm still talking and don't say bye or nothing!!!"

I finished getting dressed and sat by the window waiting. I started thinking of how long I had been attracted to Tony. He stood about five six or seven, dark brown complexion, spoke with a very sexy voice and had the most beautiful set of white teeth I've ever seen on a man. He would always try to get me to sit with him, but I had no interest in competing with all of the women he had falling at his feet as though he was royalty or something. I always fantasized about us being together and Tony being exclusively with me, but knew it was just that, a fantasy.

One Year Later

Tony and I had been in an exclusive relationship with one another for over a year. He treated me like a queen, taking me on trips and showering me with expensive gifts including the most beautiful engagement ring I had ever seen. He was ready to go to the next level and wanted us to move in together. I was reluctant at first because I enjoyed living alone with my own personal space. But he insisted that things would be more beautiful than they were now and that there were two extra bedrooms with built-in baths when I wanted my personal me time. I finally agreed and things started out just as he said they would.

One day as we sat down for dinner, Tony decided that he did not want to go to the club that we normally club at and said he was going to stay home and watch some movies. He urged me to go and have a good time. I picked up Michelle and we went to a club her cousin owns in Queens. I arrived home at about four-thirty in the morning to find Tony sitting in the recliner.

"How was the club?"

"It was nice."

"C-Lo said he did not see you there tonight."

"I wasn't there. I went to Michelle's cousin's club in Queens."

"Oh, so now you are clubbing abroad, huh?"

"Babe, it was no big deal. He just opened his club and we just went out there to support him that's all."

"Well, it is a big deal. I need to know where you are at all times."

"I beg your pardon."

"You heard me. Don't ever do that again. Are we clear?"

"Clear? I went out with my friend and you are making a big deal out of nothing?"

"Listen, do not talk back to me!"

"You are my man, not my father."

As I walked past him to exit the room, he jumped up and grabbed me.

"Take your hands off of me!" I yelled.

"What did you say, bitch?"

It was then that I smelled the alcohol that reeked from his breath.

"You been drinking. Let me go!"

Before letting me go, Tony pointed his finger in my face. His eyes blood-shot red from drinking and a lack of sleep.

"Don't you ever disrespect me again. Do you understand? I will hurt you!"

As tears rolled down my face, I was in total disbelief. The man that I had fallen in love with had a side that I had never seen before. I went into the spare bedroom and locked the door before crying myself to sleep.

The next morning, I woke up to Tony sitting on the side of the bed.

"How did you get in here?"

"I used the key."

"I don't think this is going to work out between us. I think it's best that we end this relationship. I . . ."

"Babe, I'm sorry. I was drinking and started thinking all kinds of stuff."

"That's no excuse for what you did."

"I know. Please forgive me and give me another chance."

"I am not going to be with a man that calls me out of my name or puts his damn hands on me."

"I know. Can we get through this? It will not happen again."

"It better not because if it does, it's over!"

Tony began kissing me and before I knew it, he was seducing me like never before. It was as though his body was apologizing with every deep stroke, while he whispered how much he loved me. Over the months, the verbal and minimal abuse escalated but every time, he would seduce me and convince me to stay.

(Phone rings)

"Hey, whatcha doin'? I haven't heard from you in a while."

"Chelle, I have just been chillin'."

"That's not what I heard. I thought we were girls?

"What are you talking about?"

"I am talking about Tony putting his damn hands on you!"

"It was just an argument."

"Look, every time you minimize his bullshit and keep forgiving him, it's going to keep a door open for him to think all he have to do is apologize and have sex with you."

"Who said that's what he's doing?"

"He tells Rob everything and brags about having you wrapped around his finger. I mean I hate to be the one to tell you this but he has someone else."

"Why are you doing this?" I ask.

"Because you are my friend and I should have told you a long time ago instead of listening to my man telling me to mind my business."

I did not want to believe Michelle, but my heart already knew. It's just a woman's instinct. So, I had my friend Steve follow Tony around, only to find out he was being unfaithful to me with a woman who lived on the Heights who appeared to be pregnant. I didn't want to believe it myself so I followed him one day and watched him take her to the doctor's office and then go for a walk in the park, rubbing her belly. I was numb. I wanted to jump out of the car and confront him, but I knew he would try to lie his way out of it. I rushed home and started rambling through his things and found pictures of them together and ultrasounds of the baby hidden in a shoebox inside his boot. As tears rolled down my face, I knew our relationship was over. I spread all of the pictures and ultrasounds neatly on the dining room table. I sat in the chair and waited for him to come home.

Tony walked into the room where I was sitting. His eyes connected to mine as he walked towards me.

"Babe, let me explain."

"There's nothing to explain. You are always accusing me of betraying you, but you have been betraying me."

He tried to kiss me but I turned my face away.

"Who is she? Is that your baby?"

"No."

"Then why do you have all of these sonogram pictures? You know what, it doesn't even matter anymore. You have physically, verbally and emotionally abused me and I am done. You can have that bitch!"

I went upstairs and called Michelle to let her know what was going on.

"Gurl, you can come stay with me as long as you like. Is he there?"

"Yes, he's here."

Tony burst through the door with his shirt off and his fist balled up.

"Who in the hell are you talking to?"

He slapped my cell phone out of my hand and punched me in the side of the head. I fell to the floor and was dizzy, as I felt his hands ripping my panties off. He grabbed me by my hair and dragged me to the bed.

"Get up, bitch. You leaving me, right? Right?

"Just let me go," I said sobbing

"I gave you everything!"

I tried to get up and get my phone to call 911, but Tony grabbed me around the neck and began choking me until he heard the doorbell ringing. Thanks to Michelle—she stayed on the line and brought the police to our house.

Tony was arrested for assault and battery.

I could not believe that a man I once called my PRINCE CHARM-ING possessed such a wicked, dangerous and abusive DARK SIDE.

I AM A SURVIVOR OF DOMESTIC VIOLENCE.

The Longest Wait of My Life

Katherine De la Cruz

This section would not be complete without a story representing the children of the incarcerated, whose numbers are increasing every year. Katherine was part of Herstory's "Our Story" workshop that engages 120 Educational Opportunity Program students at Stony Brook University every summer, as part of their required freshman orientation. Working to incorporate Herstory's "dare to care"
technique as they write to contribute to a movement for civil rights and economic justice, these entering students explore the ways in which their own stories might dare current and future decision makers in the larger community to care.

As Katherine explored the technique, adding a new scene each week, she was able to provide her classmates not only a riveting picture of a three-year-old watching an unimaginable crime, but of the way in which having a parent in jail casts a continual shadow of sorrow and "otherness" over the lives of children left behind. The response of her classmates, as they showed her how she had allowed them to walk in her shoes, helped break that isolation as it strengthened her resolve to use her story to help others. This story has been read to audiences interested in youth justice and used for training purposes. Katherine became very active in student affairs and has recently decided to major in journalism.

I find myself on this huge bus sitting next to complete strangers and somehow still feeling like I have something in common with each and every one of them. Looking around while I'm on an overnight bus ride, which feels like the longest ride of my life, I see people who look just as exhausted and anxious as me. At last, as the sun is rising, while I stare out the window, I've arrived at this destination that at this point is still unfamiliar to me, but I'm looking around trying to guess. All I see is a building made of brick with a fence as long as a football field surrounding the entire thing and what looks like barbwire at the top of it. The feeling of separation and coldness as I enter the building is something inevitable. As I walk in, there are a number of men and seldom women in uniform awaiting my arrival. After I go through all security measures I am finally allowed in. I go sit at a table and take another look around, staring at all the unfamiliar people I sat right next to on the bus ride here. I stop moving my eyeballs from left to right and fixate them on one target, a door in which the people that walk out are the only ones that can walk back in. This feels like the longest wait of my life and perhaps it feels that way because I have waited all my life for this moment.

A man finally exits out of the door and I automatically recognize everything about him—from the way he walks, to the form of his facial features and even his voice. He sits right across from me, only to stare and await some type of dialogue to form. I don't know where to start or even how to start; it is like sitting by a stranger.

No one would have guessed this man to be my birth father. I'm 16-years-old at this point, and finally it hits me that my father was a stranger to me. As I say "Hello" and call him by his real name instead of Dad, I keep having flashbacks of the very moment where everything changed, the reason for my visit, and the reason for him being in this place.

My memories of my father are for the most part nonexistent; I spent the majority of my childhood pretending I wasn't as affected as I really was by his lack of involvement. And the rest of my life I spent making up excuses for both my father and mother. My mother and father formed an unusual couple. They never really looked happy together, just content, and eventually you would look at them and realize they were both just putting up with one another. Through them I learned to put up. That's what got me sitting in this room, staring at my father through this transparent glass, which separated his world and mine. His world filled with limitations and my world of limitless possibilities. I found myself even beyond the resentfulness, wanting to share a portion of my freedom with him. For as long as I could remember it had been that way. It had been years and I had begun to stop missing him, perhaps he had been gone so long that I had become accustomed to living the life I was living without him.

He proceeded to ask me how I'd been, but I couldn't help thinking to myself, *Is he just asking to start a conversation?* Perhaps he actually was interested in what had happened in the last 13 years of my life at this point. So in a courteous manner I answered that I had been good, although you can only imagine what I was really thinking. After staring at each other in complete silence the guard warned us that we must begin to say our goodbyes and although I couldn't say a word, I watched my father disappear into the very door he came out of. I sat in this wooden jail chair and stared at the emptiness that just a few moments before had been his presence. As the tears ran down my face like a waterfall, I placed my hand on the glass and whispered into the emptiness, "I forgive you, Dad".

As I walked out of the prison where my father had been all my childhood, I shed some more tears and mounted back on the bus awaiting the long awkward bus ride back once again. But this time on my ride back I had a lot of reflecting to do. Somehow, although this long ride wasn't new to me, I still couldn't adjust to it all. Finally, after 15 minutes of waiting, the bus pulled away from the same building whose picture was still engraved into my mind.

As I proceeded to put headphones in my ears and tried to ignore the noise of these unknown people, I pressed PLAY on the purple iPod my mother had given me. As I listened to the music, I closed my eyes and tried to get to a tranquil zone where nothing and no one could bother me. After ten minutes I finally achieved the level of relaxation I had aimed for, only to have the calm broken by my thoughts. My favorite song had come on and with every high pitch and change of beat, the scene faded more and more, until it completely disappeared. I can't speak for anyone, but it's the worst feeling ever, avoiding remembering certain things but then having the very thing you're avoiding come up time and time again. It's like I can feel it now—the harder the sound of the drum, the more it hurt to think. I finally just let the feeling take over me and closed my eyes, envisioning a scene that was so specific and crucial to my life.

There she was, a young girl of at least three years of age, sitting on this brown and tan striped couch with her aunt, watching a popular Spanish show on a Spanish network which was quite popular where she came from. As the girl looks at her aunt she can't help but smile. Her aunt was glowing and her laughter could fill every corner of her 18-floor apartment building with sound. The young girl proceeded to the kitchen, which was down this long, narrow, dark hallway right by the main entrance to the apartment. I couldn't help but giggle at the image of the three-year-old girl, shorter than the table she was standing in front of, yet still completely filled with enthusiasm as she attempts to fill this big aluminum cup, which is her aunt's favorite, with ice tea. Before she could finish a man walked in. I could at this point describe every last aspect of him, as though I were being questioned by a police officer. He looked about six feet tall in my vision, with a navy blue sweater with a hood which covered his face and protected his identity from me. He just had walked in, didn't look anywhere besides forward, and proceeded to the living room. The young girl with terror reading all over her face stayed underneath the table. In her face you could also tell she sensed danger and from her vantage point all she could hear was six loud thumps, but it was louder than a nail to a hammer or the sound of a hammer falling to the ground.

When I began to hear these sounds within my vision, the music became louder, and it finally drove me to remove the earphones. But even after that the sound wouldn't stop. I searched deep within the vision again and replayed that very moment, and after the second time I could finally depict the sound. The man exited quickly following the noise. The young girl attempted to call her aunt's name from the kitchen and be sure she was okay, but all she heard in response was silence. The very thing that scared her at that point was the silence. So the girl ran to the living room as if she sensed something was wrong, and there it was, as sure as she said it—her aunt's body on the striped couches—but this time they were colored tan, brown and stains of red. The television and the show still on, she could hear someone's voice coming from the phone and just a body lying lifeless there.

She looked so helpless and confused, so she picked up the phone and heard a woman say, "Hello" with a voice that was too similar to that of her mother's. And sure enough it was the young girl's aunt's sister, and in an ironic shift of events, also the girl's mother.

When I realized the vision was now over, I wiped these tears that ran down my face, because I could relate to this girl as if I were living her life. This vision came to me after I visited my father in prison and I remembered just the things that happened throughout my life and how one day I was that young girl. That young girl was still inside me and the man I had just sat in front of, staring through the translucent glass, was her father, my father, our father. He was the man in my vision and the cause for everything I stood for at this point. I was that little girl who had witnessed it all.

The next thing I remember clearly was sitting in a room with the sadness and disturbing memory of my aunt lying on the couch. I remember feeling overwhelmed as I observed police officers run in and detectives taking photographs of the crime scene. I remember the police asking everyone questions and I just sat and heard all they had to say. I had the answers to their questions and couldn't communicate myself with them. Perhaps it was because I was three and no one expected me to know. But that moment was the moment in which I grew up.

I know you hear your whole life the world say that you don't know any better when you're three, but I had broken that stereotype. Better yet, my situation had broken that stereotype—not many girls go through traumatic experiences like that. My family had never agreed on much of anything except the fact that any girl who had ever witnessed that needed help. So my mother thought I should give it a try and honestly what better could I do but go to some psychologist. Knowing then what I know now I wouldn't have gone, but I was three and all I could do was obey what my mom told me to do. So that's when it all started that my father, although he had been gone all my life, was the centerpiece around every last thing I did. I only had attended two sessions of this counseling and already I thought to myself this is pointless, because no matter what, no one could take me out of that moment. It's a moment that I would carry in my memory and chest for the rest of my living days here on this earth.

I can remember sitting in the living rooms of my family members' houses and hearing them talk about the situation as if they even lived it. I think they just didn't consider my feelings because I was three. I couldn't believe how selfish they all were and it hurt me to think that they couldn't see my hurt. I spent so much time in these counseling sessions, each one getting more pointless than the one before. When were these people going to get that I wasn't crying because I couldn't anymore, and that I was honestly going to be okay? I didn't want anyone to baby me. I wanted to live my life normally without having the world feel bad for me.

In middle school I was still taking counseling sessions and I hated to tell people that, so not even my closest friends knew. I built my life around the idea that friends didn't exist and best friends aren't true friends, so I never felt left out. Around school you'd see everyone with someone else and I was always alone. Some of my best times of the day were when I could just be alone. I would try to convince the world friends don't exist and now thinking about it, maybe I was jealous that everyone had someone to talk to and I didn't. I spent so much time trying to isolate myself from the world so no one would find out about my life or what had happened to me. And this idea worked for a while, but there were times I was fed up and I'd sit in a bathroom stall in my gym locker room and just cry. I never liked to show people my emotions and somehow I couldn't help but burst out into tears.

Graduating from middle school marked the end of my counseling. You see my mother had given me the choice to stop going, so I did. The end of this very memory took me right back to the scenery I was passing on my way home, the cars zooming past us and the emptiness that submerged my existence.

Here I was on this bus thinking about every minute memory I had that built up to this memory. The more I thought the more I realized that the pictures of these memories remain instilled in my mind and the image is ever so clear. My father, although he had committed wrongful actions, always taught us to never lie or cheat and above all, even though he did wrong that day, he was a man of his word. I can still place myself in the moment, the hour, the minute, the very second in which he gave himself in to the authorities.

It was the very next day after it all had happened. I watched out of my sixth-floor apartment window as my father strolled up the hill in my neighborhood park in hand cuffs with two men in uniform escorting him. I remember waving goodbye, but not realizing what that goodbye signified. I had said bye many times before as he walked up that same hill, but I always knew he'd return, but in my heart I knew this time was different.

That hill brought back the few memories I had of my father to me. I had fallen and scraped my knees there numerous times before, so many times I had lost count. My father loved taking me to that park and chasing me around trying to teach me to ride a tricycle. As I watched tears of desperation and sorrow run down my mother's face, all I could do was hug her and hold on tight. Little did I know it'd be the last time we hugged that significantly.

At the beginning my mother spoke to no one about what had happened with my father. She stayed home and cried most of the time and I couldn't take it, I found myself wanting to alleviate her problems. It was like an emotional cut, something I couldn't put a bandage over and just leave all alone because I knew it wouldn't heal any quicker. My childhood was spent trying to relieve the pain my mother felt, knowing what my father had done and attempting to forget and help her forget. At times I felt like the adult, and it was sickening to me. I had no time for anything—all I could do was sit and think of ways to make my mother happy. So I started off doing small things for her. I would sweep and mop and even wash dishes.

And as the years progressed I started realizing the damage I had done to both my mom and myself. I let her become too accustomed to always having me around, and now it was really hitting me. As the years progressed, I continued doing all those things, but now added cooking and doing laundry to that list—basically I was doing all the things mothers are supposed to do. My mother and I never had one of those relationships where we spoke about things, or even hugged. It was one of those relationships where you love someone from afar and that's what I was doing watching her and loving her but yet never letting her know. I would never admit this to her, but I spent a lot of time feeling guilty like in some way me and my brother were at fault for my father's actions. I never asked her, but

I always felt below everyone at home, and it wasn't until I got older that I began to question myself. I would think to myself, *What am I doing wrong?* And the answer was *Nothing*.

My mother, her whole life, had problems with love and relationships and somehow after every heartbreak and breakup I found myself trying to pick up the broken pieces and put them back together. It was my fault, I'd say to myself to make me feel better, although inside I always felt like the person being taken advantage of. I was the true victim, but still I acted as though nothing bothered me and instead made sure that my mother was okay. Throughout the first couple of months of my father's imprisonment my mother faithfully would go visit him and then have me and my brother visit him too. When she finally decided she couldn't handle this relationship from the two different worlds they were in, she suddenly stopped and I started to break down inside at this point.

I never knew what it meant to me for my parents to be together but at all costs, even if they would be at each other's throats all the time, I wanted them to be together. I continued visiting my father along with my brother and that's what got me on this bus. But just as my mother did, my brother stopped coming to see him.

The first time I remember actually coming in to the jail and visiting him I was still so young, I was only six-years-old and still I felt more mature than ever. You had to have heart to enter these places and leave them the same. As I sit and remember the very first time I saw him in an all navy blue uniform, I guess it's hard to forget. I took a picture of him and it lies on the nightstand right by my bed. As I still spend my weekends cleaning my house. just as I did before. I often come across it and I dust it off and stare at it for a while. I swear it's like the more I look at it. the clearer I remember it all.

Walking through the lie detector and feeling as if they had stripped me completely naked, but I still had clothes on, that feeling of discomfort was inevitable. You can only imagine the way I felt when I had to keep reliving it. It was as if I had tripped and fallen one day and had to constantly relive the moment. It was painful and I for one couldn't take it anymore. Walking in and anticipating my father's walk to the empty table at which I sat and conversing for a few moments knowing that in an hour I would be back on that bus.

No matter how much I tried to get my mind set on how things were going to be, as I approached the exit of the jail, I always suddenly turned back to look and see if my father had come behind me and we would leave together but it never happened. Silly me thinking I could change the course of time or the events that occurred just because I was unhappy. I was selfish, but I had every reason to be in my eyes—my mother was selfish, and my father perhaps the most selfish of us all, and together they taught me to be selfish. He never really spoke much on the subject and I honestly never felt the need to bring it up, but his repeated *I'm sorry*'s told it all. I didn't see myself ever getting past the moment and ultimately that affected my relationship with my mother.

I never understood her, as she never understood me, and perhaps that was my fault. I never tried hard enough to get close to her, because I felt somehow that by helping her with all the things that worried her I was doing her a favor. I never realized just how important it would have been for my mother and me to discuss my father's actions and for me to express to her the guilt I felt, because I thought she blamed me for all the things that went wrong in her life. My mother grew accustomed to life with me helping her fixate on all the little issues that would bother her. When my twin brother and sister were now born, I should have known things weren't going to change. Once again I found myself fixing one more of my mother's issues. When it wasn't housework, it became her relationship issues, and now to add to all that was already on my shoulders, I had a baby brother and sister here.

My mother worked hard to maintain us living the life my father had accustomed us to live. She worked in this hospital right up the hill from my apartment building. It was located right up the same hill in which I had viewed my father walk up handcuffed. I couldn't help it that every time I walked up the hill I felt like I was losing a part of me. In many ways I still felt my father very much a part of me. I found myself always comparing how life would have been with him around. I found him to be my inspiration because I knew although I loved him dearly that I didn't want to be anything like him and that motivated me in school. My mother was never too concerned with grades because she grew complacent with the low grades my brother and sister brought home.

I remember the day I spent a whole two weeks on a paper and got an A+. I ran home to show my mom as she was watching her favorite Spanish soap opera, but I missed the opportunity in between her *hold on*'s and *give me a second*'s. It finally turned into that she fell asleep once more. I started honestly, believing it didn't matter to her so if she wouldn't ask I wouldn't tell. Maybe it was because my mom received an eighth grade education and she somehow was always jealous of all the things I had accomplished and she wasn't able to. My mother knew I was capable and wanted the same for my brother and sister, but they were their own persons and my mother couldn't see past all that.

It started off with small things—honors assemblies, report cards, unviewed test scores and quickly before I knew it. It was my senior year in high school and she was doing the same thing she always did. I learned to fend for myself very early in life. So for anything that had to do with being accepted to college or even scholarships I had worked my hardest to win, she never showed up. After a while I gave up, lost interest in doing almost everything, just because I knew it didn't matter to anyone.

A decade later I'm on my way, embarking on one of the greatest moments of my life; I remember the butterflies in my stomach as I began to zip up this white gown that concealed the white dress and shoes I was wearing. I remember clearly walking down this long narrow pathway, standing next to all these people that were familiar to me at this point, but sooner or later I would forget all about. The moment was coming and I could feel it as I got closer and closer to the podium. It was a moment of anxiety, which I couldn't remove myself from, it was just another thing that was out of my control.

As the stage got closer, all the people who at one point seemed minute, enlarged right before my eyes and a sense of relief took over me. All I could think about wasn't what I was going to say, but the estranged relationship I had with my father and the nonexistent relationship between my mom and me.

I approached the stairs that led to the podium and I lifted a side of this big all-white gown I had on, afraid I might trip. There I was—all these words written on paper and somehow not finding a way to communicate them through my shaky hands and low voice. It was this very moment that put me in the same situation I had been in, staring at my father through that translucent glass. Somehow I always find that happens to me when I get nervous. I began with "Good afternoon, Ladies and Gentlemen and most importantly my fellow class of 2010." After saying this I began to choke up on the stage, remembering all the amazing small moments that led to this everlasting life long memory.

I went into high school thinking I just want to do enough to get by. By my tenth-grade year I decided I'm going to do all I can to do better then everyone around me, but in 11th grade I realized I have to do enough to make myself proud and not only do better than the people who are at my level but somehow surpass their intellect, because at this point I realized the world was my competition. Better yet, my whole life I felt was an ongoing war with the world. I wasn't sure when it was time to just let everything go. Whenever I got up, I felt like the world would dig me in deeper and I began to be inspired to rise above it all.

I remember this feeling I felt at this point. I wasn't addressing my classmates as valedictorian or even salutatorian—I had accomplished what any person with leadership qualities would of loved—I had been president of the student body at my school. I know the position sounds mediocre, but being in this environment was the only time I didn't think of what I had been through all my life. I continued addressing the graduating class, telling them how proud I was of being able to say I knew each and every one of them. I always saw myself standing right in the position I was in right this second. I just didn't see the day coming soon enough. But I knew what it was going to take to get me there. I was at this point where I had become my own mom and dad and I never once let my father's absence affect where I was going in life. My constant reliving of it every time I took a step onto that bus drove me to a sea of tears in which I was constantly swimming.

Years later here I am, no longer taking those long pointless trips to the middle of nowhere to visit a stranger. Instead I'm in the place I call my home, awaiting the phone call that never happens and the letters I never receive. I give up, I say. I forgive him, I can finally say, because I grew out of the grudge against him. I'm different, I can yell, because he's my inspiration for what I don't want to become. I am who I am because I created all the parts that compose me! And I live for me, because if I don't, no one else will!

This Is Your Family Now

Jacqueline

In 2010, Herstory embarked on an exciting new program—"Youth Writing for Restorative Justice and Racial Equity"—allowing college activists to write side by side with young people impacted by the juvenile justice system. Jackie, then a freshman at SUNY Old Westbury, was one of the first pioneers in a project that sent young women majoring in psychology and criminology to craft their stories with girls in a reform school environment that—unbeknownst to us—would bring up echoes of what she herself once lived through. Ever since, she has thrown herself into helping younger people caught in the "school to prison pipeline" and children at risk.

The piece we have reproduced here captures the feelings of so many young people who are subjected to escalating levels of harsh responses from the juvenile justice system, rather than being met on their journeys by a true acknowledgement of their vulnerability and pain.

It is in listening to the vulnerability of the young people who have been caught in the system, but who, like herself, have found an inner reserve of strength and engagement, that Jackie's strength lies. As an AmeriCorps intern, she has tailored her service learning around working to educate the public about conditions for women in jail as she continues to study alternative solutions for young people at risk.

"**Y**ou can't use the phone, you can't talk to your friends, no computer, no contact with your family. This is your family now."

These are the uplifting words my CPS worker gives to me on my first day of foster care. Somehow I am being punished for having parents who did the wrong thing. Somehow I'm the bad guy. Well if they're gonna treat me like this I might as well act how everyone portrays me to be.

There is no way I'm doing all of that, and no these people will never be my family. Fuck you, Fuck them, Fuck all of this shit!

"Give me your cell phone Jackie right now!"

Run, run away from this mess is all my brain tells me. My legs start pumping until I reach the front lawn where I realize I have nowhere to run to. I have nothing. Blank. Now I'm on my back on the front lawn. *How'd I get down here?*

"Jackie! JACKIE! I went through your things—no more phone, or cigarettes. I will make it my mission to make sure that if you contact anyone from home you will pay greatly for it. You are a live wire, a monster. Enjoy your new home."

The tears fell across my cheek. My thoughts were limited to what I had to do to get out of this, get back to my home. *There is no way out! I can't find a way out! If they won't let me out, I won't let them enjoy me. They have created a new me. A girl who's young, angry and has nothing to lose. They've created a monster.*

Dear Diary,

These days, weeks, months that I've been here have brought me deeper and deeper into this black sea of depression. Its strong tide keeps sucking me deeper and deeper and keeps me there for a long time.

Experimenting with weed, alcohol and coke are no longer fun for me, they're my escape. They bring me deeper and deeper.

How deep can I go? I've already gone much deeper than drugs. The razor cuts on my arms prove that. School, what a joke! And I think I'm the new Houdini because my disappearing acts have my CPS worker in awe. Titi, aka "foster momster," doesn't care what I do. She doesn't want to help me and I don't want her help. She just wants her check and that's the end of it.

Well not really—I haven't eaten in days, not by choice, by punishment. I have no friends in this place. This nasty place. This place filled with guys who wanna have their way with you, place filled with connections to drugs, place filled with people who care about nothing but what they want. This place that I hate, but in a way fit into.

All my associates are drug dealers or druggies. All of them don't give a shit, just like me. All of them want to go deeper and deeper into their own seas, just like me. No one cares about the nights I walk back to this place, messed up beyond belief on all sorts of things at crazy hours of the night. And neither do I.

No one cares on the nights I sit in this room, stuck in my head, watering my black sea with my tears, gliding the razors across my arms hoping this time it would work and I'd end up dead. And neither did I. No one cared the other night when I did heroin for the first time. Sitting in the woods with a "friend" smoking the thick potent smoke until it was all gone.

It was great, I was gone—far, far away from the world I lived in. I felt like I was in the mountains. The sidewalk was mountains. The street lights were the bright and vibrant stars. The house was a cabin. And . . . my throw up brought me back to this mess.

This mess of a life. I didn't care and neither did anyone else. So I'll just keep swimming, deeper and deeper, all by myself.

I remember my dad told me you should never swim alone, but who would take this swim with me?   ✎

AFTERWORD

*T*ucked *along the bend* of where Routes 24 and 94 meld, *west* of Suffolk County's government buildings and Supreme Court, is Riverhead Correctional Facility, embodying the hard image any one might imagine a jail to be—check-points, steel fencing, barbed wire, concrete walls. The drive there is an extreme opposite to this façade as it's mostly composed of windy hilly roads lined with trees and pastures, and panoramic views of Long Island farmlands radiating feelings of freedom and plenty. It is before this grandeur of green open space that anxiety's hum is rising inside me, that I find myself tightening up as I think over and over: *Am I really ready? I need "special" training. How will they see me? How will they be? Will they let me in?*

I'm absorbed by the anticipation of the women I'm about to meet and the world I'm about to enter. The facts that I've never been to a jail before, that I've never met anyone who's "done time," that at this moment I'm falling victim to a slew of stereotypical images of life in jail, warding off ripples of barraging Hollywood and reality television bites—gangs, drugs, ghetto life, hard-looking and tatted-up bitches hustling and cussing loud—all push me to reason I'm not ready, that I lack the necessary skills and bravado for tempering any ensuing crisis, outburst, or raging display between "these women." *I need "special training . . ." an overview . . . drug and alcohol counseling . . . anger management . . . conflict resolution . . .*

Am I really ready? I try to bring it back to what I do know, for at this point in time by no means was I stranger to Herstory Writers Workshop; I was "dipped and dyed," as Erika often liked to say, in Herstory's unique elements and approach to writing memoir. I had started writing my own story and training in the workshops, and was already facilitating weekly Herstory Spanish language and bilingual workshops in the community and "Our Story" projects in local colleges and universities. Over the last several years, I'd become more adept and confident at daring new writers to find their "Page One Moments," at guiding them to open up into more story, or "slow down" enough so that any reading stranger would genuinely be moved and care about the person and journey on the page. But on this particular winter morning, I was more nervous than usual. My new group was to be composed not of immigrant women from the community, or young fifth grade girls, or first-year college students; I was to be meeting Linda and Lonnie's groups from "the inside."

How will they be? How will they see me? Will they let me in? But I know better. To temper another flush of uneasy fancy I recalled my readings of *Voices*—Volumes I and II—remembering them to be visceral experiences, both in feeling an unpleasant gut reaction to the cold hard facts and disparities about women in prison, and in feeling forever infused by the stories and their powerful portrayal of innocence and danger, longing and abuse, overall, the great falling and rising of the human spirit. Hope in me surges as I focus more on this, on story . . . the stories . . . the stories . . . those little windows that let us in, that let us see and hear and feel the woman and the life the factual bones let run dry. The stories . . . the stories . . . life force. This is perhaps my greatest source of comfort—my turning point—this refocus not on the teller but on the making and telling of story, on the writing and sharing it in community. It will be no different here on "the inside," I tell myself.

By the time Linda, Lonnie and I are temporarily "in the cage," awaiting the slamming shut of the gate behind us and the clanking opening of another before us, I feel more solid and anchored in story, guided more by my own humane instinct and warmly supported by my friends and colleagues. I know I am not alone, but am still worrying a little if the women will like me . . . *How will they see me? Will they let me in?*

Once in the chapel, one by one, the women arrived: all in green, some wide-eyed, some still a little groggy, some slow in their stepping while others seem even bopping. "Happy Valentine's Day!" cried out a few women as they ran open-armed to greet Linda and

Lonnie. None of us had taken special notice of the fact that it was Sunday, February 14th, but all of a sudden, here on "the inside" it was reason enough to rejoice and hug more than usual, and to smile brightly or silently cry for the loved ones left behind. In a setting where touching is prohibited and affection seriously deferred, this scene was already making me feel I was not in jail, for I was sensing nothing but acceptance and kindness, and caring and understanding; the experiencing of a space and gestures that welcomed all of us just as we were, as whole or broken as that might be. And even though the women were meeting me for the first time, they all, for the most part, hugged me, too, making me feel truly initiated and part of their Sunday writing ritual.

So the shift happened seamlessly, lifting anxiety away. I found myself in the middle of the circle no longer coerced by skewed and sensationalized stereotypes, but rather enthralled and illumed by women writing their stories, by the sheer fact they'd survived harsh and extreme circumstances and still found the courage to tell, to sing their blues and highs, to share their songs. As the women read and listened to each other I also caught closer glances of their faces and hands, taking note of porcelain smoothness, deep lines, nervous smiles, eccentric braids, chipped or rotten teeth, bitten fingernails. Some of the women seemed so young, too young and girlish to be in jail; others seemed so much older, evoking me to think "grandma" and imagine all the generations before and after her. At one point during this day, I also remember looking down and noticing one of the teen writers had crisscrossed the straps of the generic black sneakers all inmates are issued, thrilling me with the thought that individuality and creative expression and a sense of self still persist despite the confinement and oppression of the prison system.

That Sunday, like many more after it, imbued me with a greater purpose and deeper understanding about my work with Herstory and the power that stories hold in our lives and the world, more precisely their power to teach, to renew, and to transform. The opportunities to lead Herstory writing workshops in the Yaphank DWI Alternative Facility and Nassau County Correctional Facility in East Meadow, along with workshops for teen moms and alternative high school students and youth involved in PINS diversion programs, have positioned me at an interesting crux of the infamous school-to-prison pipeline, inviting me to inquire further about how these stories can impact not only our general consciousness about prison life, but our overall understanding and treatment of the men and women—and children—that end up in it; and better yet, how can these stories be used as preventive tools for keeping jails empty?

Now, when thinking about women in prison I conjure up my own organic (literally non-toxic) images of our writing circles together, I hear the echoes of their stories, defying all expectations of metaphor, tone and rhyme, for one wouldn't expect such profundity and beauty to come from jail. I go back to those readings that pulled us all in a little closer, that dared us to look at each other straight in the eyes and not turn our backs, not walk away. These are the voices and stories now humming inside me. I can only sincerely hope that after reading this expanded edition of **VOICES**, you, like me, feel the transforming power of their images and words, and dare yourself to care, for after Herstory and this sharing of stories, we are strangers no more.

Silvia P. Heredia
Herstory Facilitator for
Nassau County Correctional Facility
Teen Workshops and
Yaphank Correctional Facility

ACKNOWLEDGEMENTS

IT IS HARD to know where to begin in extending acknowledgements to everyone who has had an impact on our work in developing the *Herstory Inside* program to where it is today. We must thank not only those with whom we have worked directly, but also the many poets and writers who have done groundbreaking work in prison world-wide, who have inspired us to bring our own writing process to incarcerated women. We particularly thank Eve Ensler for her inspirational work in Bedford Hills, and for the documentary of that program, "What I Want My Words to Do to You," that ignited our intuition that if Herstory is about breaking silences, we too needed to work in the place where the silencing is greatest.

We would like to include, first and foremost, acknowledgement of the efforts and writing of an average of 200 women each year with whom we have worked since 2004. We carry them in our hearts, each and every one, and wish we could include all of their work in this volume.

We thank Linda Coleman and Lonnie Mathis for the wisdom and caring they brought into the inauguration of this project in Riverhead Correctional Facility and then in Yaphank, Silvia Heredia who later became the facilitator in Yaphank Correctional Facility and Nassau County Correctional Facility, and Lynn Doris who worked briefly with the Herstory approach with two of the incarcerated women represented here.

We again thank our mentor and teacher, Herstory's founder and artistic director Erika Duncan, for her guidance, her ceaseless energy to bring the stories of all women to the page, and her dogged determination to find continuous financial support for this project. We are forever grateful for the hard work and good humor of Herstory office manager, Gabriella Luciano, who typed for us endlessly and so very quickly.

None of this would be possible without the ongoing support and good will of Lieutenant Darlene McClurkin and Sergeant Noreen Fisher at Riverhead Correctional Facility, Captain Helen Geslak, who worked with us at Riverhead and Yaphank Correctional Facilities, and Jonathan Scherr, program director of the DWI Facility at Yaphank, and the patience and accommodation of the correctional officers in Rehab at Riverhead Correctional Facility. We thank the officers who have lovingly selected and supported the teen writers in Nassau County Correctional Facility.

As the project took shape, its funders provided us with much more than money. We extend particular thanks to Vanessa Greene for helping us to frame a theoretical basis and ensuing plan of action for taking this work into the arena of social justice, during her tenure at the Long Island Community Foundation, and for bringing us together with Clarence Sheppard and Natalie Byfield of Black Media Foundation in a film documentary project funded by Suffolk County's Office of Cultural Affairs, leading to many related projects. We thank Laurel Parker West, former executive director of the Women's Fund of Long Island, Hazel Weiser of the Society of American Law Teachers, and L. Susan Slavin, Esq., for helping to get our Education and Activism Initiative off the ground. We thank Long Island Unitarian Universalist Fund (in Long Island Community Foundation), Horace and Amy Hagedorn Fund in New York Community Trust, MS Foundation for Women, Ben & Jerry's Foundation, Chase and Stephanie Coleman Foundation, the Office of Suffolk County Legislator Vivian-Viloria Fisher and Have a Heart Community Fund for supporting our for programs in Long Island's correctional facilities, and bridge workshops in Huntington Station.

We offer particular thanks to the MS Foundation for Women and Ben & Jerry's Foundation and Dr. Laura Anker of SUNY College at Old Westbury for supporting our "Writing for Restorative Justice" program, which has resulted in Part Two of this book. The conceptual work that led to this expanded volume would never have been possible without the continued friendship, active guidance and loving friendship of Angela Zimmerman and Deborah Barrett-Anderson of the Nassau County Youth Board. We thank our board of directors for helping us to chart our direction as we moved from a writing project empowering individual women into the larger use of our "dare to care" pedagogy to change hearts, minds and policies, and most especially the late, Roslyn Muraskin, pioneer in feminist criminology who brought our work to the attention of an international audience through including us in *It's a Crime: Women and Justice,* the text that she edited over the years.

We again thank Natalie Byfield, professor of sociology at St. John's University and visiting research scholar with John Jay College of Criminal Justice, for her examination of these stories and the changes in the lives of the women who wrote them as she posited a new way of looking at restoration and guilt in victimless crimes. We thank Fran Medaglia of the Women on the Job project of the Long Island Fund for Women and Girls, who commissioned the story about looking for work that appears in this volume as part of the movement for Second Chance legislation. We thank Suzy Dalton Sonenberg and Amy Hagedorn, long-time mentors in many different roles, and Serena Alfieri-Liguori, our advocacy and justice program director, for the larger perspective and dreams they have brought to this project. We thank Robert Dembia of Eastern Suffolk **BOCES** for seeing the potential of our project to further **BOCES** educational goals, and for lending the support that helps us to bring our work to the women and adolescent girls writing in Suffolk County's jails year after year. Beyond this we thank the many large and small donors who have given to the project, and the women in prison themselves, who sewed pillows and carrying bags and other objects, asking us to sell them for whatever we could get to keep the project going.

For the publication of the first issue of **VOICES** (Part One of this volume), we thank the Women's Fund of Long Island for underwriting it as part of their Education and Activism grant. We thank MS Foundation for Women and Ben & Jerry's Foundation for making the expanded issue possible. We thank Alan Gold for designing this book and for working so closely with us to prepare it for production and Jim Harris of G&H SOHO, Inc. (www.ghsoho.com) for his personal involvement and caring work with us as the printer of this volume.

Not only the women represented here, but all of the women of Herstory Inside and Herstory Inside Out, gave us each, in their own ways, not only their stories, but new knowledge of how to develop our approach so that it could be increasingly helpful, and so that the voices that emerged might truly make a difference.

"HERSTORY INSIDE" FACILITATORS AND JUSTICE AND ADVOCACY PROGRAM STAFF

Linda Coleman has recently completed her memoir, *Radical Descent,* which tells of her transit through idealism and dogma amidst the violent revolutionary underground of the early 1970s. Other memoir pieces were published in the Fall 2007 issue of *North Atlantic Review* and the Summer 2008 issue of *Memoir (and)* . . . A Herstory facilitator since 2003, it was her dream to bring these stories of incarcerated women not only to others in similar circumstances, but also to the judges, parole officers, corrections officers, and criminology students and teachers who would have such power over their treatment. She brings her many years of nursing and study and practice of Zen Buddhism into her work as facilitator with Herstory.

Silvia P. Heredia has been working as Herstory Writers Workshop's primary Latina program facilitator, drawing on her graduate work in Latin American Literature that focuses on writing as healing to bring the Herstory technique to students in colleges, public, and alternative schools; community organizations; and "bridge-building" groups in neighborhoods where violence against immigrants has broken out. She has hosted a weekly Spanish language radio program on Radio Fiesta, WBON, reaching 120,000 listeners in three states and featuring Herstory's Latina writers from all over Long Island. She is a co-editor of *Latinas Write/Escriben,* Herstory's bilingual anthology.

Lonnie Mathis began to write with Herstory in 2000. The first book she wrote in the workshop, *Childhood Is a Relative Experience,* opens with a walk and a peek into a window that changed her life—the moment her lost childhood memories began to resurface—and takes the reader back into the world, the heart, the body, mind and soul of the little girl living in trauma. Her second book, *From the Shores of the River Denial* (in progress), opens only days later, locked away in a psychiatric ward and locked inside her own silence—"My journey into, through and up out of crazy"—offering the reader an intimate look into the breakdown and rebuilding of a life. Lonnie has been a workshop facilitator with Herstory since 2004, leading the Huntington Black, White, Brown bridge group, as well as workshops at Clubhouse of Suffolk for writers with mental illness,

Herstory's founder and artistic director, novelist and essayist Erika Duncan, has devoted her life to giving voice to stories that have been silenced and unsung. Her novels, *A Wreath of Pale White Roses* and *Those Giants: Let them Rise,* chart the search for expression. Her portraits of writers (written when she was a contributing editor for *Book Forum* and collected in *Unless Soul Clap Its Hands: Portraits and Passages*) all touch on the moment when a writer found her or his voice. This search for a spark is picked up in her front-page series for the *New York Times Long Island Weekly,* where for a four-year period her portraits of writers, artists, teachers, scientists and musicians appeared every month. Simultaneously, Duncan began to explore new ways of teaching writing, which led to numerous experiments in university and grassroots settings, and to the formation of workshops for women through the salon she co-founded in New York City, which became a first reading ground for a fair number of feminist works that have since become classics. Her latest books are *Paper Stranger: Shaping Stories in Community* and *Passing along the Dare to Care: A Mini-Memoir Course for Younger Writers.* Both of these books grew out of the Herstory Writers Workshop project, which is her creation.

Serena Alfieri-Liguori, Herstory's Advocacy and Justice Program Director, is responsible for creating and nurturing program partnerships with organizations working on social justice and legislative advocacy, where first-person testimony becomes a key tool to create change. She is also responsible for creating ways in which Herstory writers can become active participants in social justice initiatives locally and throughout New York State. Prior to joining the Herstory staff she was the Associate Director of Policy for the Correctional Association of New York's Women in Prison Project where she spearheaded legislative initiatives and policy advocacy addressing prison reform. She was the key organizer of a successful effort to create the Adoption and Safe Families Act Expanded Discretion Law, which works to secure parental rights for incarcerated parents as well as the Anti-Shackling Law, which prohibits the shackling of incarcerated mothers during labor. Serena was also the project coordinator of the Long Island Progressive Coalition's Government Efficiency Project where she oversaw a campaign aimed at ending unfair taxation in racially diverse communities. She has experienced and navigated firsthand the many challenges of incarceration, has extensive experience working with formerly and currently incarcerated people and regularly lectures on prison reform issues.

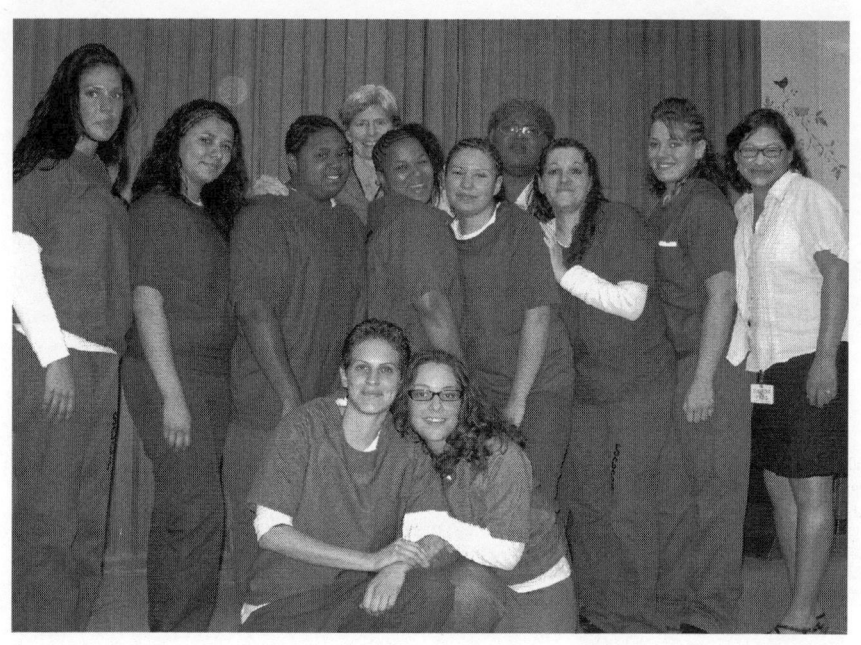

HERSTORY BOOKS AND MAGAZINES IN PRINT

These books can be ordered through our office by calling 631-676-7395 or on the web at www.herstorywriters.org, with special discounts available for classroom and conference use. All proceeds go back to Herstory's ongoing work with women who might not otherwise be able to pay for quality writing workshops.

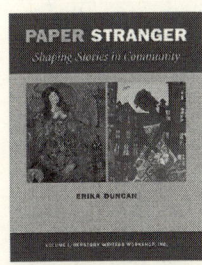

Herstory's Manual: Paper Stranger/Shaping Stories in Community, by Erika Duncan: Herstory's manual for teachers, healers and activists, provides an introduction to Herstory's empathy-based approach to memoir writing. Readings and reflections are interwoven with a step-by-step compendium of exercises and tools. **$24.95**

Passing Along the Dare to Care: A Mini-Memoir Course for Younger Writers, by Erika Duncan This collection of readings and exercises—based on what causes a "Stranger/Reader" to care—fosters dialogues across differences, diversity studies and a sense of community, as well as enhanced listening, reading and narrative skills. **$14.95**

Teaching Memoir Writing the Herstory Way. This 90-minute instructional DVD—divided into six free-standing tracks—provides, teachers, healers and activists with an overview of the empathy-based techniques that have proven effective in school, jail and community settings. It is best used in combination with our two manuals, and is being offered along with *Paper Stranger,* for teachers, and *Passing Along the Dare to Care,* for students. **$29.95**

Special Combination Package. We are offering *Paper Stranger*/Volume I, for teachers (normally $19.95), *Passing Along the Dare to Care,* for students (normally $14.95) and *Teaching Memoir the Herstory Way,* our instructional DVD (normally $29.95) at a 23% reduction from the full price.   **$29.95**

Latinas Write/Escriben, edited by Sandra Dunn and Silvia Heredia with a guest section edited by Antoinette Hertel: This 330-page bilingual collection takes the reader through sections on Immigrant Realities, Childhood, Motherhood, Faces of Illness and Faces of Love, through the voices of 23 women writing with Herstory all over Long Island and 11 women from Sutiaba, Nicaragua. Rarely do students in ESL, foreign language, sociology, writing and women's studies classes have the chance to experience literature created by people "just like them." A vital reader for community welcoming groups, book clubs, and classroom use.   **$22.95**

The Teller in the Tale: A Half-Jewish Child in Nazi Germany, by Elizabeth Heyn is the story of a half-Jewish child growing up in Nazi Germany. It traces its way through her miraculous late escape in 1941 just three weeks before the German borders close, to her coming of age as a refugee in Franco's Spain, and finally to her attempts to become a typical American teenager. Rich in the not usually documented details of everyday life for one who falls between the cracks —neither Jewish nor Gentile and thus subject to different rules—this is also the story of a mother and daughter who, due to the circumstances in their lives, need to adjust to their too-closeness, even as they find their own ways.   **$14.95**

Love Song at the End of the Day: A Journey into Alzheimer's, by Muriel Weyl. This unexpectedly optimistic memoir is a testimony to living life to its fullest, written with compassion and humor. Throughout this "love song"—which only deepens as we move from diagnosis into daily living with Alzheimer's—we find remembrances of a sixty-two-year relationship in the everyday moments that weave through this work. It is ultimately a celebration of the human spirit, a bedside book for anyone who is connected to a sufferer from memory loss.   **$14.95**

Back issues of *Latinas Write/Escriben* I and II and *Voices* I are available in magazine format for **$10** copy.